# LEARNING BY DOING

JAMES BESSEN

# Learning
# by
# Doing

THE REAL CONNECTION BETWEEN

INNOVATION, WAGES, AND WEALTH

Yale UNIVERSITY PRESS

NEW HAVEN AND LONDON

Published with assistance from the foundation established in memory of
Philip Hamilton McMillan of the Class of 1894, Yale College.

Yale University Press books may be purchased in quantity for educational,
business, or promotional use. For information, please e-mail sales
.press@yale.edu (U.S. office) or sales@yaleup.co.uk (U.K. office).

Set in Scala and Scala Sans type by Westchester Publishing Services.
Printed in the United States of America.

Library of Congress Cataloging-in-Publication Data

Bessen, James, 1958–
Learning by doing : the real connection between innovation,
wages, and wealth / James Bessen.
pages  cm
Includes bibliographical references and index.
ISBN 978-0-300-19566-8 (cloth : alk. paper)
1. Employees—Effect of technological innovations on.
2. Wages—Effect of technological innovations on.   3. Skilled labor.
4. Technological innovations—Economic aspects.   5. Economic
development.   I. Title.
HD6331.B554   2015
338'.064—dc23        2014035012

A catalogue record for this book is available from the British Library.

This paper meets the requirements of ANSI/NISO Z39.48-1992
(Permanence of Paper).

10 9 8 7 6 5 4 3 2 1

To Lauren, Neal, and Krzysztof

# CONTENTS

PART III. TECHNOLOGY POLICY

# ACKNOWLEDGMENTS

THE IDEA FOR THIS BOOK GREW OUT of the dissonance I experienced between the notions of innovation I had picked up in the classroom and my job running a software start-up. As I describe briefly in Chapter 2, I was surprised by the extent of the knowledge that I needed to acquire, as well as the amount our employees and customers needed to learn, in order to put a new technology into production. That struck me as significant and perhaps underappreciated. My curiosity led me to think about learning by doing, why it is important, and what its importance implies. Although that curiosity might not have been the best attribute for a CEO, it has led me on a course of research and study far more extensive than what I anticipated on leaving my company two decades ago and beginning academic research. The consequences of learning by doing also seem more far-reaching than I imagined.

Because my academic career path has been unusual, I am especially grateful to the people who were accepting and encouraging early on. Eric Maskin gave generously of his time and provided strong encouragement. Boyan Jovanovic provided the first airing of some of my thinking on learning by doing. Mike Meurer has been my "academic spouse" for ten years now, serving as sounding board, guide, critic, cheerleader, devil's advocate, and coauthor of *Patent Failure* and many papers. My actual spouse, Joyce, played a similar role concerning more practical matters through what were occasionally trying times.

Several institutions have been very supportive, especially Boston University School of Law, thanks to Maureen O'Rourke and Wendy Gordon. I also had brief stints at the Berkman Center at Harvard and at MIT visiting Eric von Hippel. Much of the book was initially written at the University of California at Berkeley, where I was visiting the Berkeley Center for Law and Technology, thanks to Pam Samuelson, Peter Menell, Robert Barr, and Louise Lee.

I owe special thanks to the people who read the first manuscript and provided comments: Joyce, Arthur Boatin, Emily Feinberg, Dan Fetter, Elaine Ford, Joachim Henkel, Brian Kahin, Michael Kimmage, Jeff Kuhn, Tim Lee, Megan MacGarvie, Mike Meurer, Ale Nuvolari, Rob Restuccia, Tim Simcoe, Scott Stern, and Heidi Williams. Please read the final book; it really is much, much better, thanks to your input.

Several people were essential in acquiring data and hands-on knowledge of weaving technology, including Rick Randall at the Lowell Historical National Park and Mike Christiansen at the American Textile History Museum. Tom Brush generously shared payroll data from the Lawrence Company, and the librarians at Baker Library at Harvard provided access to the original payroll registers and other historical records. Research assistants did much of the work of making data meaningful, including John McClelland, Tim Layton, Dan Wilson, and others.

Various people have shared knowledge and provided feedback in informal discussions and as commenters on papers, as editors, as coauthors, and as interviewees. They include Daron Acemoglu, Jim Adams, Philippe Aghion, Bob Allen, David Anderson, Robert Barr, Ernie Berndt, Tom Brush, Xiangdong Chen, Colleen Chien, Greg Clark, Iain Cockburn, Wes Cohen, Diego Comin, Dennis Crouch, Paul David, Joe Farrell, Dan Fetter, Price Fishback, Lee Fleming, Dominique Foray, Jennifer Ford, Claudia Goldin, Rowena Gray, Tim Guinnane, Bronwyn Hall, Dietmar Harhoff, Bob Hunt, Brian Kahin, Karim Lakhani, Naomi Lamoreaux, David Landes, Tim Layton, Bill Lazonick, Mark Lemley, Larry Lessig, Tim Leunig, David K. Levine, Frank Lewis, Brian Love, John Lyons, Bruce MacDougal, Megan MacGarvie, Christine MacLeod, Peter Menell, Rob Merges, Mike Meurer, Peter Meyer, David Mitch, Petra Moser, David Mowery, John Murray, Ale Nuvolari, Alan Olmstead, David Olson, Kevin O'Rourke, John Parker,

Lucio Picci, Mitch Polinsky, Woody Powell, Cecil Quillen, Arti Rai, Dan Ravicher, Steven Ringer, Michael Risch, Mark Rosenzweig, Pam Samuelson, AnnaLee Saxenian, Mark Schankerman, Mike Scherer, Carl Shapiro, Kathy Strandburg, Talha Syed, Grid Thoma, Stefan Thomke, Peter Thompson, Ross Thomson, Catherine Tucker, John Turner, Bruno van Pottelsberghe, Eric von Hippel, Polk Wagner, John Wallis, Heidi Williams, Jonathan Williams, Susan Wolcott, Brian Wright, Gavin Wright, Jonathan Zittrain, and many other commenters at talks at Ascona, the AEA, Beihang University, the Berkman Center, Boston University, the Center for Economic Studies at the U.S. Bureau of the Census, DRUID, Duke, the Economic History Association, EPIP, the Federal Reserve Banks of Philadelphia and San Francisco, Harvard, John Marshall Law, MIT, the NBER, NYU, PATSTAT, Pisa, Science Po, Seville, SSHA, Stanford, the University of California at Berkeley and Davis, the University of Maryland Baltimore County, the Washington area economic historians, and Yale.

All of this help yielded some papers and some unconnected ideas. Turning it into a book with a coherent focus required the critical additional help of David Miller and Lisa Adams, who also found a publisher; my wonderful editor, Bill Frucht; and an exceptionally helpful anonymous reviewer.

# LEARNING BY DOING

# Introduction

THE EFFECTS OF NEW TECHNOLOGY are all around us. We use satellites to find our location on maps, and we ask our cell phones for driving directions. Thanks to logistics, inventory management, and flexible manufacturing technologies, our supermarkets carry fifty times as many items as the grocery stores of eighty years ago, and online shopping lets us choose from an even larger cornucopia. Most of us use computers at work that are far more powerful than the computers of just a few decades ago that required large rooms with specialized air-conditioning. We work differently, communicate with each other differently, create differently, and entertain ourselves differently—all thanks to new technology. Yet there is one place the effects of technology do not appear: our paychecks.

This is today's great paradox. Since the beginning of the personal computer revolution, the median wage in the United States has been stagnant.[1] Information technology may even be hurting many white-collar workers, especially those without a college education. Voice mail systems have taken over from switchboard operators, automated teller machines do tasks of bank tellers, and computer systems have automated a whole range of routine clerical tasks. Workers in these occupations have to find new jobs or learn new skills to remain employed. Moreover, technology experts such as Erik Brynjolfsson and Andrew McAfee see these trends accelerating.[2]

It seems as if the machines have turned against us. Over the past 200 years, technology has been responsible for enormous growth in the pay of the average worker in developed nations, even for workers without advanced education. Wage earners in Britain and the United States today earn over ten times what they earned 200 years ago, after accounting for inflation, and technology is a major source of that growth.[3] Yet now technology contributes to a loss of jobs and pay for many ordinary workers, while the pay of top earners has grown dramatically.

Worse, some see the current effects of technology as a dark omen of what is to come. Thomas Piketty sees current income inequality casting a long shadow of inherited wealth for generations.[4] Tyler Cowen sees new technologies leading to a future where only elites with advanced education or specialized skills will be able to get work.[5]

But are we really experiencing a revolution in the way technology affects jobs and wages, one leading to a yawning economic gap between the educated elite and the rest? Actually, we have seen a similar pattern before. The past was not so different. There have been long periods in which advancing technology failed to provide much economic benefit to workers and when machines took over job tasks. For decades at the beginning of the Industrial Revolution, factory wages remained stagnant despite major new technologies that brought dramatic gains in output per worker.[6] Wealth was created, but it went into the pockets of the investors, managers, and a few key skilled employees. Profits grew and inequality rose, without bringing much gain to the workers. These trends eventually reversed. After decades, the pay of even uneducated factory workers rose substantially, and workers gained a substantial share of the benefit of the new technologies.

This book looks at both economic history and the current economy to understand how new technology affects ordinary workers and how society can best meet the challenges it poses. Today's technology is different from past technologies, to be sure. Yet a look at history reveals how technology increased the pay of ordinary workers and why it took decades for these wage increases to take place. This analysis provides a basis for understanding similar forces possibly at work today and for designing policies that can allow ordinary workers to prosper from technology again.

I focus on how technology affects the pay of ordinary workers rather than the inequality of wealth studied by Piketty[7] and others. These issues are related but distinct. Stagnant wages at a time of growing profits contribute to unequal wealth. However, concentrated wealth does not necessarily inhibit wage growth. In the past, technology dramatically boosted the wages of ordinary workers at times of great inequality. Concentrated wealth also threatens to undermine democracy. But billionaires are not the only vested interests promoting policies that slow the progress of ordinary workers. Wealth inequality is important, but the question here is how technology affects ordinary workers.

In particular, I argue that developing the knowledge and skills needed to implement new technologies on a large scale is a difficult social problem that takes a long time to resolve. It was a difficult problem in the past and remains so today, yet most workers will only benefit once it is resolved.[8] Resolution will take time and the right policies.

Many people fail to appreciate the complexity and slow pace of the current transition because they confuse technology with inventions and they confuse skill with education. A new technology typically requires much more than an invention in order to be designed, built, installed, operated, and maintained. Initially much of this new technical knowledge develops slowly because it is learned through experience, not in the classroom. Throughout history, workers have acquired their technical knowledge through a combination of formal training and experience. They gained much of their important technical knowledge on the job, through "learning by doing." Formal and informal experimentation aided by informal communication with others allowed workers to acquire new skills and knowledge of technology.[9]

In the past, such skills allowed even factory workers who had little schooling to command middle-class pay. Learning on the job is no less important for today's science-based technologies. Medical technicians learn new diagnostic techniques, nurses learn new care protocols, office workers learn new computer systems, and designers learn new web standards.

But when major new technologies affect many industries at once—as with mechanization during the nineteenth century or information technology today—then training large numbers of workers becomes a difficult social problem, especially during the early stages. Early technical knowledge is typically too fragmentary, uncertain, and constantly changing to be standardized. Prior to standardization, classroom education is difficult and labor markets may not reliably reward workers who invest in their training. Without robust markets and training institutions, it may take decades before large numbers of ordinary workers benefit from skills related to new technology.

In the past, these institutions eventually emerged, changing a variety of behaviors over the "technology life cycle." After decades, technologies suddenly became "disruptive"; those that had been concentrated in geographic clusters like Silicon Valley spread across the globe; and experienced workers in some new technology jobs finally saw their earnings grow.

Many occupations are undergoing such a transition today. Despite the doomsayers, technology is not replacing workers overall but is displacing them to new jobs requiring new skills. Yet few of these skills can be learned in a classroom, many skills are not standardized, and in many of the new jobs, ordinary workers have not seen rising wages. At the same time, employers complain they can't hire enough workers who already have the new skills. Technology is promoting economic inequality, but it doesn't have to be that way.

Technology does not inexorably destroy opportunities for mid-wage jobs. Even when machines take over human tasks, technology creates demand for workers with new skills. But neither does technology guarantee greater wealth for ordinary workers. The outcome depends on policy choices. Historically, U.S. policies have encouraged the development of new technical knowledge and skills among large numbers of ordinary workers. The United States led the world in education; in other areas, policy was designed to foster new skills and to encourage tech start-ups, including policies affecting government procurement, occupational credentials, employee mobility regulations, and the patent system. But too often today, policy has changed for the worse, favoring established firms and vested interests rather than advancing new technology and reducing inequality. While vested interests have long fought newcomers on policy issues, the greater role of money in politics seems to have helped tilt policy in the wrong direction in recent years.

Historically, nations differed in their willingness to provide workers with incentives to acquire technical knowledge and to thus gain some degree of economic power. These variations allowed some nations to benefit from new technology and grow rich while others benefited much less. The current economic stagnation calls for policies that will develop broad-based technical skills. The prosperity of nations depends on the institutions and policies that allow ordinary citizens to acquire technical knowledge, much of it learned on the job.

# PART I

## TECHNOLOGY

WHAT DETERMINES WHETHER AND HOW TECHNOLOGY will benefit large numbers of ordinary people? Social institutions and investments influence the pace of technological change, but they alone are not sufficient for understanding the effects of technology on wages and wealth. Chapters 1 through 4 present a view of technology as knowledge, arguing that the dynamics of knowledge are key to understanding the interaction between technology and society. Many people need to acquire technical knowledge in order to implement major new technologies. Developing new technical knowledge on a large scale is often a difficult social problem. The way societies solve this problem changes over time, and these changes shape how technology is adopted, how fast that change takes place, how new wealth is generated, and how that wealth is shared.

## CHAPTER 1

# More Than Inventions

IN THE EARLY 1840S, LUCY LARCOM BLOSSOMED as a poet. She took courses in German and botany; attended lectures by such leading thinkers as John Quincy Adams, Edward Everett, John Pierpont, and Ralph Waldo Emerson; and avidly read books from the circulating library on a variety of subjects. Still, it was as a poet—reading, writing, and discussing—that she excelled. She published dozens of poems in the *Lowell Offering*, one of several girls' literary magazines. Some of them were reprinted in national periodicals and in collections edited by Henry Wadsworth Longfellow and other leading American poets. She attracted the attention and support of John Greenleaf Whittier, who became her mentor and friend. These years launched her career as a writer and teacher.

Lucy Larcom was not a college student. She was a factory worker in Lowell, Massachusetts, the home of some of the first integrated textile mills in the United States. The Merrimack River Valley, where Lowell is located, was a center of the U.S. Industrial Revolution, a nineteenth-century Silicon Valley.

Most mill girls came from farming families from across northern New England, and they stayed in boardinghouses in Lowell during their time in the mills, which often lasted only a year or so. Lucy's family was different in that they lived in Lowell. Lucy was born in nearby Beverly, Massachusetts, the daughter of a sea captain and one of nine siblings. Her father died when Lucy was eight, and her mother moved the family to Lowell to run one of those boardinghouses. At eleven, Lucy left school and went to work in a mill to help out her family.

But she did not want to abandon her education. She resolved to "learn all I could, so that I should be fit to teach or to write, as the way opened. And it turned out that fifteen or twenty of my best years were given to teaching."[1] She taught in Illinois and at Wheaton Seminary in Massachusetts, now known as Wheaton College, where a dormitory is named after her.

Yet, although Lucy was an outstanding poet and writer, her efforts to learn were not exceptional. As she wrote in 1889,

> For twenty years or so, Lowell might have been looked upon as a rather select industrial school for young people. The girls there were just such girls as are knocking at the doors of young women's colleges to-day. They had come to work with their hands, but they could not hinder the working of their minds also. Their mental activity was overflowing at every possible outlet. . . . They were improving themselves and preparing for their future in every possible way, by purchasing and reading standard books, by attending lectures, and evening classes of their own getting up, and by meeting each other for reading and conversation.

This was not an accident. The mill owners had expressly designed the city of Lowell to be the kind of place where, in the words of one investor, "the daughters of respectable farmers were readily induced to come into these mills for a temporary period" through the lure of a rich educational, cultural, and religious environment.[2]

In 1816, Francis Cabot Lowell established a very successful cotton mill in Waltham, Massachusetts, using Yankee farm girls to operate power looms, an invention he had copied from British models. Following his death the next year, his investors sought to build a new city, named in Lowell's honor, on the site of a small farm village that had an excellent source of water power to run new mills. But the mill owners built more than factories. They also built boardinghouses for the mill girls, to be run by moral women. They made sure that every major Protestant denomination had provisions for worship. And they encouraged and supported a variety of other institutions, including twenty-three schools, the Lowell Institute, a Lyceum for lectures, a circulating library, a savings bank, and a hospital.

The owners did all this because they wanted intelligent and morally disciplined workers to run the looms. The girls they hired were not poor women desperate for work; they were the daughters of "respectable" farmers, most of whom had modest wealth or better.[3] Although Irish immigrants built the mills and canals and Irish women did domestic service in Lowell's better-off homes, the girls hired to work the looms during the 1820s and 1830s were almost exclusively of Yankee origin. They were almost all literate, at least to the level of being able to sign their names.

The mill owners' motives were not purely philanthropic. They needed bright, able workers who could learn how to use this strange new technology efficiently. Mills in other towns had failed because they had not recruited enough high-quality hands. By the 1840s, the weavers in Lowell's mills were more productive than those in English mills, which hired relatively fewer literate workers, or those in American mills that did not use such a select labor supply.[4] It would appear that the skills, knowledge, and intelligence of ordinary production workers were critical to the adoption of this new technology.

## Implementation

The behavior of the mill owners seems surprising, but it should not be unfamiliar. For similar reasons today, Google offers employees gourmet meals, on-site medical care, and a whole variety of amenities in order to attract talented people and keep them intellectually engaged. Yet the mill owners' behavior seems surprising because we often forget how difficult it was to implement technologies in the past; we forget that implementation required new skills and knowledge that took time to develop and time to learn, even for mechanical inventions. We tend to focus instead on the original act of invention.

The distinction between invention and implementation is critical and too often ignored. The key invention central to the dramatic rise of textile mills in Lowell and other towns was the power loom, a machine that partially automated the work of weaving, greatly reducing the labor required to produce a yard of cloth. The first commercially successful power looms were operated in the United Kingdom. American inventors began developing power looms around 1810, influenced by British designs. The design that eventually dominated the U.S. textile industry was developed by William Gilmour, an immigrant mechanic who had experience with textile equipment in Scotland. After Gilmour built his first loom in 1817 for Judge Daniel Lyman in Rhode Island, he shared his drawings with other mechanics, and this design was quickly adopted throughout New England.

But the widespread replication of this invention was hardly sufficient to guarantee its efficient use. Economic historian Robert Zevin notes that for at least two decades there was a shortage of people who could build, install, operate, and maintain the new machinery.[5] As late as 1845, machine shops building textile equipment suffered delays due to shortages of skilled mechanics. Because machine shops making looms and other textile equipment possessed mechanics with specialized knowledge, they were able to earn high profit margins for twenty years. The textile mills earned even higher profits. They too often could not find enough workers who knew how to use the technology efficiently, organize a factory, and train a workforce. Zevin found that mills that lacked a close relationship with a machine shop typically failed. Much of the knowledge needed by mechanics and overseers and loom fixers and weavers was highly mundane, yet for two or three decades, the difficulty of acquiring it limited the ability to operate the new technology on a sufficient scale to meet demand. Given these difficulties, it should be no surprise that the mills went to extraordinary lengths to attract and keep workers who could learn the needed skills. And the most talented mechanics and managers, called mill agents, sometimes received equity in the new companies, as is common practice among tech firms today.

Effective use of the power loom was delayed because the whole of the technology involved much more than just the original invention of the power loom. Implementation on a large scale involved several developments. First, large numbers of people in various occupations had to acquire new, specialized knowledge, skills, and know-how in order to use the technology effectively. Second, the technology itself often needed to be adapted and improved for different applications. These improvements included many secondary inventions, many of these invented by mechanics who learned of new needs and possibilities from practical experience. Third, businesses had to figure out how to best use the new technology, whom to hire, what division of labor to employ, how to organize the workplace, and how to market. Finally, because so many different people in diverse occupations needed to learn new skills and knowledge, implementation required new training institutions and new labor markets that provided incentives to learn these new, specialized capabilities.

All of this took time, yet it was quite important. The invention of the power loom was vital, but so, too, was the implementation. Indeed, the implementation was responsible for most of the economic benefit. Weavers on the first power looms could produce 2.5 times as much coarse cloth per hour as a weaver on a handloom. But over the next eighty years, improvements in the looms and in the knowledge and skills of workers generated a further *twenty-fold* increase in output per hour.

Economic historians have long understood that *most* of the economic benefit from many major new technologies does not come from the initial commercialization of the original invention but from the eventual implementation.[6] New knowledge and a long string of improvements follow for decades after the invention, continually altering the technology and the skills needed. In petroleum refining, over a forty-year period, the cost savings achieved during implementation were three times the cost saving realized on the initial installation of new technologies.[7] Improved efficiency during implementation was responsible for an eightfold increase in the amount of electric power generated per ton of coal from 1900 to 1960. If these examples are typical, then 75 to 95 percent of the productivity gains from many major new technologies were realized only after decades of improvements in the implementation. Incremental improvements and new knowledge also brought major productivity gains in metal cutting, railroad transportation, the steam engine, and the production of rayon. Even the Industrial Revolution itself, despite introducing many important innovations, showed surprisingly low productivity growth for many decades, prompting some economic historians to question whether this period should be termed a "revolution" at all.

None of these gains would have been possible without the initial inventions, but implementation was clearly important, too. Moreover, implementation is slow and difficult for reasons I elaborate over the next several chapters: much new knowledge must be acquired through experimentation or learning by doing (Chapter 2); implementation often involves a long feedback loop where each incremental improvement in the technology requires new skills, which then make further improvements feasible (Chapter 3); and the large-scale acquisition of new skills often requires new training institutions, new standards, and new labor markets (Chapter 4).

## Four Distinctions

Much thinking, both popular and scholarly, tends to ignore or downplay the significance and difficulty of implementation, making it hard to grasp how technology is affecting society today. Since implementation is the focus of this book, it is helpful to begin by outlining how consideration of implementation changes things. Four conceptual distinctions are key.

### Technology vs. Original Inventions

While scholars realize that implementing a technology involves much more than invention, others are in the grip of the popular heroic view of technology. Museums and textbooks too often highlight a misleading history of Great Inventors who brought wondrous inventions and wealth to the ignorant masses. According to this narrative, the inventions were "designed by geniuses to be run by idiots."[8] While the Great Inventors did make important contributions, it took much more than idiots to realize the benefits, including the development of skills and knowledge by large numbers of ordinary working people.

Technology is more than just inventions because implementation involves a lot of mundane technical knowledge and specialized skills, often among diverse people. Some of this knowledge is based on science; for example, semiconductors are based on quantum physics. Engineering knowledge may be required to design a large, efficient chemical plant. The design of an invention itself represents an idea, another kind of knowledge. But not all technical knowledge is so special. Joel Mokyr categorizes useful knowledge into two general types: knowledge of "what," which is descriptive knowledge of natural phenomena and regularities; and knowledge of "how," practical knowledge of techniques.[9] The latter can be very detailed and technology-specific. Much of it is also tacit—that is, not written but learned through experience or by watching others.

Some new inventions really are deployed quickly and easily, but that is not how things seem to work with many of them. Economic historians have highlighted the central role that skilled workers played during the Industrial Revolution.[10] According to Mokyr, they were

> an army of mostly anonymous artisans and mechanics, the unsung foot soldiers of the Industrial Revolution whose names do not normally appear in biographical dictionaries but who supplied that indispensable workmanship on which technological progress depended. These were craftsmen blessed by a natural dexterity, who possessed a technical *savoir-faire* taught in no school, but whose experience, skills, and practical knowledge of energy and materials constituted the difference between an idea and a product. They were mechanics, highly skilled clock and instrument makers, metalworkers, woodworkers, toymakers, glasscutters, and similar specialists, who could accurately produce parts of the precisely correct dimensions and materials, who could read blueprints and compute velocities, and who understood tolerance, resistance, friction, lubrication, and the interdependence of mechanical parts. These were the applied chemists who could manipulate laboratory equipment and acids, the doctors whose advice sometimes saved lives even if nobody yet quite understood why, the expert farmers who experimented with new breeds of animals, fertilizers, drainage systems, and fodder crops.[11]

Joel Mokyr and Ralf Meisenzahl attribute Britain's early lead during the Industrial Revolution to these craftsmen and mechanics rather than to her inventors per se.[12] A common observation during the early years of the Industrial Revolution was that the best technology was "invented in France and worked out in England."[13]

This distinction is important because technologies can take a very long time to perfect. Also, it implies a different view of the role of technology in history. In the Great Inventor account, the Great Invention has an immediate and revolutionary impact on society. A technology, as opposed to a mere invention, can also have a revolutionary impact, but often only after a long period of development—revolutions that are decades in the making.

The heroic view of technology is itself a product of the Industrial Revolution, and perhaps the origins of this view explain why it is so persistent. Before the nineteenth century, inventors were not often cast as heroes. Typically, inventions were seen as the work of the Divine Hand. Inventors merely uncovered ideas that had been left for them to uncover. For example, the invention of the printing press was seen as part of God's preparation for the Reformation.[14]

James Watt, who invented an improvement in the steam engine, was the first Great Inventor in the modern heroic mold. Historian Christine MacLeod documents how Watt's friends, relatives, assorted political allies, and, importantly, textile manufacturers conducted a public relations campaign to have a large statue of Watt placed in Westminster Abbey.[15] In the process, they changed public perception of Watt and of the rising manufacturing economy. When the campaign reached full tilt, Watt's genius was allegedly responsible for winning battles in Europe, for raising Britain to international preeminence, for the prodigious advance of wealth and population under George III, and for a revolution in manufacturing and social conditions. Economic historians have a more modest assessment. After a careful quantitative analysis, Nicholas von Tunzelmann concludes that Watt's contribution moved the timing of the Industrial Revolution forward by about one month.[16]

The public relations campaign for the statue was undertaken in part to commemorate Watt's accomplishment, at some expense to other inventors, but also as propaganda. Textile manufacturers joined the effort to lobby for a legislative ban on machinery exports—the "exceptional" nature of Watt's contribution and its central importance to the British economy meant export of machinery might endanger the wealth of the nation, not to mention textile profits.

Ever since, the hyping of new technologies and their "genius inventors" has been a standard feature of technology-related lobbying as well as the marketing of new products from the Segway to the iPhone.[17] But while inventors are surely important, the heroic version of technology is highly misleading when it comes to understanding how technology actually develops. Steve Jobs himself considered it a "disease" to think that "a really great idea is 90 percent of the work."[18]

*Mass vs. Elite Knowledge*

The Great Inventors' view of technology implies that the really important technical knowledge is held by an elite circle of inventors, engineers, scientists, and possibly entrepreneurs. Although new technology might require ordinary workers to learn new skills and knowledge, this process is seen as being accomplished easily and quickly.

However, that was not the case with the power loom, which needed mechanics and managers with specialized, hard-to-acquire skills. Nor was it the case with many other technologies that required "clock and instrument makers, metalworkers, woodworkers, toymakers, glasscutters," and others. Nor was technical knowledge an issue only for managers, craftsmen, and mechanics. The skills of the "unskilled" weavers were not easy to acquire. Even William Gilmour, who built his loom and associated machines for Lyman, could not get them to run properly until a weaver showed him how. As Lyman's son recounted,

> Mr. Gilmour, a thorough machinist, was entirely unacquainted with the practical operation, and the company had no one, at first, to start the machinery; they began to grow discouraged. The warper worked badly, the dresser worse, and the loom would not run at all. In this dilemma an intelligent though intemperate Englishman, by trade a hand weaver, came to see the machinery. After observing the miserable operation, he said the fault was not in the machinery, and he thought he could make it work; he was employed. Discouragement ceased; it was an experiment no longer. Manufacturers from all directions came to see the wonder. To this day, the same loom, with trivial alterations, is in use in all our mills.[19]

Clearly, some significant knowledge was needed to run the power loom, and surely much more knowledge and skill was needed to run it efficiently. The inventor's knowledge alone was not enough.

Even when mills could hire experienced managers, mechanics, and craftsmen, they still could fail to use the technology efficiently unless ordinary workers were properly trained. By the early twentieth century, British textile equipment manufacturers were shipping power looms and other textile equipment around the globe. Mills in India, China, and elsewhere not only used the same equipment as British mills, but they were often run by experienced British managers aided by British master weavers and spinners and engineers. Nevertheless, their output per worker was far less than that of the English or American mills because their workers—using the exact same machines—lacked the same knowledge and skills. Western weavers were 6.5 times more productive.[20] The English and American cotton textile industries held a sustained economic advantage for decades, despite paying much higher wages. Eventually, of course, other nations developed the knowledge and the institutions to train weavers—first Japan and more recently China.

It takes a long time for technical knowledge to be developed, longer for it to spread, and even longer for institutions to emerge, such as new labor markets, that allow ordinary workers to benefit from their new knowledge. Such learning on a mass scale was and is a difficult problem for society.

Perhaps because it is difficult to acquire, technical knowledge is central to the economic well-being of large numbers of people. Such specialized knowledge allows workers to demand high wages in the labor market, providing the means for large numbers of workers to share in the benefits of new technology. In Part II (Chapters 5 through 7), I explore the link between technical knowledge and the wages of ordinary workers, how this link explains the long wait before weavers' pay rose during the nineteenth century, and why wages are stagnant today.

### Knowledge vs. Ideas

Scholars recognize the importance of implementation and commercialization at one level. Yet much of the economic theory of innovation—the theory used to formulate innovation policy—is oddly one-sided, abstracting away from realistic considerations of technology implementation. Innovation theory focuses on the need to provide incentives to inventors and to firms, but it largely ignores the incentives for ordinary workers to invest in learning new skills in order to implement major new technologies.[21] Both are important.

The central insight of mainstream innovation theory is familiar: under some conditions, competitive markets provide too little incentive for inventors and firms to invest in research and development (R&D) compared to the level of investment that would be best for society. The standard argument warns that firms will invest too little if the ideas behind inventions can be replicated at low cost.[22] If rivals can reproduce an invention at low cost, they will enter the market, driving down prices and profits. Prospective inventors, anticipating little profit, will invest too little in R&D. This "market failure" can be remedied with policies that increase innovators' incentives: giving them subsidies and grants, awarding prizes for successful innovations, or granting patents so that they can earn above-normal profits by excluding rivals from the marketplace.[23]

This theory yields valuable insights, but it is incomplete because technical knowledge involves much more than just easily reproduced ideas.[24] If all technical knowledge could be replicated at low cost, then employees should be able to acquire their knowledge at low cost, too. But often that does not happen; the design of the power loom was easily replicated, the knowledge to implement it was not. For decades during the early Industrial Revolution, markets failed to deliver a sufficient supply of mechanics, mill managers, and weavers needed to make the replicated invention work.

That is, markets can also fail at developing new implementation knowledge. Frequently, during their early stages, major new technologies lack the institutions to train workers. Also, labor markets often fail to provide sufficient rewards initially. One common problem is a "coordination failure": early-stage technologies typically have many different versions. For example, early typewriters had different keyboard layouts. Workers choose a particular version to learn and firms invest in a particular version, but they need to coordinate their technology choices for markets to work well.[25] As we shall see in Chapter 4, this market coordination won't happen unless new technology standards are widely accepted, and sometimes that takes decades.

In other words, innovation can suffer from two distinct problems: markets can fail to provide strong incentives to invest in R&D, and they can fail to provide strong incentives for learning new skills. Underinvestment in R&D is not the only problem affecting innovation. It might not even be the most important problem. The early textile manufacturers had large profits and healthy incentives to invest in innovation; skills, however, were a problem. Many other technologies experienced similar circumstances during their early stages, from Bessemer steel production to wireless communications (see Chapter 11). There is simply no justification for focusing innovation policy exclusively on remedying underinvestment in R&D, especially since most firms report that patents, which are supposed to correct this underinvestment, are relatively unimportant for obtaining profits on their innovations.[26]

The policies needed to remedy labor market failures are quite different from those needed to encourage investment in R&D; these policies are also particularly relevant now. Part III of the book discusses some policies that can encourage broad-based learning of new technical skills, including vocational education, government procurement, employment law, trade secrecy, and patents.

### Dynamic vs. Static Technical Knowledge

The problems of labor markets were eventually resolved, sometimes after decades. Training institutions and labor markets do develop over time and when they do, the economics of technology changes. The concern about easy replication of ideas matters in the long run. A new encoding technique for wireless communications, for example, might be difficult to replicate when the technology is new and subject to great uncertainty, conflicting standards, limited formal training, and imperfect labor markets. But it might be easy to replicate when introduced into a well-established telecommunications industry employing trained and experienced engineers and technicians.

The insight here is that easily replicable technical knowledge is frequently the product of a long evolutionary process. Replicable knowledge doesn't just happen; it is made. Institutions, policies, and economic incentives combine in a dynamic process that changes the nature of technical knowledge, and in the process, whole industries may be overturned. This notion of dynamic change implies a sort of life cycle of technical knowledge that explains several patterns of innovation:

- Formal vocational education is difficult to conduct during the early stages of a technology, but easier later on, when knowledge becomes more standardized. Conversely, workers who are more adept at learning, perhaps because they have more general education, are more valuable early on. But as a technology matures, demand for workers with advanced general education often declines, while the supply of workers with vocational education rises.

- The difficulty of training workers using early-stage technologies often limits the scale of production. In this situation, large firms may have no great advantage over small firms. Later, when knowledge is standardized and large-scale production becomes feasible, new technologies can disrupt established technologies. Also, large firms can have a marked advantage over small producers because they own substantial complementary assets. This helps explain the observed association between small firms and new technologies.

- During the early stages, when formalized instruction is limited, person-to-person exchange is especially important for spreading knowledge. Also, because relatively few people acquire knowledge of the new technology initially, innovators can often safely share their knowledge even with rivals, giving rise to open styles of innovation. As technology matures and more people are able to copy new developments, innovators have stronger reasons to guard their knowledge.

- Early-stage technologies often tend to be highly localized. Because person-to-person knowledge exchange is so important early on, often involving hands-on demonstration of experimental techniques, early developments progress better in "technology clusters" like Silicon Valley. Much of Silicon Valley's growth can be traced to job-hopping of technical personnel. More mature, standardized technologies, on the other hand, are more readily transferred elsewhere because formalized instruction makes remote knowledge acquisition more feasible. Thus offshoring tends to involve mature technologies.

- Robust labor markets for workers with technology-specific skills depend on the standardization of those skills. Workers benefit when the knowledge they learn on the job is valuable to employers other than their own. That requires that other employers use essentially the same technology; that is, the technology is standardized.

This connection, it turns out, was a critical requirement that had to be met before workers in the Industrial Revolution could benefit from their knowledge.

Chapter 4 explores this life cycle and also relates it to other life cycle notions in the literature. This life cycle is important because it affects policy. As the economics of technical knowledge changes over time, so too does the optimal policy. Too often technology policy is assumed to be static, one policy to fit all situations. Instead, policies need to adapt to the maturity of the technology or to at least achieve some balance between start-up and mature technologies. As we shall see, this is often difficult. Laws and regulations that might work well, say, for the mature chemical industry do not necessarily work well for software start-ups. Moreover, balanced policy can be difficult because of political economic concerns. Mature technologies are often associated with well-established firms and occupational groups threatened by new disruptive technologies. Start-up technologies often have little political clout by comparison, making balance challenging to achieve.

A rich picture of technological development emerges when we consider the major role of the knowledge needed to implement technology. Inventions don't determine the fate of society on their own. Instead, the implementation of major new technologies depends on the willingness of large numbers of ordinary workers to acquire new skills and knowledge over an extended period of time. Social institutions and policies affect how this learning plays out, how well a nation adopts new technologies, and how much those ordinary workers share in the economic benefits. To understand this dynamic, we must first understand why implementation is so often difficult.

## CHAPTER 2

# The Skills of the Unskilled

TECHNOLOGY IMPLEMENTATION IS CHALLENGING because large numbers of workers need to acquire new skills and technical knowledge. I argue that this was true in the past and that it is also true today. However, the view that ordinary industrial workers had critical skills surely conflicts with the view of many historians, who presume just the opposite: that American textile mills created a new class of *unskilled* workers. For example, in his book *The Work Ethic in Industrial America*, Daniel T. Rodgers asserts that the technological breakthroughs of the Industrial Revolution replaced skilled work with unskilled: "The cotton mills, with their banks of semiautomatic looms and spinning frames and their simple machine-tending tasks, stripped so far of skill and judgment that raw recruits and children could do them, had set a pattern for factory work at the outset of the industrial transformation."

Economists also often presume that technology was "de-skilling" during the nineteenth century, as exemplified by the transition from the artisan workshop to the factory. In Europe, craftsmen had worked in guilds since medieval times. These guilds provided training through apprenticeship programs, and they controlled entry into the trade and other aspects of marketing and production. In the de-skilling narrative, technology allowed unskilled factory workers to replace skilled artisans. This narrative is a bit misleading for two reasons: first, the guild system and traditional artisan apprenticeships were in decline well before the advent of large-scale mechanization. Prior to mechanization, the artisan workshop had been substantially replaced by nonmechanized "manufactories" where workers, many with little or no apprenticeship training, performed narrow tasks.[1] Second, most early factories in the United States produced goods that had formerly been made at home, not in workshops.[2] That is, the factory did not so much replace the artisan workshop as it replaced household work, at least for many decades. For example, the number of weavers working in small workshops in the United States continued to grow through 1880 while the amount of household weaving sharply declined.[3]

Although the artisan workshop seems to inform common notions of skill in manufacturing, the word "skill" has several shades of meaning. The journeymen and masters of the guilds differed from factory workers in many ways aside from their productive abilities. We are concerned here with the notion of skill as the capabilities of a worker that help generate wealth, especially from new technologies. But there are other notions, and it is necessary to distinguish them.

For one, journeymen and masters occupied distinct middle rungs in the social hierarchy; factory workers did not. "Skill" sometimes connotes social class. Nineteenth-century observers tended to assume that factory workers had low skills and intelligence. For example, Charles Dickens, always sensitive to social distinctions, visited Lowell in 1842 and reported several "surprising facts" back to his English readers: the factory girls played pianos, they nearly all used circulating libraries, and they published quality periodicals.[4] He expected his readers to find these facts surprising because such activities were considered "above the station" of factory workers.

Also, the work of craftsmen may have been more fulfilling than work in the factories. Factories often had a finer division of labor than workshops: workers performed a narrower set of tasks and had far less autonomy. Karl Marx argued that the new technologies separated the act of thinking from that of manual labor, as did nineteenth-century social critics John Ruskin, Thomas Carlyle, and William Morris; technology was "turning . . . almost all handicraftsmen into machines."[5] More recent social critics, such as Harry Braverman and Stephen Marglin, highlight the loss of control of factory workers, leading to worker "alienation."[6] These are valid concerns, but they do little to inform us about the knowledge and skill factory workers needed to perform their jobs. A narrower set of tasks does not necessarily imply less productive ability.

Finally, artisans learned their skills formally as apprentices. Apprenticeship provided a form of certification, while skills learned in factories were not typically credentialed. Factory workers received only brief periods of formal training, if any: for weavers in cotton mills, training typically lasted only two or three weeks. Apprenticeships typically lasted five or seven years.[7] On the other hand, factory workers learned in informal ways. This learning would last longer than their brief formal training periods and it could involve costly expenditures. Thus, even though factory skills may not have been formally taught, it does not mean that factory workers acquired no skill. To understand the relationship between technology and skill, we need to think about more than just formal, certifiable skill acquisition.

Economists' common practice of defining "skilled workers" as those with four years of college is particularly misleading. In our meritocratic society it is perhaps too easy to associate skill with educational credentials. The skill needed to work with a new technology often has little to do with the knowledge acquired in college, and attitudes about less educated workers might reflect prejudices similar to the ones Dickens saw among his readers. This view is clearly anachronistic when we try to understand the skills involved in the Industrial Revolution.

## Learning by Doing

How, then, can we tell if factory workers learned substantial skills informally on the job? One way is to look at the average hourly output—the productivity—of workers as they gained experience.

Figure 2.1 shows the learning curve for a group of weavers hired at a cotton mill of the Lawrence Company in Lowell during the 1840s and early 1850s. It shows the average number of yards of cloth that each weaver produced per hour (the vertical axis) against the number of months the weaver had been on the job. These weavers did not have significant previous

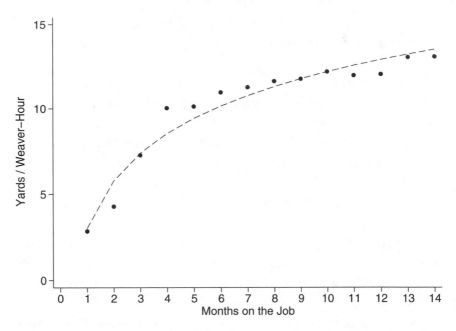

Figure 2.1. Learning curve of newly hired weavers at the Lawrence Co., 1842–1855. (Bessen, "Technology and Learning by Factory Workers.")

experience, and the first month shown is the month after they completed two to three weeks of training. We can see that the weavers rapidly improved during the first few months. After that they continued to learn, but at a slower rate.[8]

What accounts for this substantial increase in productivity? Part of the learning curve simply involved getting used to the noisy, complicated environment of a weave room with leather drive belts spinning and looms clacking away. Part of it was acquiring specific knowledge, such as how to tie a weaver's knot. Part involved practicing manual operations to find faster movements—for example, to quickly replace an empty shuttle. Other aspects included technical knowledge acquired through experimentation, such as learning how to adjust the tension on the warp so as to minimize broken threads; planning skills, such as coordinating work on multiple looms; and developing the ability to monitor the looms for minor errors and flaws. To the new hire, the job was daunting. One factory girl wrote this fictionalized account of a weaver's first day:

The next morning she went in the mill; and at first, the sight of so many bands, and wheels, and springs, in constant motion was very frightful. She felt afraid to touch the loom, and she was almost sure that she could never learn to weave; the harness puzzled and the reed perplexed her; the shuttle flew out, and made a new bump upon her head; and the first time she tried to spring the lathe, she broke out a quarter of the threads.[9]

But the story's heroine became more productive over time, as did, presumably, her creator. The weavers acquired specific knowledge about how to work with the looms; much of it was tacit knowledge, learned through experience or by imitating others.

The learning curves show that weavers acquired skills on the job. But how significant were these skills compared to, say, those of craftsmen? It might seem impossible to measure skill, but economists have a neat trick to do so: they measure the *investment* made in acquiring the skill. Assuming that markets properly compensate workers and employers for the investments they make in learning, greater investments correspond to greater returns and greater economic value of the skill.

And learning curves imply an investment. Look first at the weavers' pay. They were paid on piece rate, meaning they received a fixed amount for every standard-sized piece of cloth they produced. The workers' monthly pay was thus proportional to the number of yards shown in Figure 2.1, assuming they worked the same number of hours per month. During the early months, they would have earned very low wages, far less than what they could have earned doing alternative work, such as teaching school or making straw hats at home.[10] These newly hired weavers faced an "opportunity cost." They were willing to accept temporarily lower wages on the prospect that they could earn higher wages later on, after they had acquired sufficient skill to be more productive. The opportunity cost can be thought of as an implicit investment. Economists call it the weaver's investment in "human capital." The extra wages the weaver could earn later on—that is, the amount by which her wages exceeded the wage in alternative work—can be thought of as the return on human capital.

The mill also experienced an opportunity cost during the early months. A portion of the mill's capital was tied up in equipment dedicated to the newly hired weaver. During the early months, that capital earned less profit than the standard rate of return from other investments. This opportunity cost represents the mill's investment in the weaver's human capital, made on the prospect that after the worker was trained, the mill could earn an above-average return on its capital.

Other learning was going on as well. Figure 2.1 shows data for a group of weavers who worked just over a year. But most hires did not last that long: during the 1840s and 1850s, only about a quarter of new weavers stayed at the mill for six months or longer. Many left because they learned that they did not like factory work or could not earn enough from it. Others were let go because the overseers decided they lacked aptitude for weaving. In both of these cases, implicit investments in skill acquisition went unrewarded. Nevertheless, here, too, was an investment in learning.

Thus both the weavers and the mills made implicit investments in weavers' acquisition of skill and knowledge. The magnitudes of these investments can be calculated from the payroll ledgers of the Lawrence Company mill. My best estimate for the total investment made for each fully trained weaver during the 1840s and 1850s is about $162, which was roughly equal to one weaver's annual pay.[11] Moreover, as I will explore later, the human capital investments in weavers actually increased over the nineteenth century as more and more of the weavers' tasks were automated.

These investments are comparable to the human capital investment made by craft apprentices in the United States at about the same time. Apprentice carpenters required an investment of about $165; masons, about $253.[12] This finding is especially striking when you consider that the weavers were largely young women whose alternative employment opportunities, compared to those of the young men who became carpenters and masons, were limited and low-paying.

The mill owners were, of course, aware of the greater value of experienced weavers, and they took steps to keep them employed. One mill manager wrote in 1859 that if the mill could induce the weavers to stay for eighteen months, even though their contracts were only for a year, "They will be worth more to us the last six months than they are the first twelve."[13] It does appear that ordinary factory production workers such as weavers had substantial skills, contrary to the conventional wisdom.

The myth of de-skilling is no more accurate in other industries. While skill requirements fell in some jobs in some industries when new technologies were introduced, other jobs required greater skill. Indeed, it is hard to find a clear example where a new technology was uniformly de-skilling during the nineteenth century. Some technologies generated whole new skilled occupations. New machines such as the "self-acting mule," an automated spinning machine, begot the occupation of the "semiskilled minder" who tended these machines, and the Linotype machine begot the skilled typesetter. Similarly, semiautomatic bottle-making machines required workers with new skills. In the rubber tire industry, mechanization mainly reduced the numbers of unskilled workers who conveyed materials within the plant, but had little effect on skilled workers. In canning, mechanization allowed skilled cookers in canneries to be replaced by less skilled workers, but many unskilled jobs were also mechanized. The introduction of steam power to merchant shipping reduced the demand for able-bodied seamen but increased demand for skilled engineers, carpenters, and mates. Electrification increased the demand for clerical, numerical, planning, and people skills but reduced demand for dexterity-intensive jobs. And although a number of historians have described the introduction of interchangeable parts as a means of replacing skilled machinists with unskilled operatives, the technique depended very much on the skills of "artificers" who adjusted the parts to make them fit, and these skills took considerable time and effort to develop.[14]

In many manufacturing industries, the ranks of skilled artisans working in small workshops were thinned considerably over the nineteenth century. But this trend was not entirely the direct effect of technology. It actually began before extensive mechanization: artisan workshops were replaced by "manufactories" where a finer division of labor only required workers who performed more specialized tasks.[15] Adam Smith's famous pin factory was one such workshop. The bottom line is that technology in the nineteenth century did not eliminate the need for skill. It just created new, specialized skills that were mostly learned on the factory floor.

## The Broad Reach of Technology-Specific
## Skills and Knowledge

Is this still true? Today's workers have more education, and today's technologies are more sophisticated. Perhaps learning on the job is no longer so important.

That is not my experience. The biggest shock I had in starting a software company was just how important informal learning is. The difficulty of developing new knowledge among our employees and among our customers is what prompted me later to embark on research into learning on the job.

In 1983, I wrote what turned out to be the first WYSIWYG (what-you-see-is-what-you-get) desktop publishing program and put it into production at a weekly English/Spanish newspaper in Philadelphia. The paper was serving a growing Latino population, and in addition to being a freelance computer programmer I had a day job as the paper's business manager. The ads typically came in at the last minute, right before deadline, and were difficult to compose, especially on the simple equipment we could afford. I realized that I could write a program on one of the newly available personal computers that would let us compose the text on a computer screen and output it to our phototypesetter in one piece. This process would save time and, I thought, it might also be something we could sell or offer as a service to customers of typesetting.

The program ran on the first IBM-PC, with a luxurious 64K of RAM and a special graphics card. I tried, unsuccessfully, to sell the program to a typesetter manufacturer. Failing that, I was left with plan B: I set up a company to sell the program directly to small newspapers, magazines, catalog publishers, printers, job typesetters, and others. We packaged up the disks, wrote a manual, and started shipping product, expecting to move quickly to a new, improved version with added features not included in the first release.

Then the phone started ringing with support calls. Most of our customers had never used a computer before. We had to train them. Customers also had to learn our program and, more important, adapt it to their particular work needs. Often, we had very little knowledge of how our customers wanted to put our product to use. We began providing them tools to tailor the product, and we made changes to accommodate their needs. For example, one customer found he could produce high-quality typeset business forms with our software. This application was a well-paying niche market. He could simply draw the forms on the PC and then let his low-end typesetter print them out, even if it took all night to run. But he discovered that the photo paper in the typesetting machine sometimes slipped, ruining the output. He needed a specialized feature, which we created for him, that exposed the photo paper in a single pass so that it would not slip.

Adapting to the new technology often involved difficult organizational changes for our customers. Desktop publishing gave designers and editors greater control over a page's appearance. They did not need to wait for page proofs to approve layouts, and extensive re-keyboarding of text was eliminated. This meant that customers often had to develop new ways of working, changing job titles and workflows, and to learn new organizational systems in order to exploit the technology most efficiently. For example, when the Sears catalogs went into production with our products, job responsibilities changed radically and many jobs were eliminated. Before, outside layout artists faxed proofs to employees, who took them to the in-house art directors to mark up changes and then faxed them back; after, the layout was done in-house and art directors could make changes themselves interactively on their computers. Art directors and layout artists had to learn new skills and new ways of working together. All of these different kinds of learning meant that our company and our customers both made substantial human capital investments—often much greater than the cost of the technology itself—in order to use the software productively.

Most of the knowledge we gained was specific to the technology, the applications, and the organizations involved. Little of it could be obtained in classrooms; it had to be learned on the job. Customers could take courses to learn basic computer skills, and many did. We organized classes to teach the basics of our program, but customers had to learn on their own how to adapt it to their highly customized applications, and we had to learn something about these applications to understand how to improve our software. Because the new technology often facilitated organizational change, users also had to develop and learn new organizational rules. So, although our customers had much more education than nineteenth-century factory workers,

their effective use of the new technology still required a substantial investment in human capital on the job.

This was starkly different from the picture of innovation I had learned
in the economics classroom. In that stylized depiction, inventors come up
with ideas for inventions and these ideas are highly valuable by themselves.
The difficult and time-consuming development of new skills and knowledge I found critically necessary seldom gets mentioned.

Of course, anyone who has lived through the installation of a major new
computer system at work has some inkling of the significance of on-the-
job learning, perhaps a very serious inkling. Almost always, these systems
have long, slow, sometimes painful learning curves. For example, an economic analysis of the transition from mainframes to client/server computer
systems in the 1980s and 1990s found that adopters of this new technology made very substantial investments as they learned, adapted, and reor-
ganized their work.[16]

Moreover, the new organizational structures made necessary by new technologies often require substantial learning on the job. Economists have found
that computer use is associated with a variety of changes in workplace organization. Organizations decentralize; they move to team-based work, with
new incentives, occupations, and task assignments; workforce training is
increased; and computers often come with new products, services, and
customer-supplier relationships.[17] Many of these changes require learning
by employees or sharing of knowledge about production or about the needs
of customers and suppliers.

Where workers cannot acquire new skills to take advantage of these new
ways of working, information technology can fail. In the late 1990s, Erik
Brynjolfsson and Lorin Hitt made a study of a medical products manufacturer that had installed a computer-integrated manufacturing system in response to customer requests for greater customization. The manufacturing
company also tried to implement new workplace practices. But many workers, especially older ones working on the production line, had difficulty learning their new roles and the new rules of operation. This forced the company
to begin anew with young workers who were unencumbered by knowledge
of the old practices. Only then did it succeed. The authors concluded, "While
other firms could readily buy similar computer-controlled equipment, they

would still have to make the much larger investments in organizational learning before fully benefiting from [their investments] and the exact recipe for achieving these benefits was not trivial to invent."[18]

New capabilities often require new ways to understand customer needs and new ways to use technology to meet those needs. This can involve substantial learning. One study found that each dollar invested in computer hardware was associated with $10 of additional investment in organizational or human capital.[19] Moreover, the nineteenth-century pattern of mixed de-skilling and up-skilling is repeated with computer technology. Computers eliminate routine tasks, such as those performed by many clerks or by people re-keyboarding text, but they increase nonroutine tasks such as customer service, computer programming, and product design.[20]

Nor is such learning restricted to information technology. Workers using a wide variety of different technologies show learning curves much like those of the cotton weavers. These learning curves have been plotted for heart surgeons, insurance salesmen, steelworkers, and assembly-line workers. Atul Gawande writes eloquently of the challenges surgeons face in becoming qualified to deliver quality care. Learning by doing is key: "Surgeons, as a group, adhere to a curious egalitarianism. They believe in practice, not talent. People often assume that you have to have great hands to become a surgeon, but it's not true. . . . Skill, surgeons believe, can be taught; tenacity cannot."[21]

Learning through experimentation is also an essential part of science, and highly educated scientists acquire critical knowledge through experience. A series of studies have examined the role "star scientists" play when universities license their technologies to commercial ventures. In semiconductors, biotech, and other fields, the ongoing personal participation of these scientists is crucial for a start-up's success, presumably because these scientists have acquired valuable knowledge through experience.[22]

Learning curves have also been found for thousands of new manufacturing plants. In these cases, the curves plot the output per worker of the entire plant instead of individual worker productivity. Plants employing new technologies have often seen output per worker double or more than triple in a matter of months.[23] Plant learning curves came to the attention of management consultants during the 1960s and 1970s; they promoted strategies in which firms used the learning curve with new plants to achieve lower costs and to dominate a market.[24]

Of course, when a plant begins production, individual learning is not the only factor affecting productivity. For instance, plants might make additional capital investments as they ramp up. But much of the aggregate increase in output per worker in the plant appears to come from learning by individual workers. Plant learning curves are, in fact, associated with wages that increase with experience. That is, as the plant becomes more productive, workers' pay goes up.[25] As workers become more productive through learning on the job, employers are willing to pay them more to keep them from leaving.[26] The very common pattern of wages rising with experience suggests the prevalence of human capital acquired on the job.

Learning curves have even been measured in agriculture. During the Green Revolution in the 1960s, farmers in rural India became more productive in the use of the new seed varieties with experience.[27] A number of studies in developing nations have also found learning to be critical to technology adoption.[28]

More generally, economists have found that human capital is responsible for a great deal of the variation in wages from one person to the next.[29] As much as 77 percent of the variation in wages is "explained" by differences in workers' experience and individual characteristics, including innate abilities and schooling.[30] But only a small part of the variation in workers' human capital comes from differences in formal education. Differences that occur before school, such as birth weight and family traits, might account for some of the variation in human capital. But the research also suggests that much human capital is acquired on the job.

In summary, a wide variety of evidence suggests that learning by doing plays a large role in today's economy. It is often critical for the successful application of new technologies, and it is responsible for a substantial portion of the higher wages paid to people who work with these technologies.

## Turning the Tide

Technology-specific learning played a powerful role in the American victory in World War II. Two months after the Japanese attack on Pearl Harbor, President Franklin Roosevelt issued a directive vital to the war effort: he called for the construction of 24 million tons of merchant shipping capacity. These ships were critical to worldwide military operations and also provided an economic lifeline to Britain. But they were often vulnerable to German submarine warfare. According to a 1951 history of the wartime merchant marine effort,

> When Hitler met with his admirals in September of 1942 to survey the submarine war, he confidently asserted that American shipyards could not build ships faster than they were being sunk. The Presidential directive of 24 million tons for 1942 and 1943 was dismissed as mere propaganda. In fact the race between construction and sinkings in 1942 was nip and tuck, but the submarines were defeated whereas the shipbuilders achieved their goal. They not only fulfilled the Presidential directive of 24 million, they built 27 million tons in 1942 and 1943.[31]

The largest element of this building program, the construction of 2,708 Liberty cargo ships, each carrying 11,000 tons of cargo, employed mass production techniques on an unprecedented scale. The design of the ships was broken into roughly 100 components that were prefabricated and then assembled quickly on the shipway. Welding rather than riveting was used to save time. Few of the workers had any experience in shipbuilding, and of those who did, few had used these methods. War planners soon observed dramatic learning curves in ship production. Shipyards achieved up to a fourfold increase in output per worker over the course of the war, and the average assembly time per ship dropped from 186 days to as little as 19 days. While some of the increased output came from additional capital investment, much of it was the result of new knowledge and skills.[32] Some of it reflected the acquisition of new skills by individual workers, and some came from small innovations that were then shared. The standardization of the design meant that a jig designed by one worker to improve the cutting or shaping of a part could be used by other workers in the same shipyard or in other shipyards around the country.

If Hitler's estimate of American ship production had been right, Germany would likely have won the Battle of the Atlantic, Britain might have fallen, and the outcome of the war would have been very different. His assessment was not unreasonable, given standard shipyard productivity or the initial attempts to build Liberty ships. Learning by doing made all the difference.

Similarly, dramatic increases in output per worker were realized in other areas, such as aircraft production. Historians cite U.S. war production as a key advantage that led to victory. Clearly, much of the output of war production was only realized through the substantial acquisition of technology-specific skills learned through experience. Learning by doing amplified the U.S. advantage in natural resources.

Learning by doing has played an important role in history, it plays an important role in a large number of occupations, and it is an important determinant of wages. Learning by doing was important even for supposedly unskilled factory workers; their human capital investments were comparable to those made by skilled craftsmen.

But does this mean that learning by doing is implicated in the long delays associated with implementing major new technologies? Although the learning curves for the cotton weavers and for the Liberty shipbuilders were largely complete after only two years or so, there are two reasons why learning new skills was a major impediment nevertheless. First, as the technology kept changing, skills had to be relearned (as Chapter 3 explores). Second, what matters to a mill, to an industry, and to society generally is not how long it takes to train an individual worker, but what it takes to create a stable, trained labor force. Few workers stayed in the cotton mills for anywhere near two years during the 1830s; most workers left after a few months. Even though training times were short, labor turnover made it difficult to build an experienced labor force. A robust market for skilled weavers was needed to deliver that stable workforce and, as we shall see, this too took decades.

## CHAPTER 3

# Revolutions in Slow Motion

WE ARE SUCKERS FOR "REVOLUTIONARY breakthroughs."

Dean Kamen works forty miles up the Merrimack River from Lowell, in a converted textile mill in Manchester, New Hampshire. He has spent his adult life developing inventions. While still in college, in the 1970s, Kamen developed the first infusion pump that automatically delivered medications to diabetics. He also designed a portable dialysis machine and built a wheelchair that could function on steps and rough terrain.

By 2001, Kamen was already well established as an important inventor of medical devices. Then he had an invention of a different sort, a real breakthrough that could dramatically affect the lives of millions. In December 2001, after months of public speculation and rumors about a secret project code-named "Ginger," he introduced the Segway on *Good Morning America*. The Segway Human Transporter is a two-wheeled, self-balancing motorized scooter that carries an upright person at up to ten miles per hour on sidewalks and roads. A torrent of publicity followed the announcement. *Time* magazine described the invention as "reinventing the wheel," and technology pundits called it "as big a deal as the PC" and "maybe bigger than the Internet." Kamen claimed it would replace the automobile in cities, and Steve Jobs predicted that future cities would be "architected" around it.

Some of this publicity was merely the hype that accompanies many new tech products. We believe this sort of pitch because technology has dramatically transformed society in the past, so we get excited about new possible

37

transformations. That makes a compelling story for people who want to be in the vanguard of important changes. Hype aside, a focus on breakthrough ideas is misleading. No cities will be architected around two-wheel scooters any time soon. Perhaps the Segway will someday be widely adopted, but a decade after its introduction, it is more ridiculed than praised.

Yet, from a historical perspective, that derision is not entirely fair. During the 1890s, the automobile was widely ridiculed as a rich man's toy. Since then, cities as well as suburbs have indeed been architected around it. The automobile's revolutionary effect did not happen overnight, nor was it the result of a single "genius" idea that directly transformed society. Single technological ideas don't transform society; knowledge does. The automobile became revolutionary only after a large number of incremental innovations improved the technology and a large body of mundane, detailed knowledge developed among assembly workers, drivers, mechanics, road builders, and others. And this transformation took many decades.

Major new technologies typically go through long periods of sequential innovation, where a string of improvements, new knowledge, and new skills are developed one after the other. Central to this process—and for why it takes so long—is learning by doing. Engineers, mechanics, and ordinary technology users gain new knowledge and skills through experience.

## Decades for Overnight Success

Decade-long delays are not at all unusual. Technology after technology, many decades passed before an inventive idea was first commercialized, then it took even more decades before the product was commercially successful, and even more before major benefits flowed to workers and consumers. Many recent innovations in information technology were anticipated decades ago. Applications of artificial intelligence, first discussed during the 1950s, are coming to fruition now. The convergence of television (as we call it today) and two-way communication was first described as early as the 1870s in science fiction and popular literature. In 1878, *Punch's* Almanack published a cartoon showing a "telephonoscope," allegedly a

**Table 3.1** Time to Commercialization

| Invention | Year First Patentable | Years to First Commercialization | Years to "Shakeout" | Total Years |
|---|---|---|---|---|
| Ballpoint pen | 1938 | 7 | 28 | 35 |
| DDT | 1874 | 68 | 12 | 80 |
| Fluorescent lighting | 1859 | 74 | 2 | 76 |
| Freon refrigerant | 1931 | 2 | 36 | 38 |
| Gyrocompass | 1852 | 56 | 55 | 111 |
| Jet engine | 1791 | 153 | 17 | 170 |
| Magnetic recording | 1898 | 41 | 26 | 67 |
| Nylon and Perlon | 1930 | 9 | 34 | 43 |
| Penicillin | 1928 | 16 | 7 | 23 |
| Radar | 1904 | 31 | 17 | 48 |
| Radio | 1900 | 15 | 51 | 66 |
| Space rockets | 1925 | 19 | 23 | 42 |
| Streptomycin | 1921 | 23 | 23 | 46 |
| Television | 1905 | 35 | 33 | 68 |
| Transistor | 1948 | 7 | 13 | 20 |
| Xerography | 1937 | 13 | 25 | 38 |
| Zipper | 1891 | 32 | 63 | 95 |
| MEAN | | 35.4 | 27.4 | 62.7 |
| MEDIAN | | 23 | 25 | 48 |

*Sources*: Jewkes, Sawers, and Stillerman, *Sources of Invention*; Kitch, "Nature and Function of the Patent System"; Gort and Klepper, "Time Paths."

concept from Thomas Edison, for transmitting real-time visual images simultaneously with sound.[1] During the 1950s, AT&T began developing the Picturephone, which it introduced at the 1964 New York World's Fair. But the Picturephone was too clunky and expensive. More attempts were made with PCs during the 1980s and 1990s, but video chats and phone calls have only recently become widespread. Skype, Google Hangouts, and the Face-Time feature on the iPhone are the same idea as the Picturephone, with enhancements.

Table 3.1 summarizes the delays associated with some important inventions. Often the person who originally conceived a general invention idea is forgotten. But eventually, the idea is developed to the point that it can be patented, although inventors do not always do so. Then, typically after two or three more decades, the idea is commercialized for the first time. One study of forty-nine major inventions found that the average time from first patentability to first commercialization was twenty-nine years.[2] (Some examples are shown in the table.) But the first commercial application of an invention often fails, and even if it does succeed, it might represent only a marginal improvement over older technologies. Typically, other firms will enter the market, with innovations that improve on the original. This cycle of entry and improvement can also last decades. Eventually, the entry of new firms slows, as does the pace of new innovations. Firms begin exiting the industry or they merge. An industry "shakeout" occurs when many firms exit, leading to a mature phase of industry growth. Another study of forty-six major inventions (including many that were also in the earlier study) found that the average time from first commercialization to industry shakeout was about twenty-nine years.[3] Thus it is not at all unusual for five or six decades to elapse from the time an invention first meets the requirements needed to be patentable to the time the market is mature.

What took so long? In almost every case, innovators were involved in long trial-and-error experiments. Sometimes these were formal laboratory experiments and other times, informal learning by doing. In a few cases, such as the discovery of the antibiotic properties of penicillin, serendipity played a part, but even in that case, painstaking experimentation was needed to isolate the active ingredient from the mold and to figure out how to mass-produce the antibiotic. In other cases, commercialization had to wait for improvements in complementary technologies. The gyrocompass needed precision machining; the jet engine needed advanced metallurgy. These technologies went through their own long, slow learning process.

## Complexity

Why is so much trial-and-error learning needed? Because technologies are complex.[4] Typically, new technologies demand that a large number of variables be properly controlled. Henry Bessemer's simple principle of refining molten iron with a blast of oxygen works properly only at the right temperatures, in the right size vessel, with the right sort of vessel refractory lining, the right volume and temperature of air, and the right ores. Even very old and simple technologies, such as machines for spinning yarn out of cotton fiber, require the control of a large number of parameters. Yarn can break as it is wound onto the spindle of a spinning machine. The risk of breaks varies with temperature and humidity, which change throughout each day, the quality of the cotton inputs, the fineness of the yarn being spun, and the amount of twist put into the yarn. The tension on the yarn must be carefully regulated. Too little tension and the yarn will snarl; too much, and it will break. In the worst situations, hundreds of threads can break at once. These variables mean that for a spinner to operate new machinery efficiently, she needs significant skill and knowledge of a complex environment.

The source of this complexity seems basic to the human condition. It is often asserted that creativity uniquely distinguishes humans from other species. That is not quite right. While it is true, for example, that primitive humans came up with the idea of using stones as tools, monkeys and sea otters also use stones as hammers and for other uses. What really distinguished the early humans from other species was not conceiving technology ideas, but *perfecting* those ideas to deal with the complex natural environment. Humans, too, probably began using stones to hammer. But by the Neolithic period, they had developed scores of different stone tools—axes, adzes, chisels, arrowheads, burins, and other types—each optimized to solve a specific problem. Moreover, they made these tools using optimized production techniques—stone knapping techniques that archaeology graduate students have a hard time mastering after a semester of trial and error. This sophisticated specialization allowed early humans to make stone tools to handle a wide range of problems. Ultimately, it is the complexity of nature—or of what humans want from nature—that makes technology complex.

Complexity explains in the first instance why learning by doing takes time: complicated technologies involve many parameters that must be controlled. Finding efficient combinations of these parameters takes a lot of searching. As a consequence, knowledge of new technologies is often initially tentative and uncertain: Much of the knowledge is gained through experience and experiment and cannot be easily communicated; much of it may be tacit.

Thus Henry Bessemer developed and demonstrated a new process for producing steel, but at first none of his licensees could get the process to work. The scientific knowledge of the day provided little guidance. Bessemer had to search for what was different at their steel plants and, one by one, test the differences. He eventually found that the ore he had used was low in phosphorus while the licensees were using ores with higher phosphorus, and this made the difference. But even where the base of scientific knowledge is better developed, as in aeronautics or chemistry, the ability to build an airplane or chemical plant is still heavily dependent on experimentally derived knowledge, for example, from wind tunnel testing or tests on chemical plant components.[5]

Experimentation is important not just for engineers, managers, and mechanics. Often the people who use and maintain a new technology need to acquire skills and knowledge that go beyond what inventors and mechanics know. As we have seen, a wide range of ordinary workers, from weavers to welders to computer users to surgeons, acquire knowledge to use new technology by learning on the job.

## Sequential Innovation and Economic Feasibility

Yet the success of major new technologies does not typically depend on the outcome of just a single experiment. Bessemer needed to solve the problem of what ore to use, but there were other problems to solve as well, including how to design the optimal vessel for producing steel and how to construct a steel mill for optimal production. Because technologies are complex, implementation required many different experiments. Complex processes were broken into modular steps, complex products were broken into modular components, and these steps and components were each targets for improvement.

Often, a long series of improvements occur over time; that is, innovation is sequential. This was the case in weaving. The twentyfold increase in cloth output per weaver over the course of the nineteenth century after the initial power loom was largely the result of sequential innovations. Some of these inventions completely automated tasks the weavers had performed by hand. Others involved partial automation: they made certain tasks faster or reduced their frequency. Inventors took out over 3,500 patents on loom technology during the nineteenth century. Many of these patents were for specific adaptations or applications, such as carpet weaving; a handful of inventions (not all of them patented) realized major improvements in output per worker.[6] And about a quarter of the increase in cloth output per weaver came because the weavers themselves became more efficient—they had better skills and could work more productively.

Not all technologies exhibit such extended sequential innovation. Once discovered, small molecule chemical and pharmaceutical products often go into production with relatively little additional development, although regulatory approval for pharmaceuticals requires clinical trials. For example, scientists at Geigy discovered the powerful insect-killing properties of DDT after a couple of decades of research into insecticides. But this chemical had already been synthesized in the nineteenth century and the chemical engineering knowledge and skills needed to produce it commercially were already well established. DDT went into large-scale production relatively quickly, building, in a sense, on earlier generations of sequential innovation in chemical engineering and synthesis.

When major new technologies do not have such broad shoulders to stand on, as is typical, then long sequential innovation may be more representative. This was the case with textile processing and a wide variety of nineteenth-century mechanical technologies; it was the case with electrical technologies during the early twentieth century; it is the case with many information technologies today. For these important technologies, the implementation delays were very much matters of sequential innovation.

Yet the slow pace of sequential innovation is not determined purely by the technology. While technical advances might sometimes wait until new engineering knowledge is developed, frequently the delays arise for *economic* reasons. Even when inventors know how to make an improvement and have all the capabilities and tools, that improvement might not get commercialized until significant profits are expected. Many incremental innovations apparently provide little value until the technology has already developed substantially. And that development may well depend on the learned skills of ordinary workers.

## The Remainder Principle

Consider, for instance, the economics of a weaving invention called the "warp stop motion." The mechanical principle of this invention was known long before inventors were motivated to work out the practical details. A warp stop motion stops the loom when it detects that a warp thread is broken. The warp on a loom is the set of threads that run the length of the loom. These threads are under some tension, and occasionally they break as weaving progresses. When a warp thread broke, the weaver had to stop the loom, find the broken ends and tie them together, check and fix any defects in the cloth, and restart the loom. During this time the loom was idle. The longer the loom had been running with a broken warp thread, the longer it took the weaver to get things running again. Hence there was an advantage to stopping the loom as soon as a break occurred.

Since the early nineteenth century, mechanics had created stop-motion devices for a variety of machines, but they had not developed effective stop motions for detecting warp thread breaks. Clearly, this device did not need to wait for general advances in engineering knowledge or for some propitious discovery. The principle and the need were well understood. Instead, the warp stop motion was not implemented until the economic value grew large enough to motivate inventors to invest in its development and mill owners to adopt it.

The payoff from this invention grew as the looms produced more cloth per weaver-hour. Consider the arithmetic. Suppose that the warp stop motion reduced the time a weaver needed to fix a single warp thread break by a mere six seconds, and one warp thread would break, on average, for every three yards of cloth woven on a single loom.[7] At the speed the original handlooms ran in 1810, this invention would allow the weaver to produce just an additional three yards of cloth in an entire year. The value of these three additional yards does not begin to offset the cost of setting up the warp stop motion. By 1833, however, after some of the weaver's tasks had been automated, each weaver was able to tend two looms that ran substantially faster, and the output per weaver was greater. Now a saving of six seconds per break would allow a weaver to produce 100 additional yards of cloth per year. By 1883, a half-century later, more tasks had been automated and the warp stop invention would allow these weavers to produce over 600 additional yards per year. Moreover, as automation allowed weavers to tend more looms, it became harder to monitor the looms closely enough to catch warp breaks quickly, before a large amount of defective cloth had been produced.

Thus by the 1880s, the payoff from this invention would have been significant. The payoff calculation involves more than the amount of extra cloth produced, of course. It depends on the level of wages relative to the price of woven cloth, the cost of developing a stop motion and testing the many different versions of stop motions in order to find the best, and the cost of setting up a stop motion in production. But given the wages and prices and the availability of skilled mechanics in North America in the late nineteenth century, 600 yards of cloth per year would cover a lot of costs.[8]

With the introduction of the Northrop loom in 1895—which automated the task of filling the weaving shuttles with bobbins of yarn—the output per weaver multiplied even more, and the returns on a warp stop motion were even greater. This is just when we see patenting activity on these devices start to take off. Before 1880, no more than three patents were granted for warp stop motions during each decade. In the 1880s, six patents were granted on warp stop motions; in the 1890s there were 97, and from 1900 through 1909, 211 patents were granted. Then, with successful designs in wide use, patenting levels fell off.

William F. Draper, whose company commercialized the Northrop loom and made a number of the warp stop inventions, wrote in 1903 that "warp stop motions are old in theory but undeveloped in practice as before the [Northrop loom] was invented there was slight necessity for their use, the weaver necessarily being near a few looms all the time where oversight was easy."[9]

Thus greater automation increased the potential payoff to mill owners adopting the warp stop motion. An invention that would not have been commercially feasible in 1803 or 1833 became feasible by 1883 and critical by 1903. This illustrates a broader rule I call the "remainder principle": as technology reduces costs or increases performance on one task in a process or one component in a product, the value of performance on the remaining tasks or components increases. Automate other steps in weaving, and the value of fixing warp threads increases. Spin cotton faster and cheaper, and the value of weaving increases. Increase the speed of computers and lower their cost and the value of software increases.[10] The principle applies to individual components of a single machine as well as to broad processes composed of complementary steps.

These interactions happen because technologies are modularized in complementary parts: complex technological processes are broken into steps and complex products are broken into components in order to manage the development and sharing of knowledge more efficiently.[11] Each module is complementary to the rest, so that improvements in one module increase the payoff to an invention that improves the performance of another module. The warp stop motion and many other inventions had to wait for technology to develop before they became valuable targets for inventors.

## Skills and the Long Cycle of Sequential Innovation

The warp stop was not a feasible target for inventors until weaving had reached a high level of output per weaver. Yet that level of output depended not only on earlier inventions but also on new skills developed in response to those inventions. At the turn of the twentieth century, weavers in India, China, and Japan used the same equipment as Western weavers, but only achieved a fraction of the output per weaver. Clearly, the payoff would have been much smaller in those countries and perhaps not feasible at all.

Nor was this learning a one-time thing. As the machines changed, so too did the skills needed to operate them. The ongoing stream of sequential improvements meant that weavers had to periodically learn new skills. The realization of the productivity potential of new improvements depended on the ability of the workforce to learn on the job repeatedly.

For example, by 1840, weaving technology had improved sufficiently that weavers could potentially handle three or four looms each. But that was not initially obvious, and for several years the mills made no attempts to assign more looms per weaver. Experiments with three looms per weaver began in Lowell in 1842, during an economic depression. At the time, James Montgomery, a mill manager and commentator who was familiar with textile technology in both the United States and Britain, felt certain that weavers would not be able to keep up with three machines. And at first he was right.

The mills had to slow down the looms to give weavers time to attend to all the necessary tasks. But over the next year and a half the weavers—already experienced on the earlier configuration of two looms each—learned to handle three looms running at the same speeds that had been used for two looms. Within a few years, some weavers were operating four looms each. These new skills contributed to a major increase in output per worker by the 1850s, during a time when there was little additional improvement in the equipment.

The same economic logic that made it attractive for mills to invest in a warp stop motion also made it attractive for them to invest in greater workforce skills as the performance of the technology improved. Suppose that with some effort, a weaver could teach herself a new skill—maybe a difficult but very quick method of knot-tying—that would allow her to fix a thread six seconds faster. Would it be worthwhile to either her or her employer to learn this skill?[12] The same arithmetic applies to her skills as to the invention of a warp stop motion. If it's 1833 and she operates a single handloom, this skill would allow her to produce only three additional yards of cloth in a year. It would hardly pay to invest much time learning the new skill. But her granddaughter in 1883, working on five looms at a time, could produce an additional 600 yards of cloth per year. It would be worthwhile spending significant time trying different techniques and experimenting with different knot-tying motions in order to improve her skill at fixing warp breaks. As technology automated more and more weaving tasks over the course of the nineteenth century, the economic incentives for developing better skills increased on the remaining tasks. The mill owners would be willing to invest in human capital or to provide incentives (via piece rate) to encourage the weaver to invest in acquiring these skills.

And invest they did. Recall from Chapter 2 that the total investment, made by the employer and the worker, in getting a worker up to speed can be measured from the learning curve data. From the 1830s to the 1850s, the human capital investment roughly tripled (from $47 to $162) as the number of looms per weaver increased from two to four. Then the human capital investments roughly doubled again by the 1880s, when weavers handled five looms each. Although the later weavers performed fewer tasks, they had a much greater investment of human capital. They performed some of the same tasks with greater skill because the increased output made it economical to do so. Their skill set was narrower, but deeper.

This finding runs counter to common thinking. A naïve view holds that if technology automates more tasks, then less skill is needed, because fewer tasks remain to be learned. Karl Marx, who shared this view, argued, "Along with the tool, the skill of the workman in handling it passes over to the machine."[13] That is, with progressive mechanization, technology would reduce the need for skilled workers. But that is not how things worked; technology was not de-skilling in general. Technology's effect on skills was double-edged. Automating some tasks decreased the need for skill associated with those tasks; on the other hand, a greater rate of output increased the need for skill on the tasks that remained. In weaving, the latter effect dominated, raising demand for skilled workers over the nineteenth century. Computer technology has a similar double-edged effect: computers reduce demand for routine skills, but they increase demand for nonroutine skills.[14] Although some technologies eliminate more skilled jobs than they create, the remainder principle ensures that technologies are not uniformly de-skilling.

## The Slow Feedback Loop

Incremental improvements to major new technologies thus often work in a long, slow feedback loop: innovations followed by periods of learning. After an innovation, new knowledge is acquired about how best to use the innovation, which designs work best, and how to install and maintain the technology. Workers who use the new invention acquire the skills needed to draw the maximum benefit from it.

In some cases, this new knowledge provides ideas for new improvements.[15] Often, inventors get ideas for improvements from working with the technology. For example, Ross Thomson has shown that patents on sewing machine improvements followed from efforts to sell this new technology.[16] Sometimes, new inventions brought complementary organizational changes, which also involved learning and experimenting. Altogether these learning by doing processes increased the output per worker, which, in turn, permitted further incremental innovations. Inventors begin working on the next generation of innovations and the cycle begins anew.

As the looms gradually became more productive, all sorts of new improvements in weaving gradually became economically valuable. The first improvements were those with the biggest absolute payoffs—inventions such as the automatic loom temple, which automatically kept the edges of the woven cloth straight, and the weft fork, which stopped the loom if the weft thread broke. These improvements further increased the productivity of the looms, making yet more improvements profitable to develop.

Meanwhile, complementary technologies such as steam power were going through their own cycles of improvement. The slow development of these technologies affected the pace of weaving technology. Some weaving advances were not feasible unless the looms were run at faster speeds, but it was not feasible to run the looms faster until power became cheaper. Thus improvements in weaving also depended on advances in water turbines and steam engines, and the mills' demand for more efficient power generation spurred improvements in these technologies. These technologies were interdependent. Each one's cycle of learning and invention affected the development of the other.[17]

Weaving technology benefited from a steady stream of improvements that, over the course of the nineteenth century, generated a fiftyfold increase in output per weaver. Output per weaver doubled roughly every nineteen years and has continued to grow at a roughly constant rate since.[18] Like semiconductor chips following Moore's Law, the productivity of textile technology grows exponentially, although at a slower pace.[19]

Other technological revolutions also took decades to achieve overnight success. For example, the first electrical generating stations opened in 1881, but electrification had little effect on economic productivity until the 1920s. Economic historian Paul David explains that to realize the benefits of electricity, large numbers of people had to figure out not only how to install, operate, and maintain new electrical equipment, but also how best to design new factories, change workflows, and reorganize production.[20] It took time and experimentation to develop this new knowledge and to train managers and architects on these new methods.

A similar pattern seems to be at work with information technology. During the 1980s and 1990s, computers were widely deployed in many industries, but these industries did not seem to show the benefits of increased productivity. Some firms, however, achieved major benefits from computers, especially those that engaged in new organizational practices that facilitated employee learning and sharing of knowledge between work teams, customers, and suppliers.[21] These practices include workplace training, meetings where nonmanagerial workers can voice concerns, and redesign of workflows to facilitate decentralized decision making by nonmanagerial workers. Computer systems, too, develop incrementally and with critical learning at each advance.

The dynamic combination of complementary and sequential innovation helps explain why the software industry was so innovative before software was patentable. The future payoffs are sometimes so great that innovators can benefit by sharing their knowledge today.[22]

Major new technologies become "revolutionary" only after a long process of learning by doing and incremental improvement. Having the breakthrough idea is not enough. But learning through experience and experimentation is expensive and slow. Experimentation involves a search for productive techniques: testing and eliminating bad techniques in order to find good ones. This means that workers and equipment typically operate for extended periods at low levels of productivity using poor techniques and are able to eliminate those poor practices only when they find something better. However, there is sometimes a better way. If knowledge can be standardized and formalized so that it can be taught in classrooms and recorded in textbooks, then learning can happen faster and at lower cost.

## CHAPTER 4

# Standard Knowledge

AS A PROMISING STUDENT FROM SIBERIA, Dmitri Mendeleev showed early interest in the natural sciences, but he had difficulty gaining admission to a university in Moscow or St. Petersburg. After several rejections, in 1850 he was finally accepted at the Pedagogical Institute in St. Petersburg, where his father had studied, in a program that trained science teachers. His career progressed, and in 1867 he was awarded tenure at the St. Petersburg University when a professorship in chemistry opened up there. This new position required him to teach a course in inorganic chemistry, something he had not previously done. In preparing the course, he could not find a suitable textbook for his students. So he decided to write his own: *The Principles of Chemistry.*

At the time, chemistry was a heavily empirical field with few strong theoretical principles to organize knowledge. Students had to memorize a large number of experimental results. Although chemists analyzed the elements in terms of "atoms," there was little sense of what an atom really was or any certainty that it even existed. To help make sense of this empirical knowledge for his students, Mendeleev developed an organizing schema. He wrote a notecard for each element, listing its properties, and then organized them according to the experimentally derived atomic weight of the element. He noticed, as others had noticed, that there was a repeating pattern to some of these properties. Displaying each repetition as a separate row in a two-dimensional table, Mendeleev created what we now call the Periodic Table of the Elements.

This simple change in the representation of chemical knowledge did much more than help Mendeleev's students. It had two far-reaching consequences, one well known, the other less so. First, where the table had "holes," Mendeleev famously predicted that elements would be found to fill these holes; he also accurately predicted the chemical properties of these elements based on their positions in the table. Second, and less well known, the periodic table made educating new chemists faster and easier by standardizing chemical knowledge. Students no longer needed to study and absorb hundreds of seemingly unrelated experimental results. Instead, they could readily infer chemical properties from the highly formalized representation in the periodic table.[1] Mendeleev's textbook went through thirteen editions and was translated into French, German, and English.

Other aspects of chemical knowledge were standardized around the same time, including basic techniques of organic analysis and synthesis. Together, this new representation of chemical knowledge transformed chemical education and, with it, the nature and structure of the chemical industry. These changes included:

- The scale of education. At the beginning of the nineteenth century, chemists were trained essentially as apprentices in leading scientists' laboratories. But such laboratories were few, and they typically trained few students.[2] By reducing the cost and time involved, standardization facilitated the training of chemists. By 1899, there were 20,000 chemistry students at German universities and polytechnic schools.
- The scale of industrial research and thus the scope of the industry. Large numbers of trained chemists permitted the creation of large R&D laboratories pursuing bigger projects. For example, in 1884 the Bayer Company employed only eight or nine chemists to do production testing. In 1889, the lab was engaged in research to take advantage of the expanding new science, and a decade later it employed 144 chemists.[3] This "industrialization of invention" was critical to the synthesis of indigo dye, perfected in 1904.

- The labor market for chemists. A robust market for chemists developed in Germany as large numbers of credentialed chemists trained at universities and polytechnic schools came on the market to be hired by chemical firms.
- The geography of education and innovation. Before key knowledge was standardized, the education of chemists depended mainly on person-to-person communication in a few labs. Innovative activity was clustered around these labs. Standardized knowledge was more amenable to instruction through textbooks and other formalized means of training, which facilitated the geographic dispersion of chemistry education as well as innovative activity.[4]
- The use of patents. More accessible knowledge meant that it became easier for new firms to enter the market for any particular chemical, intensifying competition and causing firms to rely more on patents to protect their innovations. The use of chemical patents soared after the 1860s.

The standardization of chemical knowledge during the 1860s had far-reaching effects, and it is not hard to find other examples. The standardization of technical knowledge gives rise to distinctive patterns of economic behavior.[5] It accelerates the development of complementary knowledge, quickening the pace of sequential development and changing the scale and nature of learning. This transforms industries, markets, and the ability of workers to benefit from their skills and knowledge.

## What Is Standardization of Technical Knowledge?

Standardization of technical knowledge occurs when knowledge is simplified by limiting the range of technical parameters used to describe and implement the technology. Standardization makes knowledge easier to acquire and communicate by reducing the essential amount of information that must be conveyed. For example, using the periodic table, a chemist can infer the chemical properties of an element by knowing a single fact, the element's atomic number. Elements with atomic numbers that fall into the next to last column of the periodic table (known as halogens) react with hydrogen to form acids. Before the periodic table was created, the chemist would need to learn chemical characteristics element by element—that fluorine reacts with hydrogen to form hydrofluoric acid, chlorine reacts with hydrogen to form hydrochloric acid, and so on. The periodic table is an example of scientific abstraction, where a large body of experimental or observational data is summarized in a simple principle. Essential characteristics can be determined from a few simple facts. Other examples include Newton's Laws of Motion and Maxwell's equations on electromagnetism.

Standardization of knowledge takes place in a variety of other ways. "Codification," writing knowledge down or recording it in a specific language, is a form of standardization that simplifies the description of technical knowledge.[6] Another common form is the technical standard—a norm or requirement to limit the range of technical parameters used in the implementation of a technology. These limits might apply to inputs used, such as a requirement that low-phosphorus iron ore be used in the Bessemer process for steelmaking. Technical standards might apply to the products produced, such as standard cotton cloths with a given count of threads to the inch. They might also apply to conditions of operation, such as requiring a certain level of humidity to spin cotton yarn.

Technical standards can be formally documented standards promulgated by a firm, like the PostScript standard published by Adobe for driving computer printers; they may be formally endorsed by government bodies, like the GSM mobile telephone standard mandated by the European Commission; or they may be developed by industry standard-setting organizations like the Internet Engineering Task Force (IETF), a voluntary association of engineers that sets standards for the Internet. Or they can be informal, becoming standards only by virtue of their common acceptance. The QWERTY layout for typewriter keyboards, for instance, is not mandated by any formal body.[7] Finally, to the extent that standards are embodied in organizations, they are often part of "standard operating procedures" that formally or informally describe the routines that organizations follow.[8] These routines are also a form of technical knowledge.

The informational advantages of standardized knowledge go beyond facilitating training. They also affect markets. For example, most commodity markets depend on technical standards to convey quality, safety, and other characteristics. Wheat varieties are controlled so that buyers of "hard red spring wheat," for instance, know that it has between 13 and 16 percent protein content, certain milling characteristics, and other qualities.

Technical standards also facilitate market coordination of complementary products. Compatibility standards allow independent producers to make components that work together. Internet standards, for instance, allow makers of networking hardware and software and creators of websites to develop their components independently but remain assured that they will all work together. Much of the economics literature on technical standards focuses on compatibility standards and the problems of coordination. Sometimes multiple standards, sponsored by different groups of firms, will compete for dominance, like the VHS and Betamax standards for video recording.[9] These competitions can delay the emergence of a single dominant standard.

Finally, it is more helpful to think of *degrees* of standardization. Standardization typically simplifies the representation of a portion of the knowledge of a technology, but additional knowledge must still be acquired through experience. For this reason, formal standards are revised over time; dominant designs like the Wintel architecture (Windows operating system running on an Intel microprocessor) for personal computers are regularly enhanced with new versions and more features.

## Some Effects of Standardizing Knowledge

Standardization can transform industries as it transformed the chemical industry in the nineteenth century. Consider these aspects, which I described in Chapter 1:

1. The nature of training. Because standardized knowledge is simpler, it can be more readily taught to larger numbers of students or trainees and thus more readily replicated. When knowledge has also been codified, students can learn it from textbooks and classroom lectures. These methods of teaching and learning are more efficient than one-off learning by doing. Hence the periodic table meant that core chemical knowledge could be learned in the

classroom rather than by trial and error at the lab bench. Of course, chemists still learn from experiments involving individual exploration—the periodic table standardized only part of chemical knowledge.

2. The scale of training and of production. Reduce the cost of training, and it becomes economical to train more people. Train more workers, and it becomes economical to use more workers in production or research. Standardization of chemical knowledge facilitated the training of chemists in universities and polytechnic schools in Germany, which in turn facilitated the growth of larger research laboratories.

3. Geographic dispersion. Before technical knowledge can be taught in classrooms or acquired from textbooks, it usually must be learned first through hands-on experience under the guidance of people who have already mastered it. For this reason, technical knowledge that is not highly standardized tends to be developed in geographical clusters like Silicon Valley. When that knowledge becomes more standardized, direct experience and person-to-person mentoring become less important, and the knowledge can be more easily acquired at a distance. At this point it becomes possible to export the technology around the globe. Semiconductor processes developed in Silicon Valley were only later exported to Taiwan and Singapore.[10]

4. Intellectual property strategy. Sharing of new knowledge is usually critical for the development of new technologies. When knowledge cannot be readily communicated through formal documents, it must be shared largely through person-to-person communication. In an environment where employee job-hopping, worker migration, and informal worker-to-worker communication are the main vectors of knowledge sharing, intellectual property policies such as trade secrecy laws and employee noncompete agreements sharply limit the spread of information. When knowledge is more standardized, it can be shared through formal documentation and thus subject to licensing restrictions and patent protection without necessarily inhibiting communication. Strategies that firms

employ regarding the exclusivity of technical knowledge often change with standardization.

5. Labor markets. Just as it affects markets in commodities, standardization is also important in labor markets. In particular, it facilitates the development of labor markets that compensate workers for specific skills related to new technologies.

These effects of standardization can overturn industries.

## Disruptive Innovation

On a December day in 1994 in Orlando, Florida, Gerald M. Levin, chairman of Time Warner, stood before an audience of 500 reporters, guest observers, and technology executives and turned on the world's first interactive TV system. This, he told them, was "an irreversible step across the threshold of change. . . . One day, all publishers of information will have to understand the implications of interactive television." It would be the next breakthrough technology.

This combination of television, electronic communications, and digital computing held a host of promises. Soon, people would shop for groceries or clothing, check their bank account balances and transfer funds, or play video games against remote opponents, using only their TV sets and remote controls. A printer would let them print coupons and other images straight from their screens. Movies, shows, and broadcast news would be available on demand, with the option to pause, fast-forward, or rewind at will; hockey or baseball games would offer viewers a choice of multiple camera angles. The long-anticipated dream of "digital convergence," Levin promised the assembly, was finally coming true.

During the 1950s and 1960s, technology companies had talked about the convergence of communication, computing, and television technologies, but attempts like the AT&T Picturephone had all failed. The earlier hardware had been too costly and slow. But now, Levin and others realized, the hardware existed to make convergence work.

This promise of a breakthrough technology—and the prospect of charging consumers for it—set off a frenzy of activity by computer, telephone, and cable television companies in the early 1990s. John Markoff, technology reporter for the *New York Times*, called it a battle for "control of the access to all the video entertainment and new types of electronic information that enter and leave the home."[11] Firms invested heavily in software and fiber optic cable, and in developing new cable-control boxes and sophisticated servers. The Orlando project required more lines of computer code than NASA had used to put astronauts on the moon. To enhance their chances of playing on the winning team, firms rushed to join in—according to trade newsletter *Digital Media*, the major firms formed at least 348 alliances.

Yet by the time of the launch, a rival to interactive television had emerged— the Internet. In 1994, the Internet was a limited and primitive alternative to cable television. But it improved dramatically. By the beginning of 1997, a little over two years after the launch, Time Warner saw that the Internet would surpass interactive television and that most of the possibilities that its product offered would eventually be available online. The company pulled the plug on the Orlando project in May 1997.

How could so many bright executives at so many well-managed, well-funded companies have gotten it so wrong? It is tempting to say that they bet on the wrong technology, that the Internet was superior to interactive television and somehow these executives failed to appreciate the technical differences. But differences in the base technologies are not to blame. Under the covers, interactive TV and the Internet are hardly different at all. The cable-control box used in interactive television is a microcomputer, and the cable connection used in Orlando closely resembled the broadband cable service Time Warner now offers its Internet customers. Interactive TV used a remote control as its main input device instead of a keyboard or mouse, but in many interactive television systems these devices could be added. These differences do not explain so fundamental a gap in acceptance.

Moreover, this was not a case of a large established firm sticking with the conservative technology—Levin and his cohorts knew that interactive video technology, in either incarnation, was revolutionary. They bet big on a breakthrough "disruptive" technology.

Clayton Christensen pioneered the notion of "disruptive innovation."[12] Well-managed firms are sometimes overtaken and replaced by firms with new technologies. Often the established firms could have invested in the new technology but did not because initially the new technology was inferior. Start-up firms instead employ the new technology, often in niche markets. As the implementation of the technology improves, it becomes more competitive in the broader market, eventually surpassing the old technology and the incumbent firms. The key to disruption is technological improvement that comes from better implementation, and standards are often key to dramatically changing the nature of implementation. Many managers seek to bet on breakthrough technologies, as Levin did. But harnessing disruption may be more about establishing the most effective way to promote broad-based learning.

Consider online shopping. Here is an account of Time Warner's offering from 1994:

> Perhaps the most impressive service under development is grocery shopping, a service developed by Shopper Vision, a small start-up company in Norcross, Georgia. In a simulation, viewers were able to select a store, then browse through video images of each aisle.
>
> They could then start with a wide view, then scan particular rows left to right, and then pull particular products off the shelf. Using the vast computer-processing power of the Silicon Graphics set-top communications device, a person would be able to turn the product around, read the labels, check the price, and buy it. The system would also let people look for products by category or brand name. For a $10 fee, Shopper Vision will process the order—regardless of size—and have it delivered to the home.
>
> Sandy Goldman, president of Shopper Vision, said the service should become available in Orlando in about six months and will offer 20,000 products from three retailers—the Winn-Dixie supermarket chain, the Eckerd Drug Company, and the Drug Emporium chains. Shopper Vision hopes to generate its revenue from delivery fees, fees charged to participating supermarkets, and advertising that will run on the video service.[13]

A revolutionary idea in its time, but limited and narrow compared to what the Internet offers today. Shopper Vision involved only three retailers. There were no mom-and-pop merchants selling specialty hot peppers or gourmet coffees. And the capabilities, though impressive, may not have been the right ones to facilitate online shopping. There was no way for retailers to offer other information or incentives to customers or to solicit customer input; no place for evaluation of products by customers or experts; no tool to automatically compare prices of products offered by competing retailers; no ability to hold auctions for used or overstocked items; and no easy means to search for products. We now know that such features are what make online shopping attractive to consumers. We also know that, so far, online grocery stores have fared far worse than online retailers of books (or pornography). Our present online marketplace is far more vibrant and diverse than the best and brightest at Time Warner or Silicon Graphics or Shopper Vision could have imagined.

Time Warner failed because it attempted to launch a highly complex technology while maintaining strict control over who could access, modify, and therefore innovate with it. The approach is not surprising, given that Time Warner viewed the "real" contest, as John Markoff noted, as being about who would control this information channel into the home. Time Warner gave little thought to changing the actual information that would come over the channel. Shutting out market rivals also meant limiting learning by doing.

Gerald Levin did not lack technological imagination; his vision was bold and futuristic. Nor did he and his allies lack technical competence. But they lacked *social* imagination. The Internet easily surpassed their efforts because its social structure gave developers and users vast opportunities for learning by doing. The Internet facilitated *mass innovation* from the bottom up, while the Time Warner effort, though substantial, was tightly controlled from the top. The Internet allowed tens of thousands of people to experiment with new ideas to improve the implementation. Most of these ideas failed, but the successes were stunningly effective and often unanticipated. The collective effort was far greater than anything Time Warner and its allies could generate, even though they could throw around billions of dollars. More important, the Internet harnessed the energy of a far more diverse group of people, and this diversity was particularly fertile for innovation. Many of these innovators would never have passed muster at Time Warner or its allies. But by collaborating online they proved far more adept than Time Warner at developing useful and attractive services.

Why did the Internet facilitate learning on a large scale while Time Warner's effort did not? The Internet was built on open standards: key elements of the knowledge about its hardware and plumbing were standardized, and these standards were made freely available. They were (and are) managed by standards organizations such as the IETF, which covers key aspects of the way Internet devices talk to each other, and the World Wide Web Consortium (W3C), which covers the basic software for handling web pages. These organizations selected key features of the hardware and software plumbing and published formal specifications. Standardization reduced the time and cost of acquiring the knowledge needed to participate in Internet and web development. By making it easier to learn by doing, standardization accelerated the development and sharing of critical new knowledge on a large scale. Because the standards were open, large numbers of unaffiliated developers and consumers could participate in the learning experiments taking place on the Internet.

Time Warner's bet on the breakthrough idea of interactive television failed because the company missed the bigger picture. It missed all the new knowledge that had to be developed. The open standards of the Internet, by facilitating learning on a very large scale, permitted the real breakthrough. Widely shared standards were key to the disruptive power of the Internet.

## Standards and Labor Markets

Standards can overturn industries. They also change labor markets, affecting skills, jobs, and wages. This aspect of standards-based disruption is central to the puzzle of stagnant wages. The Internet and World Wide Web opened up all sorts of new jobs requiring a whole new range of skills. I will look more closely at one of these opportunities in Chapter 7. It is perhaps easier to see the impact of standards on jobs in a more discrete technology.

Consider, for example, how the emergence of a widely accepted standard opened up new career paths for Margaret Kelly and many other young women during the early twentieth century. In 1911, Kelly became the highest-paid female government official, taking the position of acting director of the U.S.

Mint, a position just below that of cabinet officer. "Miss Kelly's appointment marks an epoch in the history of the advancement and development of woman in the business world," declared Congressman Edward Taylor of Colorado.[14] Her exceptional career began fifteen years earlier when she took a civil service job as a stenographer in the Treasury Department.

The occupation of stenographer was a new one for women. It had not been available to Margaret's mother or to earlier generations of women. Large numbers of women were able to become stenographer-typists, changing the nature of the office workplace and advancing the opportunities available to women.[15] G. K. Chesterton was one of many who saw the connection between women's rights and stenography, quipping, "Ten thousand women marched through the streets of London saying: 'We will not be dictated to', and then went off to become stenographers."[16]

Some forms of stenography—also known as shorthand—had been in use since ancient times. In the nineteenth century, authors such as Charles Dickens had used it as a sort of personal productivity tool. But until the 1870s it was hardly used in commerce, and even then almost exclusively by male clerks, who took shorthand dictation and then recorded documents in longhand. That changed in 1873 with the introduction of the first commercially successful typewriter. The typewriter was much faster than transcribing into longhand, and thanks to carbon paper, it also made duplicating easier. These benefits facilitated an organizational change that created a new occupation for many young women. During the nineteenth century, clerks and secretaries were mainly male employees who were familiar with the entire operation of the firm. The job of secretary was frequently a stepping stone to a management position.[17] The typewriter allowed a new division of labor in the business office: a businessperson could dictate to a stenographer-typist who would record a document in shorthand and later type it up. This person did not need a comprehensive understanding of the business, just proficiency in shorthand, typing, spelling, punctuation, and grammar. The job could be done by a young woman with a high school diploma and a six-month course in shorthand and typing. As firms began using stenographer-typists during the 1880s, large numbers of schools were created to teach these new skills. There were 276 such schools or private instructors by 1882, and over 1300 by 1890.[18]

But like other young women considering this new career, Margaret had to choose among courses that were not equivalent. Each typing course used just one model of typewriter. Different typewriters had different keyboard layouts, and so learning to type on one keyboard was of no value toward obtaining work using another manufacturer's typewriter. In New Hampshire, where Margaret grew up, only two schools offered training to young women during the early 1890s, one on the Remington typewriter, which had the now-familiar QWERTY layout, and one on the Hammond typewriter, which had a different layout. Margaret chose instead to attend a school in Boston, where typing schools offered training on no fewer than five different models of typewriters.

Incompatible keyboard standards limited the market. Employers who had bought Remington typewriters would not hire typists trained on Hammonds. This restricted the employment opportunities for typists trained on any one model of typewriter and reduced the incentives for young high school graduates like Margaret to invest in training. Some women were unwilling to pay much for the training; others looked for different work.

During the 1890s, a common standard emerged. In 1890, the Hammond Company, which had developed an "Ideal" keyboard that it claimed was technically superior, offered the QWERTY keyboard as an option on its newest model.[19] Other manufacturers followed suit, and by 1900, QWERTY was the dominant layout.[20]

The emergence of a common standard unified the labor market for typists and enhanced the value of their skills. The number of stenographers and typists in the United States soared from about 200 in 1870, when the profession was all male, to over 800,000 in 1930, when 96 percent of working stenographer-typists were female (see Figure 4.1).[21] Standardization of typewriters played a critical role in creating a labor market that allowed nearly a million young women to earn good wages. It was not the only factor that contributed to the adoption of the typewriter, but it was critical.

The typewriter, too, was a disruptive innovation and standardization was key to its disruptive power. The stenographer-typist was not as capable as the male secretary; she did not know all aspects of the business, nor was she typically groomed for a management position, notwithstanding the occasional promotion of women like Margaret Kelly. Thus the new business

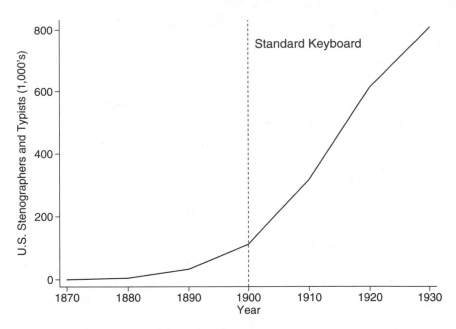

Figure 4.1. The market for typists soars after standardization. (Edwards,
*Comparative Occupation Statistics of the United States, 1870 to 1940,*
tables 9 and 10.)

model was, from this perspective, inferior. But typists could perform a few
tasks particularly well, namely, transcribing and duplicating documents.
And standardization meant that effective training was accessible to large
numbers of people so that the new business model could be employed on
a large scale. In doing so, it opened up many opportunities for women in
the workforce.

The emergence of a widely accepted standard was critical to the effectiveness of the labor market for typists. The dominance of QWERTY meant that
employers could more easily find typists with the right skills and typists
could more easily find employers with the right equipment. This matching
benefit of standardization is a common feature of specific skills associated
with major new technologies. Economists call this benefit a "network
externality"—when a typist chooses to learn a specific keyboard layout, not
only does she benefit, but the labor market improves for all other typists
who have learned that layout. Economists have recognized the importance

of network externalities for new technologies, but they have largely analyzed it with regard to strategic behavior. Yet these same network externalities have important implications for the emergence of robust labor markets for new technology-specific skills, including possible delays in the emergence of dominant standards.

## The Life Cycle of Technical Knowledge

The "revolutionary" impact of the typewriter had to wait both for the technology to develop sequentially and for a dominant standard to emerge. Yet the emergence of a dominant standard sometimes takes decades. After the introduction of the QWERTY keyboard, in 1873, it took roughly twenty-five years before most typewriter manufacturers offered it, either as their only keyboard or as an option.[22] A study of the emergence of "dominant designs" finds common delays of two or three decades.[23]

Why do standards sometimes take so long to emerge and to be widely accepted for major new technologies? There are two problems. First, given the ongoing process of sequential innovation, time is needed for the technology to become sufficiently mature and sufficiently stable to make the investment in developing a standard worthwhile. For example, Henry Bessemer patented his steelmaking process in 1856, but it took another fifteen years before a standard plant design and process for high-throughput production emerged in the United States.[24] It took time to conduct the necessary experiments in order to have an effective standard. It did not make sense to sink this investment cost until the technology was sufficiently well developed to meet demand. Early on, the process was too uncertain and unreliable.

Standardization was delayed because formulating a standard involved significant fixed costs. The necessary experiments were costly, and once the standard was accepted—by sinking costs into new plants—it would be difficult to change. That is, these investments are sometimes irreversible. Given irreversible investments, firms wait until the technology is sufficiently profitable before investing in standardization. Moreover, if technology changes rapidly, they will not make an investment in a standard that will soon be obsolete. A rapid rate of change in a technology—or in complementary technologies, organizations, and markets—provides an additional reason to wait.[25] Not infrequently, standards are promulgated prematurely and soon abandoned.

Standards are not always formulated by the firms or consumers who will adopt them. Government bodies, trade associations, and independent standard-setting organizations all participate. Also, sometimes the standardization of knowledge occurs in universities, as with chemistry. For some of these bodies, profitability is not an issue and hence is not necessarily an obstacle to investing in a standard. However, even in many of these cases, the *adoption* of the standard might involve significant investments, which can cause delay.

But a second problem also causes delay: multiple standards often emerge, making it harder for any one of them to become widely accepted. Multiple standards are, perhaps, inevitable given the complexity of technology—there are just multiple ways of doing things. But given competing standards, it often takes time to settle on one or a few choices, as was the case with typewriter keyboards. This is a well-known problem of coordinating economic behavior among competitors. Because learning costs were high, typists were reluctant to invest in learning to use a model that did not have a large installed base.[26] Instead, they might wait to see which keyboard layout emerged with the largest base of adopters.[27] Competing manufacturers, meanwhile, might seek to build a large installed base around their particular keyboard layout. In such a "standards war" they might be reluctant to coordinate on a single standard—those manufacturers with bigger installed bases would be more reluctant to give up their competitive advantage, thus further delaying the emergence of a common standard.

Not all standards take that long to become dominant. During the 1980s, for example, new standards for computer modems came out every few years as modem speeds increased (300 baud, 1200 baud, 9600 baud, etc.). The difference between this example and typewriters can be explained by switching costs. The cost of learning to use a new modem is small; the cost of learning a new keyboard layout is significant and the knowledge is not transferable. Because typing required an irreversible investment, changes were approached with greater caution.

In general, then, widely accepted standards might take time to develop when the costs of learning associated with the standard are substantial. This will tend to be the case with major new technologies—new technological "paradigms" or "regimes" that involve a lot of new knowledge and hence substantial switching costs, including the costs of switching from older technologies.[28]

Delays in standardization mean that behavior around technical knowledge will change gradually as such major new technologies develop. A "life cycle of technical knowledge" emerges naturally when standardization of major new technologies is delayed. Early-stage technologies—those with relatively little standardized knowledge—tend to be used at a smaller scale; activity is localized; personal training and direct knowledge sharing are important; and labor markets do not compensate workers for their new skills. Mature technologies—with greater standardized knowledge— operate at large scale and globally, market permitting; formalized training and knowledge exchange are more common; and robust labor markets encourage workers to develop their own skills.

These life cycle changes can have far-reaching effects. The typewriter changed the nature of office work and the role of women; the Internet changed culture. Scholars have identified a number of other regularities that tend to occur as technologies mature: product innovation gives way to process innovation; the number of innovations and revenue initially grow rapidly, then later slow; firms initially enter the industry, to exit later as a mature industry goes through a "shakeout"; and established incumbents are replaced by disruptive innovations that overturn industries.[29]

These phenomena involve more than just the standardization of knowledge.[30] But standardization plays a key role: it explains how technical knowledge becomes more easily replicable so that technologies can be implemented on a large scale, generating new wealth and long-term economic growth. By facilitating markets for new skills, standardization also allows that wealth to be shared. But life cycle delays in standardization and the long cycle of sequential innovation also explain why workers' benefits from new technology are sometimes postponed for decades.

# PART II

## WAGES

NEW TECHNOLOGY CREATES THE POTENTIAL for increased wealth, but that does not guarantee that most people will benefit economically from new technology. Stagnant wages sometimes accompany new technology, as is happening today. Chapters 5 through 7 explore the role that evolving technical knowledge plays in generating wealth for large numbers of workers and why the generation of widely shared wealth can take decades.

## CHAPTER 5

# When Does Technology Raise Wages?

WHILE VACATIONING AT MATLOCK IN DERBYSHIRE during the summer of 1784, an English clergyman named Edmund Cartwright struck up a conversation with a group of gentlemen.[1] They began discussing the new technology being used to spin cotton yarn in the gentlemen's home city of Manchester. Cartwright, the Oxford-educated son of a Nottingham landowner, had a parish in rural Derbyshire. He was naturally concerned with the well-being of his parishioners and made efforts to help them, advising them on medical remedies and cultivation techniques. The conversation with the Manchester gentlemen raised a fresh concern: the new spinning technology would soon produce so much yarn that the cottage weavers in rural England would not be able to keep up with demand. Textile manufacturers would have to get their yarn woven on the Continent, where weavers were paid less than in England; before long, manufacturers would have little need for the costlier local weavers. The new technology thus threatened to undermine English farmers and workers, who relied on weaving for part of their livelihood.

Weaving is an ancient technology, shared since prehistoric times by cultures around the world. On the handlooms used in the eighteenth century, it was still a slow and laborious process. Cartwright convinced himself that he could build a loom that would partially automate this process, allowing English weavers to meet the demand for cloth and thus keep the business. It turned out to be much harder than he expected. The machines he designed did not work well. The textile business he founded using these looms was a failure. But other inventors built on what Cartwright had started. By the end of the nineteenth century in the United States, a weaver using power looms could produce fifty times as much cloth in an hour as a weaver on a handloom.

Did this technology save the English poor, as Cartwright hoped, or did it destroy them? Several decades after Cartwright went bankrupt, Karl Marx wrote of the tragedy of the handloom weavers who he claimed were driven into dire poverty and starvation by competition from power loom factories. A debate about whether new technology helps or harms most people has been going on for centuries. Cartwright's invention did not, in the end, save his parishioners. Instead of maintaining part-time weaving as a supplement to farm income, it helped shift weaving to the factories. But neither was Marx right. Generally speaking, handloom weavers notwithstanding (more on them later), the evidence has largely put Marx on the losing side of the larger debate. Over the last 200 years, technologies such as the power loom have driven a dramatic increase in the wages and wealth of average workers in Britain, the United States, and other developed nations. British workers today earn over ten times what their ancestors earned in 1784, after accounting for inflation. Technology is the main source of that gain. In spite of this record of success, the question of whether technology harms or helps most people is not settled. It seems especially relevant today because a whole new generation of technology has apparently failed to boost the average worker's economic well-being; workers may even have been harmed.

Much of today's debate reflects what we think we know about the past. Does technology boost wages, or does it replace workers with machines? Does technology eliminate skills, undercutting wages, or does it increase skills and wages? Does the globalization of technology also undercut wages? The interplay of invention, wages, jobs, skills, and globalization in textile weaving, the technology that provoked Cartwright's imagination and Marx's censure, provides an illustrative account. It is helpful to begin by understanding how technology boosts wages in theory.

## Why Did Wages Grow in the Past?

For centuries prior to 1800, incomes of ordinary people in Western societies remained roughly the same, sometimes rising, sometimes falling, but all within a relatively narrow range. Economic historian Gregory Clark suggests that even Stone Age hunter-gatherers might have had better living standards than ordinary laborers in 1800 because the agrarian economies of 1800 were much more unequal.[2] Then, beginning with the Industrial Revolution, living conditions began to improve steadily.

Wages were able to grow so much because output per worker grew strongly as well. The size of the economic "pie" increased, so there was room for increasing workers' pay. Not all of the extra output they produced went into the pockets of ordinary workers, but we can understand the source of wage growth in two parts: first, why output per worker grew so much, and second, why workers significantly shared in that output in the form of higher pay.

### More Output Per Worker

Textiles illustrate this growth in output. In 1902, a weaver in the most advanced U.S. cotton mills could produce about fifty times as much coarse cloth in an hour as a handloom weaver could produce in an hour of weaving in 1800. Economists identify three main sources of growth in output per worker: growth in the amount of capital (buildings, equipment) per worker, better technology, and better worker skills.[3] Each corresponds to a narrative about the sources of growth:

1. Capital accumulation. Initially, in agrarian economies, little investment went to industry. As industry grew and as financial markets developed, the supply of funds for investment grew, driving down interest rates and thus making investment cheaper relative to wages. This made it profitable to provide more equipment per worker; with more equipment, a worker could often produce more output. For example, if a weaver working a single loom was idle while the machine performed automatic functions, then it might be profitable to add a second loom. The cheaper the cost of

financing that additional loom, the more profitable it would be to increase the capital per weaver.

2. Technological change. Inventors came up with new ways of doing things. For example, loom improvements allowed the machines to automate some tasks previously performed by the weavers. This meant that a weaver could tend more looms and thus produce more. This kind of technical change is called "labor saving."

3. Better skills. More skilled weavers could handle more looms and run them with less downtime. Sometimes, greater skills were associated with greater effort as well: it took effort to acquire the skills, and some skills enabled workers to work more intensively. Economists often associate skills with education, but education levels did not change much until the twentieth century in the United States. Indeed, for weavers, the workforce was initially literate, but later, more illiterate weavers were hired.

How important were each of these stories? They are hard to disentangle. In cotton weaving, the 1902 weaver operated eighteen looms while the handloom weaver of 1800 operated only one. But that does not mean capital accumulation was necessarily driving growth. In each story, there might be more machines per worker, but for different reasons: in the capital accumulation story, more machines were used because they were cheaper relative to wages; in the other stories, weavers needed less time to tend each machine, so they were freed to operate more machines.

Following Abramovitz and Solow, economists have developed methods of "growth accounting" using aggregate data in order to obtain generalized measures of productivity.[4] However, these "multifactor productivity" measures do not accurately capture the contribution of technology because they are based on strong assumptions about technology that do not necessarily apply.[5] Indeed, economists have shown that they can't disentangle these stories just using aggregate data without making strong assumptions.[6]

Fortunately for the case of cotton weaving, we have detailed knowledge of the technology as it changed over time.[7] We know how much idle time weavers had, how long it took them to do various tasks, and how often those tasks occurred. Using such information, one can construct an "engineering production function" that shows how the mills actually responded to changes in interest rates and prices, how different inventions affected the amount of labor time a weaver needed to spend on each loom, and how output grew with weaver skills. This function definitively shows the sources of the increase in output per worker or, equivalently, the decrease in the amount of labor time needed per yard of cloth. A handloom weaver in 1800 took nearly forty minutes to weave a yard of coarse cloth using a single loom. A weaver in 1902 took less than a minute on average while operating eighteen Northrop looms. Of the roughly thirty-nine-minute reduction in labor time per yard, capital accumulation due to the changing cost of capital relative to wages accounted for just 2 percent of the reduction; inventions accounted for 73 percent of the reduction; and 25 percent of the time saving came from greater skill and effort of the weavers.

Technology was, by far, the most important factor driving the growth in output per worker in cotton weaving. Skills were important, too, but the role of capital accumulation was minimal, counter to the conventional wisdom.[8] It is possible that pure accumulation was a more important factor in the growth of output per worker in other industries or that it might be more important today. However, for the nineteenth century, textile processing was not just one among many growing technologies; it was the most important one. Gregory Clark estimates that over half of the productivity growth in England during the Industrial Revolution derived from the textile industry.[9]

While this analysis challenges the older view that output per person grew largely as the result of greater investment, it does fit with modern economic growth theory. Paul Romer highlights the importance of the replicability of inventions: because productive inventions could be replicated with little cost and used simultaneously in different production facilities, dramatically greater output could be achieved from the same inputs.[10] Although I have emphasized that technology—as opposed to inventions—is not necessarily reproduced at low cost, Romer's insight is nevertheless valuable, with the caveat that it might take some significant learning before technical knowledge can be reproduced; technology is still a source of growing output per person because of the replication that does occur.

The analysis of weaving also highlights the importance of worker skills and effort. Lacking direct measurement of worker skills, economists have tended to rely on education as a proxy measure. This analysis demonstrates, however, that because skills can be acquired through experience, education may be a poor proxy; weavers with little education acquired significant skills that were substantially important to the growth of output per worker.

The growth in output per worker provides growing resources that society can use to increase the real pay of workers. Some economists, such as Tyler Cowen and Robert Gordon, worry that technology no longer increases output per worker today as rapidly as it did in the past and that this is responsible for stagnant wages.[11] There is evidence that the growth in output per hour, measured using the gross domestic product (GDP), has been slower in recent decades. The Bureau of Labor Statistics reports a measure of real output per hour for the nonfarm business sector. From 1947 to 1980 this index grew at 2.4 percent per year; from 1980 to 2013, it grew only 2.0 percent per year. Robert Gordon predicts this growth will fall to 1.3 percent per year in coming years. Gordon's predictions are controversial, and there is also some controversy over whether the GDP statistics fully capture output in today's information-intensive economy. Erik Brynjolfsson and Andrew McAfee argue, contrary to Gordon, that technology is starting to increase the growth rate of output per worker significantly.[12] This debate is beyond the scope of this book. Nevertheless, even if Gordon is right, something else must be mainly responsible for the stagnant wages of ordinary workers. The median wage has not been growing at a rate anywhere near 1.3 percent per year, let alone 2.0 percent per year. In other words, the economy is generating growing output per person, but that output has not been going into the pockets of ordinary workers in recent decades. Ordinary workers have simply not been sharing in that growth to any substantial degree.

### Workers' Share

Figure 5.1 shows the decline in workers' share of the economic pie. The solid black line in the figure shows total employee compensation—wages plus benefits—as a share of national income.[13] The dashed line excludes the top one percent of wage earners, thus representing more ordinary

Figure 5.1. Employees' share of the economic pie declines: Employee compensation (wages + benefits) as a share of national income. (Bureau of Economic Analysis, National Income and Product Accounts, http://www.bea.gov/iTable/index_nipa.cfm; Saez and Piketty, "Income Inequality in the United States, 1913–1998.")

workers. After trending higher for the fifty years since 1929, the employee share has fallen sharply during the last three decades, especially after the top wage earners are removed. Data are available for the United Kingdom and France going back to the early nineteenth century. These data show an even longer trend prior to the recent reversal. The employee share of income fell during the Industrial Revolution but trended upward from about 1850 to 1980 before reversing.[14]

The decline in the workers' share of income, especially for the bottom 99 percent, explains why the median wage has stagnated despite substantial growth in output per person for the last three decades. Something changed around 1980. Some economists such as Joseph Stiglitz attribute a major role to the political influence of the wealthy.[15] Globalization may have played a role as well as increased industry concentration. Some research attributes the primary role to changes in technology. The trend is not confined to the United States, but is global, suggesting that technology is a major factor.[16]

In any case, the last three decades are not the first time that labor has seen its share of national income decline. As we shall see in Chapter 6, workers' wages were stagnant at the beginning of the Industrial Revolution while output per worker grew, shrinking their share of income. Later, wages started increasing, too, increasing workers' share of income until 1980.

But what determines workers' share of national income generally? Greater output per worker explains the increase in the aggregate wealth of a nation, but it does not tell us how or whether that wealth "trickles down" to most citizens of the nation. The wealth might, as Marx predicted, accrue instead to a narrow capitalist elite.

The easy replicability of inventions actually suggests the possibility of this outcome. If economic growth comes largely from the frictionless replication of inventions, then in a global economy, new ideas can be used anywhere in the world. New inventions can be employed in remote places where workers are willing to accept subsistence wages. These inventions might increase the wealth of a few entrepreneurs and investors, and possibly inventors, but they would not increase wages, either in this country or abroad. Inventions can increase output, but there is no guarantee that the benefits of that output will be shared among the many.

Is this what is happening today? Economists have developed macroeconomic theories as to why this scenario has not played out in the past, but these theories are neither highly persuasive nor widely accepted. In seeking to explain how the aggregate wealth of a nation "trickles down" to the average worker, economists have mainly looked toward capital accumulation. The pattern of growing capital per worker that we saw with textile technology is also seen in many other technologies and in aggregate data. Some economists have focused on how the changing cost of capital goods (including interest rates) relative to wages induces firms to invest more capital per worker.[17] The key parameter determining this behavior is called the "elasticity of substitution between capital and labor," which describes how sensitive firms are to reallocating the capital assigned per worker in response to relative price changes. However, economists don't agree on whether the elasticity of substitution between capital and labor is large or small, nor do they have an explanation as to why it should be large or small in general.[18]

Moreover, this simple parameter does little to explain the pattern observed during the nineteenth century. In weaving, the price of capital relative to wages had little role in the growth of output per worker, so it would be surprising if it had a major role in the division of that extra output. Furthermore, the engineering production function analysis shows that the elasticity of substitution between looms and weavers was quite low. But according to the theory, this finding implies that greater capital per worker should have led to a growing share of income going to workers. In fact, the opposite occurred. For decades at the beginning of the Industrial Revolution, both capital per worker and output per worker grew but workers gained little. The problem is that these models do not paint a robust picture of technology or the associated skills that workers acquire in order to implement new technologies.

Economists Claudia Goldin and Lawrence Katz consider the link between capital accumulation and skills by pointing out that capital-intensive technology creates demand for certain skilled workers.[19] They call their hypothesis "capital-skill complementarity." They, too, see the growth in capital per worker as central, but they argue that more investment in capital requires more skilled workers to install, maintain, and repair this additional capital equipment. In their view, technology increases capital, and greater capital, in turn, increases the demand for skilled maintenance labor, thus increasing wages. But this hypothesis cannot explain more than a marginal contribution to the increase in the wages of average workers over the last 200 years. Only 4 percent of the workforce has jobs in installation, maintenance, and repair occupations, and many of these workers are not highly paid. This is not much more than the share of such workers in the early textile mills. If we add the people who make the new capital goods (including engineering and computer occupations in recent years), the total comes to 7 percent. Clearly, the demand for this small group of workers in specialized occupations cannot explain the dramatic growth in wages for the average worker for a century prior to 1980. The notion that skills are needed to keep the machines running is important, but there is little reason to think that those skills are limited to a few specialized occupations; as history tells us, ordinary workers such as weavers also needed skills to keep the machines running.

Perhaps it is more promising to look at the broader role of knowledge needed to implement new technology. Some economists have recognized the importance of technology-specific knowledge,[20] but they have not developed a detailed understanding of how that knowledge changes over time and how this affects the economics. In a sense, economics lacks a good explanation for capitalism's greatest apparent success against Marxism. This is a significant shortcoming at a time when the link between new technology and the wealth of the masses seems to be broken. Yet economics does have a good micro-level explanation for why some workers earn more than others. This explanation concerns human capital, the investment people make in skills and knowledge.

## The Paradox of Technical Knowledge

Question: How do workers benefit from inventions that can be easily replicated around the world?

Answer: By having related knowledge and skills that *cannot* be easily replicated.

Workers earn high pay when they have technology-specific knowledge and skills. This observation is plainly evident in any help-wanted listing. All of the high-paying jobs that are advertised require some sort of education, either a college degree or specific vocational training. And to the distress of many recent graduates, the good jobs also usually require experience, implying that important knowledge and skills are learned on the job. This casual impression is confirmed by econometric studies of human capital. But job-specific knowledge is largely related to technology, broadly speaking. New technologies require new knowledge and skills that are not easy to communicate.

Thus while the idea of using machinery to automate weaving contains great potential for producing more output per worker, the idea alone is not enough. Producing cloth efficiently on a large scale also requires detailed knowledge of how to build high-performance looms, how to organize factories, and how to run the looms efficiently. Because this new knowledge was difficult to acquire and yet critical to profitability, mill owners were willing to pay a premium to those workers who had acquired it. Although it took decades, large numbers of ordinary weavers acquired skills and knowledge on the job that allowed them to earn these higher wages.

Today there is ample evidence that a very large share of what workers earn derives from technical knowledge and skills. Experienced workers often earn 30 percent or more than new hires.[21] Economists estimate that 77 percent of the variation in pay between workers arises from differences in experience and individual characteristics, including training.[22] It is therefore not hard to see how major technological changes can affect the share of income that goes to workers. The recent decline in labor's share of income could be explained by changes in workers' returns to experience. If technology makes old skills obsolete, then the pay of experienced workers will fall relative to new hires. In Chapter 7, we will see that substantial changes of this sort have occurred in some economic sectors. Conversely, the pay of experienced and trained workers can rise as new skills become established, increasing labor's share of income.

Technical knowledge is not, of course, the only factor affecting wages. Because borders restrict the flows of immigrants, capital, and sometimes technology, even the least skilled workers might earn more in one country than in another. But over decades and centuries, these factors are not that significant in determining the availability of technology. Advanced textile-manufacturing equipment was available worldwide by the beginning of the twentieth century, but what mattered more than availability was whether a nation had the skills and knowledge to make effective use of that technology and how much workers shared in its benefits. When such technologies deliver fiftyfold increases in productivity, the effect of immigration restrictions is minor. Culture and institutions also differ from country to country, affecting, for example, the hours and effort that workers are willing to put in at a given wage. But these differences alone are minor compared to the differences brought by technology. Likewise, government regulation can directly affect wages, for example, with minimum wage requirements.

Historians also highlight the role of unions in bringing higher wages to working people. The labor movement has played an important political role, pushing for the eight-hour workday, child labor laws, health and safety laws, and more. But empirical evidence suggests that the direct effect of unions on wages is limited. Union workers earn about 15 percent more than comparable nonunion workers.[23] Moreover, this premium is not independent of worker skills. Union power depends to a degree on the technical knowledge and skills of workers. The ability of steelworkers, say, to mount an effective strike depended in part on the union's ability to maintain solidarity and exclude strikebreakers, but it also depended on the difficulty of replacing workers' specialized technical knowledge and skills.[24] Over the long run, the latter was quite important. Indeed, textile workers saw their wages rise during the latter part of the nineteenth century even though textile unions were small and ineffective. Bessemer steelworkers earned much higher wages than craft ironworkers, and they worked an eight-hour day despite consistent defeats for the unions over the first decades of Bessemer production.[25] Today, nonunion blue-collar steelworkers still command relatively high salaries, presumably thanks to their skills and knowledge. Unions certainly were important, but their long run impact is significantly a product of their members' technical knowledge and skills. When that knowledge becomes obsolete, unions can rapidly lose power, as the once-formidable International Typographical Union did (see Chapter 7). But technical knowledge is the key, both with and without unions.

This, then, is the paradox of technical knowledge: technology creates aggregate wealth for a nation because new ideas can be replicated at low cost, but technology creates wealth for the *people* of a nation by requiring new technical knowledge that *cannot* be easily replicated. Replicating ideas allows more output from the same inputs, but ordinary people don't share in that added output unless they have valuable knowledge that is somewhat scarce. When technical knowledge requires a significant human capital investment, it can earn significant returns.

Although human capital is a source of popular wealth, that wealth does not always flow to workers. As Gary Becker explained in his seminal work on human capital in the 1960s, workers may have skills and knowledge, but under some circumstances the benefits of those skills and knowledge flow to their employers, increasing profits instead of wages.[26] Employers

sometimes make the investments in human capital and they earn the returns on those investments as long as trained workers stay employed. In
these situations, wages can remain unchanged while output increases and
profits grow. This point is important for understanding how technology
affected wages in the past, and how it may be producing wage stagnation
today.

## CHAPTER 6

# How the Weavers Got Good Wages

IN OCTOBER 1836, HARRIET HANSON (later married to William Robinson) led the women in her room in one of the Lowell mills on a walkout, joining as many as 1,500 other women in a procession through town. This was only the second major strike in Lowell.

Harriet's family came to Lowell to run a boardinghouse after her father died, much like Lucy Larcom, who later became her friend. Harriet acquired an elementary school education and began working in the mills at age ten to help her family. Like Lucy, Harriet would later resume her education, studying French, Latin, and English composition and grammar. She became a poet, an author, and an active suffragette, founding the National Woman Suffrage Association of Massachusetts. But in 1836, at the time of the strike, she was only a girl of eleven.

The mill managers announced an increase in the price of room and board at the company boardinghouses, effectively reducing wages for most women in the mills. This immediately sparked a discussion of a strike among the factory workers, despite the failure of a walkout to prevent a wage decrease two years earlier. Harriet later recounted her role:

> My own recollection of this first strike (or "turn out" as it was called) is very vivid. I worked in a lower room, where I had heard the proposed strike fully, if not vehemently, discussed; I had been an ardent listener to what was said against this attempt at "oppression" on the part of the corporation, and nat-

urally I took sides with the strikers. When the day came on which the girls were to turn out, those in the upper rooms started first, and so many of them left that our mill was at once shut down. Then, when the girls in my room stood irresolute, uncertain what to do, asking each other, "Would you?" or "Shall we turn out?" and not one of them having the courage to lead off, I, who began to think they would not go out, after all their talk, became impatient, and started on ahead, saying, with childish bravado, "I don't care what you do, I am going to turn out, whether any one else does or not"; and I marched out, and was followed by the others.

As I looked back at the long line that followed me, I was more proud than I have ever been since at any success I may have achieved, and more proud than I shall ever be again until my own beloved State gives to its women citizens the right of suffrage.[1]


The young women exited the mills, shutting them down, and they marched through town to Chapel Hill to hear "incendiary" speeches by labor reformers, including one by a mill girl. The strikers had a significant impact on the mills because workers had been in short supply even before the strike. The strikers themselves were well organized and the strike lasted weeks.[2]

Nevertheless, in Harriet's view, "this strike did no good. The dissatisfaction of the operatives subsided, or burned itself out, and though the authorities did not accede to their demands, the majority returned to their work, and the corporation went on cutting down the wages."[3] The failure was personal as well. Although Harriet was permitted to return to work, the mill agent fired her mother from her job running a boardinghouse because she had not prevented her daughter from participating in the strike.

Nor were subsequent strikes successful during the nineteenth century, although Lowell saw a major textile strike in 1912. During the nineteenth century, the labor movement was perhaps more successful as a political movement. In the 1840s, the Lowell Female Labor Reform Association was formed and began a petition demanding that the workday be limited to ten hours. Some 2,500 women signed the petition, although it was not successful. Nevertheless, this political agitation set in motion forces that led Massachusetts to become the first state to limit the workday to ten hours for women in 1874. Nevertheless, labor activity did not succeed in raising weavers' wages; they remained stagnant at a time when productivity was growing rapidly, and for many years the mills made phenomenal profits.

This pattern ended after the Civil War, when weavers' pay grew rapidly, ending decades of stagnant wages. Weavers continued to earn modestly good pay through the twentieth century. Weaving was a career that paid middle-class wages, even though most weavers lacked a high school diploma and about half were women. They were eventually compensated for their skills, but it took a while.

## Engels' Pause

This puzzle is, in fact, more general. Many manufacturing workers during the Industrial Revolution had important new skills and knowledge, but at first their wages did not reflect these skills. Marx's dire view of the effect of technology on workers' wages was *initially* right.

Economic historian Robert Allen has described the first six or seven decades of the British Industrial Revolution as "Engels' Pause."[4] Friedrich Engels wrote in 1844 that the industrialists "grow rich on the misery of the mass of wage earners."[5] And indeed, for six or seven decades at the beginning of the Industrial Revolution, output per capita grew rapidly while wages did not. The capitalists and middle classes pocketed the difference. New technology brought greater productivity and higher profits, but also greater inequality and stagnant wages. Other observers at the time, including Ricardo and Malthus, assumed that flat wages were a feature of capitalist economic development. Yet not long after Engels wrote *The Condition of the Working Class in England in 1844*, things changed. For the remainder of the nineteenth century, wages grew rapidly, and workers received most of the benefit of new technology.[6]

A similar delay occurred during the Industrial Revolution in the United States, and it shows up in the wages of weavers. Figure 6.1 shows the hourly wages of weavers and spinners in the mills of Lowell, adjusted for inflation. Despite the importance of skills, weavers' wages did not begin increasing

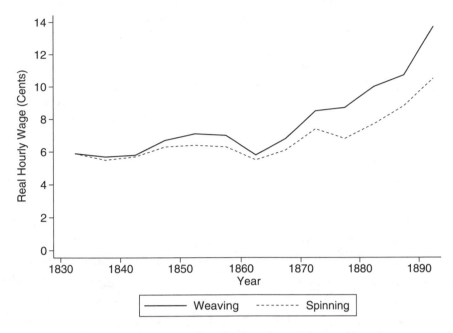

Figure 6.1. Weavers' pay rises sharply after a long delay: Real hourly wages
for weavers and spinners in Lowell (in 1860 dollars).
(Bessen, "Was Mechanization De-Skilling?")

until the 1870s. From 1830 to 1855, their real daily wages increased by only
about 14 percent while their hourly output increased roughly 80 percent.[7]
After the Civil War, however, things changed. By 1900, weavers' real wages
had more than doubled. They increased by 112 percent over the level of 1830.[8]
A small part of this increase came from a general rise in wages, perhaps
from a growing demand for labor generated by an expanding economy or
by the growth of the West.[9] Nor can the increase be attributed to changing
demographics. The weavers were still mostly women, although now mostly
Irish and French Canadian immigrants.

   Most of the increase in wages came because the weavers were paid more
for their skills. This can be seen by comparing weavers' wages to those of
spinners in the same mills. The spinners were demographically similar to
the weavers in the Lowell mills, but their jobs involved considerably less
skill.[10] That means that the spinners' wages more closely reflected the

Table 6.1 Weaver's Pay and Experience

|  | Weaver's Pay Premium to Less Skilled Job (Spinning) | Share of New Hires with Experience | Experience Premium |
|---|---|---|---|
| 1830s | 1% | 18% | 19% |
| 1850s | 8% | 65% | 51% |
| 1880s | 47% | 87% | 117% |

*Source*: Bessen, "Was Mechanization De-Skilling?"

general demand for female labor; the weavers, on the other hand, received a wage that reflected both the general demand for labor plus the specific demand for their skills. The difference between weavers' wages and spinners' wages thus reflects a portion of the weavers' pay that can be attributed to their skills. The total portion of weavers' pay that can be attributed to skills was larger than this difference because the spinners had some skills as well. Nevertheless, the growth in the gap between the pay of weavers and spinners shows a growing share of weavers' compensation coming as a return on their skills.

During the 1830s, weavers earned about the same as spinners (see "Weaver's Pay Premium to Less Skilled Job" in Table 6.1). They made relatively small investments in learning and earned only a small experience premium.[11] But by the 1880s, women weavers earned a 47 percent premium over women in the spinning departments. Thus the benefits of this powerfully productive technology did flow to the weavers, but only after a delay of five or so decades from the first mill in 1816.

The growing value of experience also implies greater returns on skill. The third column of the table shows the pay of an experienced weaver compared to an inexperienced one. During the 1880s, the relative pay of experienced weavers was higher because the weavers earned much lower pay during their first months on the job as they were learning; this was their human capital investment. Once they had experience, they were effectively paid a return on this investment in the form of higher wages. The substantial growth of this experience premium indicates the much greater returns to skill paid to weavers in the 1880s.

## Wages and Alternative Employment

Why did it take several decades for weavers' pay levels to reflect their skill? The simple answer is that most weavers had limited alternatives for using their skills during the 1830s and 1840s. Even though they had important skills, they could not credibly threaten to leave if they were not paid enough. Few other jobs for young women paid as well. The mills in Lowell set wages jointly, and mills in other towns did not hire significant numbers of trained weavers, nor did they offer premium wages to lure them away.[12] It would have been risky to seek work elsewhere. The mills thus did not need to pay much of a premium to keep weavers from leaving. As long as they did not reduce wages too much—the mill agents were acutely aware of this danger—they had available a ready supply of new trainees.[13]

But while untrained workers could be quickly hired, there was little market for *trained* weavers—the mills hired relatively few experienced workers. As Table 6.1 shows, only 18 percent of new hires had previous experience during the 1830s. But the supply of experienced weavers grew: by the 1850s, 65 percent of new hires had experience, and by the 1880s, 87 percent did.[14] By then, trained weavers had a more effective threat than a walkout: they could readily get a job in another mill. Other employers were willing to pay a bit more to hire away an underpaid experienced weaver because it saved them training costs. Competition among employers meant that experienced weavers could finally get substantial compensation for the skills that they had acquired. Spinners and other less skilled workers had no comparable threat because their training costs were not so great. Thus weavers' pay went up relative to less skilled workers (column 1 shows how much more weavers were paid compared to spinners) who were easier to train, and also relative to untrained weavers (column 3 shows how much more experienced weavers were paid compared to inexperienced ones).

Although the weavers' labor action in the 1830s proved ineffective—subsequent strikes in Lowell were no more successful—the weavers later did achieve major pay increases. In other industries, of course, unions did sometimes help workers earn greater pay. But even then, the strength of unions often depended on the difficulty firms had in replacing skilled workers.

## Waiting for the Market

Why did it take so long for a robust market for skilled weavers to develop? We are accustomed to thinking of new markets emerging rapidly, more or less as soon as a new product emerges or a new need is identified. But that view is true only for standardized products. However, the specific skills associated with a major new technology are not standardized at first, which limits the market. Initially, these skills are *always* limited to specific employers. At the first power loom mill in Waltham, there was no market for skilled weavers because no other mill had power looms.

As more mills began using power looms, the market still remained limited for some time. There was a chicken-and-egg problem. Weavers were not willing to pay for their own training (perhaps by accepting below-market wages while they were learning) unless doing so gave them a secure prospect of higher wages later on. But mills could not credibly offer a wage premium to trained weavers unless it was profitable to do so, and there are reasons why it might not be. First, if the technology were not standardized, each firm would have somewhat different looms, different products, different inputs, and different ways of working. If workers needed substantial retraining, the investment required of the mill could be almost as much as training someone with no experience. Second, it might be difficult to tell which weavers at another firm were really skilled. Without standard training and some sort of certification, prospective employers could not rely on credentials or on reference letters to verify a weaver's proficiency. Third, an employer who wanted to get out of the business of training most new employees had to be able to hire a sufficient number of experienced weavers on the market. Lack of standardization limited competition between the mills.

The market for experienced weavers was limited in the 1830s because the pool of experienced workers living around Lowell was small and because neither operations nor training were standardized.[15] During the 1830s, the markets for textile equipment were fragmented. For example, the machine shop that made looms for the Lowell mills sold few looms to other mills in New England, and other mills used different loom designs.[16] Different mills also used different types of labor supplies and were organized differently (see the discussion of the Waltham and Rhode Island "systems" in the next section on standardization).

Markets do exist for unstandardized products, but they rely on mechanisms such as reputation to convey information about the services provided and consumer needs. For experienced weavers with established reputations, such a market did exist. Many of these weavers were hired as "dayhands" who did not do piece work but trained new hires or assisted other weavers. For example, Betsy Merriam was hired in the Upper Weaving Room at Lawrence Company Mill No. 2 and was paid a weekly rate about 30 percent higher than what experienced weavers would earn on piece work. It may have helped her reputation that she had the same last name as that room's overseer, Darius Merriam. Reputation, once established, can help a worker earn substantially more than workers without reputations. In the extreme case, workers with good reputations become "superstars" and earn far more than others.[17]

But most weavers did not have the same opportunity as Betsy Merriam to earn high wages until a robust labor market developed after the Civil War. This commoditization of the labor market for weavers reduced the relative opportunities for the select weavers like Betsy Merriam who had established reputations—dayhands in 1883 earned about the same per week as experienced weavers working on piece rate—but it gave most weavers more opportunity.

### Waiting for Standardization

Why did it take so long for weaving skills to become standardized? We have seen that a number of factors can delay the standardization of technology. The QWERTY keyboard, for instance, took several decades to emerge as dominant. A variety of factors, beyond the geographical distance between mills, contributed to the delay in the standardization of weaving skills:[18]

1. *Rapid obsolescence.* Ongoing technological changes meant that the needed skills kept changing as mills tried new looms, new products, and new improvements in the manufacturing process. Especially during the early years, when the technological improvements had the greatest absolute effect on weavers' activity, there were large changes in weavers' skills. A weaver good at working on two looms might not easily adapt to working in

a mill with four improved looms per weaver. In 1842, when the mills changed from two looms per weaver to three, weavers who were experienced on two looms went through a second learning curve before they reached their former levels of productivity.

This meant that during the early years, weavers trained at one mill could not necessarily work proficiently at another. Eventually, however, the technological changes became more incremental. A core of basic skills was transferable from one mill to another, and the costs of retraining for the specific needs of each particular mill were relatively less. While the transition from two looms to three demanded new abilities to monitor and coordinate activity across more looms, changing from four looms to five was easier.

2. *Competing standards.* In order to create a robust labor market it is not enough to have *a* standard; the standard must be widely accepted. We saw that competing standards, such as VHS and Betamax for video recording, sometimes delay the emergence of a dominant standard. Textile technologies also had standards wars, for example, between "ring spinning," in which yarn was spun continuously onto rotating spindles, and "mule spinning," in which yarn was alternately spun and wound onto a large carriage of spindles. Other variations in standards may have arisen from different equipment configurations, different qualities of cloth, and different organizational practices. During the early decades, looms were not off-the-shelf products but were custom-built for each mill.

The standardization of knowledge after the Civil War was aided by institutions founded to share knowledge and coordinate standards. The New England Association of Cotton Manufacturers was formed in 1865 to exchange technical and management knowledge. The first technical school for textile managers and workers opened in Philadelphia in 1884, and the first one in New England opened in 1895. Knowledge exchange and formal training helped standardize the technology from one mill to another. The cotton manufacturers' association helped develop notions of best practice not only for the configuration of technology but also for labor practices and worker training. The schools helped instill these common practices in rising managers, technicians, and workers, and also established a basic set of weavers' skills. The emergence of a core of technical knowledge meant that weavers trained at one mill could readily work at another, and a robust labor market could function.

3. *Organizational change.* New technologies often bring a restructuring of occupations and industries, and changes in work organization. Until both the technology and work organization stabilize, it is difficult for a robust labor market for skilled workers to develop.

Often, the standardization of technical knowledge creates opportunities for different ways of training people. In chemistry, university training replaced laboratory apprenticeships. The cotton mills made major changes in the way they acquired a labor force. The first cotton mills in the United States, which only made yarn, were organized in the so-called Rhode Island system.[19] Whole families were recruited to live and work in mill villages, often with company housing and a company store. The family typically received a plot of land to work but committed to supply a certain amount of labor to the mill—often the labor of children supervised by one of their parents.

This system imposed serious limitations on skill development. The mills did not control which family members worked in the mills. Children were less likely or slower to acquire new skills than literate adults. And the families who were willing to settle into such situations were generally poor and, in the words of one mill owner, "often very ignorant, and too often vicious."[20] It was hard to build a high-quality workforce.

This was followed by the Waltham system, used by the first integrated spinning and weaving mills. These mills hired literate young Yankee women recruited from farms—often well-off farms—across northern New England. The women lived in boardinghouses in the mill town, typically working there for only a year or two. This labor supply was much better suited to the acquisition of new skills on the job.

But as the mills sought to deepen their investment in weavers' skills during the 1840s and 1850s, the Waltham system proved less than ideal. With deeper investments, the mills needed to keep the weavers employed for longer periods in order to recoup their investments. Although literate farm girls could acquire skills quickly, they were less likely to stay employed for long periods. By the 1850s they had other opportunities, such as becoming schoolteachers. Moreover, once they left the mills, they often left town and were not available to be rehired.

In the 1840s, the mills began hiring a different sort of worker: permanent residents of the mill towns who were often immigrants and frequently illiterate. These workers might take longer to acquire their skills, but once they did, they would stay employed longer. Even after they left employment, because they lived in the town they were often available to be rehired later, so the mills could again benefit from their skills. The mills gradually disbanded their support for boardinghouses, and slowly a local pool of experienced weavers developed. This pool was an essential prerequisite to a well-functioning labor market for skilled weavers.

### Sharing the Pie and Expanding the Pie

The emergence of a robust market for skilled weavers in New England not only led to a dramatic increase in wages of textile workers—refuting Engels—but it also led to a much more effective way for workers to acquire skills and knowledge on a large scale. Standardization meant both that workers shared more in the benefits of new technology, and that new technology could be used more widely.

During the early years, with a limited market, weavers invested little in their own skills because they could not count on earning higher wages later. Most of the investment was made by the mill owners, who earned a return on this investment by making greater profits with fully trained weavers. Later, when a robust market for skilled weavers had developed, each weaver could invest in developing her own skills by accepting lower pay during the initial months on the job, but she could reasonably expect to recoup that investment through higher wages over the remainder of her career.[21]

This change also facilitated a deeper investment in human capital. The mill owner, expecting the weaver to stay at his mill for only a year or so, would not invest much in weavers' training because he had such a short time to earn a return on the investment. And without a robust labor market, the weaver had little reason to put much effort into learning.[22] But with a robust labor market, a weaver, investing in her own human capital, could look forward to higher pay and a long career, possibly at many different employers, perhaps with spells out of the labor market. This greater payoff and longer time horizon provided a stronger incentive for weavers to invest in their own human capital. The deepening returns to experience, as shown in the last column of Table 6.1, demonstrate that weavers did, indeed, make bigger investments and earn bigger returns.

Standardization did not bring technological change to an end or even slow it down. Weaving technology continued to make major improvements throughout the nineteenth century and into the twentieth. And weavers did need to learn new skills—for instance, to adapt to the new automatic loom introduced in 1895. But these skills could be learned in the context of an existing labor market. New standards were quickly established for the new machines, and the basic organizational structure of the workplace changed little, allowing labor markets to quickly adapt to the new technology.

## Technology and Jobs

But while textile workers were paid more, weren't there fewer and fewer textile workers who could earn these higher wages? Marx's concern about the handloom weavers was that factory technology would replace manual workers and eliminate their jobs.

Much of the technology of the Industrial Revolution automated tasks formerly performed by manual workers. In the cotton mills, machines performed some of the weaver's tasks, such as propelling the shuttle across the loom or winding the woven cloth onto a roll. Less labor was needed to produce a yard of cloth. Weavers, with time freed up on one loom, could now be assigned to work on more than one machine. Would this replacement of human labor by machines generate a permanent loss in jobs, leading to widespread unemployment and misery?

No. Technology did not create permanent unemployment because while machines replaced humans on some tasks, they also created new demand for workers. Some of the new jobs were in the same occupation, others in new occupations or different industries. These new jobs required workers to acquire new technology-specific skills, which was often slow and difficult. But the net effect of technology in the past was to *displace* workers, not permanently replace them. Workers had to move from one set of technologies and organizations to another, from one set of knowledge and skills to another. Even though machines performed more and more tasks, there was no long-term shortage of jobs because there was always something else to do.

Consider how this worked in weaving. During the Industrial Revolution, cotton spinning was one of the first industries automated. Automation led to a huge drop in the price of cotton yarn and, correspondingly, a huge increase in the demand for cotton cloth. At first, this demand was met by weavers working at home on handlooms, often to supplement their income from agriculture. But eventually weaving, too, was automated. Power looms were used in factories, weaving ever more efficiently and driving down the price of cloth. This competition also drove down the earnings of handloom weavers. Marx saw the deterioration of their pay as the "tragedy of the handloom weavers": "History discloses no tragedy more horrible than the gradual extinction of the English handloom weavers, an extinction that was spread over several decades, and finally sealed in 1838 [a depression year]. Many of them died of starvation."[23]

Marx seems to have assumed that the handloom weavers had no other options, but the economic historian John Lyons looked carefully at the condition of the handloom weavers in England and found that, in fact, they moved to urban districts where family members obtained jobs in the mills.[24] While the power loom eliminated jobs at home, it created new jobs in the mills. The handloom weavers were certainly poor, Lyons concludes, but they were not the great losers of the Industrial Revolution. They bore the costs of a technological transition but otherwise did not fare so differently from other workers. Marx's mistake was to observe the labor-saving effect of technology on one occupation in one industry without noticing the offsetting increase in jobs in other occupations, industries, and sectors.

For over a century, labor-saving automation in weaving actually created jobs. Over the nineteenth century in the United States, the amount of coarse cotton cloth a weaver could produce in an hour increased fiftyfold.[25] In other words, automation eliminated 98 percent of the weaving labor required to produce a yard of cloth. Yet 98 percent of weavers did not lose their jobs.

Instead, their numbers grew substantially, quadrupling between 1830 and 1900. Why? Because automation also increased demand. With progressively lower costs, prices fell, consumers demanded more cotton cloth per capita, and there was more demand for weavers.[26] That growth in per capita consumption continued until the 1920s—at which point, apparently, consumers wanted little additional cotton cloth even at lower prices, partly because they preferred new synthetic fibers for some uses, partly because they only had limited demand for textiles of any sort. Since the 1920s, the number of cotton textile jobs has declined, while output per worker continued to increase by about 3 percent per year.[27]

This pattern is typical of major new technologies. In the early phases, many consumers typically are priced out of the market. Price reductions then increase demand, often rapidly. If this demand response is strong enough, the price reductions following labor-saving innovations will increase demand so much that the net number of jobs increases. In economics jargon, this happens when demand is sufficiently elastic.[28]

But when most consumers do not want much more of the good even at lower prices, jobs in the sector will decrease. Labor-saving technology eventually acted to decrease the number of weavers, but only after it had spurred more than a century of job growth.

Even then, the total number of jobs in the economy did not fall, because there were major unmet demands in other sectors. We have seen this happen before, too. For example, in 1800, before the Industrial Revolution, 74 percent of the labor force worked in agriculture. Technology dramatically reduced the amount of labor needed to produce our food, prices fell to the point where most demand for food was met, and agricultural jobs, as a percentage of the workforce, fell into the low single digits. But lower food prices also meant that workers had more money to spare for other things, and the increased demand for other goods and services created new jobs in other sectors.

Marx's error should serve as a caution. Just because a technology can eliminate much or even most of the labor needed to produce a unit of output, it does not follow that jobs will necessarily disappear in the affected industry or, even more, in the economy as a whole.

The key point is that in a competitive economy, the effect of technology on jobs depends on demand. As long as technology does not *completely* replace humans, the outcome does not depend entirely on how much or how rapidly machines take over human tasks. What also matters is how much technology increases demand, by reducing prices, improving quality, or adding new product features. As long as technology continues to satisfy important new needs and as long as some human tasks are not automated, technology will not entirely replace humans.

## Technology and Globalization

Technology has another effect on jobs. It facilitates globalization, especially when technical knowledge becomes highly standardized.

Consider, again, cotton textiles. During the early twentieth century, British textile machinery manufacturers exported their technology around the world, including to India, China, and Japan.[29] But the technical knowledge needed to install, manage, and operate this technology, along with the necessary institutions and organizations to allow large numbers of workers to acquire this knowledge, did not appear in these countries for many decades. Cotton textile workers in China, India, and Japan in 1910 had the same machines as those in England, but their productivity was far less than that of the English or American workers because they lacked the same knowledge and skills.[30] Even when English managers ran mills in India and China, productivity tended to be low because the English managers had to adapt their knowledge to a different environment and culture.[31] During the 1930s, Japan became the first developing nation to achieve high levels of productivity, and it began exporting yarn and cloth, mainly to Asian markets. Others took longer: some large developing nations are still catching up. A recent study showed that Indian textile mills today can make major efficiency gains by applying such basic managerial methods as tracking inventory and measuring machine downtime.[32]

But Japan's entry into world markets had little effect on the American textile industry. The United States did not even become a net exporter of textiles until the 1920s, when domestic demand for cloth started to level off.[33] Even to this day, the United States exports more textiles than it imports,[34] thanks to an industry that has remained competitive by investing in technology and by specializing in more advanced fabrics while basic products like simple cotton cloths have migrated offshore.[35] While maturing technologies facilitated the offshoring of jobs, many of the workers were displaced to jobs producing fancier or more advanced goods.[36]

Nevertheless, globalization *has* eliminated textile jobs during recent decades mainly because of globalization in the less technically sophisticated *apparel* industry—overseas clothing makers are more likely to also use cloth made overseas. But imports of apparel did not become significant until the 1980s and especially since 2000, with large-scale production in China. This led to significant American job losses in both the textile and apparel industries, but not until almost a century after the basic technology was exported around the globe.[37]

## Learning from History

Edmund Cartwright invented the power loom to aid his rural parishioners who wove to supplement their farm income. Weaving technology did not remain a major source of income for Cartwright's parishioners, but neither did it drive anyone to starvation. After a delay of decades, factory weavers saw rising incomes, and weaving became a path for relatively uneducated workers, mostly women, to enter the lower middle class. Even in the late 1970s, weavers—two-thirds female, most with less than a high school education—earned about the median wage. Despite labor-saving technological improvements and globalization, weaving provided employment for substantial numbers of people for nearly 200 years, and the absolute number of weaving jobs grew over the power loom's first century.

This is, of course, just a single case study. Many other factors affected workers' wages during the nineteenth and twentieth centuries, and not all technologies developed the same way. Other technologies and occupations saw different patterns of development. Some, like textile spinning, did not involve as much learning on the job and consequently did not pay as well.[38] In others, such as typewriting and steelmaking, the market for skilled labor took less time to develop—but that time was still some decades.[39] Other technologies addressed niche markets so that technological improvements did not create the potential for major job growth.

Nevertheless, weaving provides some important lessons. Weaving technology took over most of the tasks that humans performed on the looms, yet the number of jobs increased for 100 years, thanks to growing demand for cotton cloth. Nor did technology eliminate the skills of weavers that provided a basis for higher earnings; thanks to the remainder principle, nonautomated skills became more valuable. Yet it took time, new training institutions, and new labor markets before weavers became highly compensated for those skills.

## CHAPTER 7

# The Transition Today:
# Scarce Skills, Not Scarce Jobs

AT A LARGE DISTRIBUTION CENTER north of Boston, a robot lifts a shelf holding merchandise and navigates it through the warehouse to the workstation of an employee who then picks the item needed for an order and places it in a shipping box. The distribution center, run by Quiet Logistics, a company that fills orders for sellers of premium branded apparel, is featured in a *60 Minutes* episode, "Are Robots Hurting Job Growth?"[1] Incoming orders are processed by a computer that sends picking requests to sixty-nine robots. The robots deliver storage units to roughly a hundred workers, saving the workers the task of walking through the warehouse to find the items.

This is work that warehouse workers do in other distribution centers. Steve Kroft of *60 Minutes* poses the following question to Bruce Welty, CEO of Quiet Logistics:

> Steve Kroft: If you had to replace the robots with people, how many people would you have to hire?
> Bruce Welty: Probably one and a half people for every robot.
> Kroft: So it saves you a lot of money?
> Welty: Yes.

Robots have long been a staple of science fiction. "Now they're finally here," Kroft tells us, "but instead of serving us, we found that they are competing for our jobs. . . . If you've lost your white-collar job to downsizing, or to a worker in India or China, you're most likely a victim of what economists have called technological unemployment. There is a lot of it going around, with more to come."

The robots perform tasks that humans previously performed. The fear is that they are replacing human jobs, eliminating work in distribution centers and elsewhere in the economy. It is not hard to imagine that technology might be a major factor causing persistent unemployment today and threatening "more to come."

Surprisingly, the managers of distribution centers and supply chains see things rather differently: in surveys they report that they can't hire *enough* workers, at least not enough workers who have the necessary skills to deal with new technology.[2] "Supply chain" is the term for the systems used to move products from suppliers to customers. Warehouse robots are not the first technology taking over some of the tasks of supply chain workers, nor are they even seen as the most important technology affecting the industry today.[3] Information technology has been transforming supply chains for decades, often taking over tasks previously performed by shipping clerks and others. Systems track items from source to customer, keeping inventories at optimal levels and minimizing shipping time and cost. RFID (radio frequency identification) tags allow items to be tracked automatically, eliminating much clerical work. These technologies allow today's retail stores to offer a far more varied selection than in the past, often at lower prices, and to respond quickly to changes in demand. They have changed the retail landscape, for example, powering the growth of Walmart, a pioneer in adopting some of these technologies.

Yet although these technologies eliminated some jobs for clerks and warehouse laborers, they also created new jobs by creating new capabilities. However, these new jobs require specialized skills among both the managers and technicians, who typically have college degrees, as well as among the less educated operational occupations. Workers who have these skills, often learned on the job, are in short supply.

Moreover, industry experts see the need for skilled workers increasing in the short run and persisting for at least another decade. Working with industry trade associations, academic experts issued a "U.S. Roadmap for Material Handling and Logistics," arguing that

Despite the potential of dramatically improved processes and technology for material handling and logistics systems in the coming years, much of the work in the industry will continue to be done by a human workforce in the year 2025. Moreover, other aspects of this [technology], such as mass personalization, will require levels of operational flexibility that can only be handled by a skilled and creative workforce. In other words, people will continue to be vital to the industry in 2025.[4]

As with weaving and other nineteenth-century technologies, automation of some tasks increases the value of the remaining tasks, even as new or deeper skills are needed. But workers with those skills are not readily available, nor do robust labor markets initially provide the right incentives for workers to acquire those skills. The supply chain industry experts contributing to the U.S. Roadmap say that a key challenge is to "overcome a perception that joining [the industry] might not result in a career with suitable rewards." Prospective workers are not likely to make investments in new skills if they don't know "where a particular job might lead them." The experts call for training programs with a new curriculum and certifications to standardize emerging job classifications. In their view, training certifications are essential to standardizing skills that will enable labor markets to provide long-term rewards: "On-the-job training will be required of companies in any feasible long-term solution. Nevertheless, there is a need to build a network of certifying bodies to incorporate certifications from associations and related programs in place today." The experts call for training programs, including on-the-job training that will generate 70,000 such certifications per year. As in the past, developing broad-based standardized skills is critical to employing new technology and creating well-paying jobs for large numbers of workers.

These problems posed by technology are not unique to supply chain workers. In their book *The Second Machine Age*, Erik Brynjolfsson and Andrew McAfee make a strong argument that technology is transforming work in a wide range of occupations. They write, "There's never been a worse time to be a worker with only 'ordinary' skills and abilities to offer, because computers, robots, and other digital technologies are acquiring these skills and abilities at an extraordinary rate."[5] In the past, new technologies tended to automate blue-collar jobs. Now information technology has begun automating white-collar jobs, and the new technologies will increasingly automate even professional jobs. Already computers can diagnose breast cancer from X-rays and predict survival rates at least as well as the average radiologist.

There is no doubt that technology is transforming work, but the question here is exactly how. The two perspectives described—one held by *60 Minutes* and the other by industry managers—represent two different views of how technology is affecting jobs in the current economy. Both views recognize that technology takes over some tasks that humans performed. But one view contends that technology is not only taking over tasks, it is now eliminating work overall. Machines are *replacing* workers, leading to fewer and fewer jobs, especially for those without high levels of education. In this view, technology-induced unemployment keeps the median wage stagnant. A large pool of unemployed workers competing for too few jobs drives wages down.

In the other view, technology doesn't replace workers; it *displaces* workers to jobs with somewhat different skill sets. Sometimes these new skills are employed in the same occupation; sometimes they are employed in new jobs in other occupations. But in this view, technology is not causing an endemic shortage of jobs except in very mature industries. Instead, wages are stagnant because it is difficult for many workers to acquire the new skills and labor markets do not fully compensate workers for those skills. In this view, skills are scarce and labor markets are incomplete; in the other, jobs are scarce.

## Replacement or Displacement?

The difference between replacement and displacement is important because it affects policy. If technology is replacing workers, then there is little that policy can do to overcome economic inequality short of drastic redistribution. Moreover, the future may be one where only the most educated workers have access to good jobs. Such extreme economic inequality might lead to political instability or to the end of liberal democracy. This view represents a historical break in the role of technology, which has raised the economic welfare of many over the last 200 years. This view foreshadows extreme political stress on the capitalist system, if not collapse.

On the other hand, if technology is mainly displacing workers rather than replacing them, the future, perhaps after a lengthy transition, might not be so different from the past. But achieving that future depends critically on putting in place the policies that will encourage broad-based develop- ment of new skills. As we shall see, government policy in recent decades has mainly moved in the wrong direction. For this reason, understanding the nature of our current predicament is crucial to developing the right pol- icies now.

In fact, the evidence shows that information technology today is displac- ing workers, not replacing them. I look first at case study evidence and then at aggregate data. Perhaps the future will be different from the recent past, but a close look at actual trends in the labor market suggest a difficult tran- sition is underway today rather than a sharp break with history.

*Are Robots Stealing Our Jobs?*

The *60 Minutes* episode notes several other occupations affected by tech- nology. Ticket kiosks at airports have replaced airline ticket agents, "bank tellers have given way to ATMs, sales clerks are surrendering to e-commerce, and switchboard operators and secretaries to voice recognition technology."

It might seem obvious that if ATMs do the work of bank tellers and ac- counting software does the work of bookkeepers, there will be fewer jobs for bank tellers and bookkeepers. But that reasoning is fallacious. We can test the argument about automation by looking at the actual changes in em- ployment in some of these occupations. Table 7.1 shows these changes over the last decade.[6]

Even with the Great Recession, the number of bank tellers increased despite ATMs, the number of bookkeepers increased despite accounting software, and the number of retail salespersons grew robustly despite e-commerce. Combined, these occupations added three quarters of a mil- lion new jobs. The number of typists and switchboard operators declined, but their decline was offset by a corresponding increase in the number of

Table 7.1 Are Robots Replacing Humans in These Jobs?

| Occupation | Change in Employment, 1999–2009 |
|---|---|
| **Supposedly Replaced, Employment Grew** | |
| Bank tellers | 123,440 |
| Bookkeeping, accounting, and auditing clerks | 138,000 |
| Retail salespersons | 480,460 |
| TOTAL | 741,900 |
| **Supposedly Replaced, Displaced to Other Occupations** | |
| Word processors and typists | −161,840 |
| Switchboard operators, including answering service | −101,590 |
| Secretaries, except legal, medical, and executive | 215,590 |
| Receptionists and information clerks | 64,440 |
| TOTAL | 16,600 |
| **Actually Replaced** | |
| Reservation and transportation ticket agents and travel clerks | −79,840 |

*Source*: Bureau of Labor Statistics, Occupational Employment Survey, http://www.bls.gov/oes/.

secretaries and receptionists. In other words, machines did not replace them, but their work was displaced to different occupations. If the widespread use of ATMs, accounting software, and word processing had really replaced workers, these groups of occupations would have shown drastic declines. Of these examples, only travel ticket agents appear to show an uncompensated decline. And even here, computer technology did not really replace human labor; it just transferred labor from airline employees to airline customers.

These examples do not make a strong case for technological unemployment, even if technology took over certain tasks. Certainly, ATMs, accounting software, and so on did allow machines to perform tasks formerly performed by humans, and so changed the nature of those jobs. But, as in the case of weaving, that does not mean that these technologies necessarily led to fewer jobs, even within the occupation most directly affected.

The simplistic story that machines steal jobs is appealing, but several examples suggest it is not an accurate account of what is going on in several occupations.

### The Case of the (Non-)Missing Bank Tellers

Consider tellers and the ATM. The first ATMs in the United States were installed by the Seattle First National Bank in 1971. By 1976, the country had over 5,000 ATMs, and installations accelerated after that.[7] By 1984, 42 percent of U.S. families had ATM cards. The banks initially used these machines as a way of providing better service and also reaching a wider geographic area at a time when the expansion of bank branches was restricted. But bankers also saw the potential to eliminate costs. Richard Rosenberg, vice chairman of Wells Fargo, wrote in 1980 that electronic transactions would reduce the number of bank branches and the remaining branches would have "few, if any, support staff members."[8]

But the number of tellers did not shrink. Instead, as Figure 7.1 shows, when the number of ATMs surged beginning in the mid-1990s, the number of tellers employed actually rose slightly.[9] Banks have now slowed their installations of ATMs, yet the number of teller jobs shows no evidence that these machines have replaced human tellers. If machines such as the ATM were really generating large-scale unemployment by replacing workers, we should see a dramatic drop in the number of tellers employed accompanying the surge of ATMs. We do not.

How could this be? For several reasons, the demand for teller services increased as some of those services were taken over by machines. In the average urban market, the number of employees used to operate a branch declined from about twenty in 1988 to a little over thirteen in 2004. But this meant it was less expensive for a bank to open a branch, leading banks to create more of them. The number of urban commercial bank branches increased 43 percent between 1988 and 2004, offsetting the decrease in employees per branch.[10]

ATMs also made many banking transactions more convenient for customers. It is hard to remember what a chore banking was for customers in the 1970s, with scattered branches and restricted hours. With the greater convenience of the ATM and deregulation of many restrictions, the

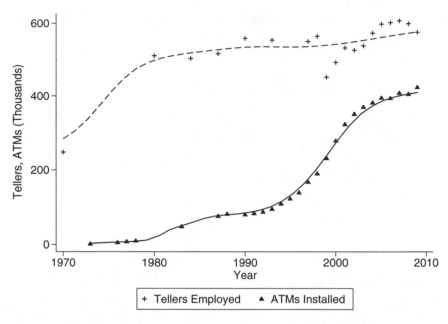

Figure 7.1. Adoption of automated teller machines did not reduce teller jobs. (Ruggles et al., Integrated Public Use Microdata Series: Version 5.0; Bureau of Labor Statistics, Occupational Employment Survey, http://www.bls.gov/oes/; Bank for International Settlements, Committee on Payment and Settlement Systems, various publications [see p. 243, note 9]).

number of banking transactions soared. But ATMs could not handle all bank transactions, including those of small businesses with high cash needs. Nor did all customers feel comfortable using ATMs. Some people preferred to wait in line for tellers. Although ATMs allowed banks to process many more transactions per teller, demand for teller services provided by humans did not disappear.

Bank deregulation also opened up markets to more competition by allowing banks to compete across state boundaries. The lower cost of operating a branch also encouraged banks to spread outside their states. Once they had to compete more for customers, convenience and quality of service mattered more. While some banks saw ATMs as replacements for tellers, others found greater success using tellers as part of the "customer service team" that sought to draw customers to more profitable services, such as invest-

ment management. This was called "relationship banking." Bank management journals now talk about the ways of reducing teller turnover, employing
enough tellers to minimize wait times, and using them to create a "wow
customer experience."[11] And what is the major new feature offered on the
latest ATMs? A live video link to a real teller.[12]

Thus the story that machines replace labor and reduce overall employment and wages is too simplistic. Just as with weaving, machines could perform some tasks, but they increased demand for other tasks. ATMs could
perform simple transactions, but by allowing banks to increase the number of branch offices, they raised demand for tellers who performed other
tasks. The effect of technology on jobs is simply more dynamic and more
complicated than many people recognize. Computers are taking over tasks
done by bank tellers and by workers in many other occupations, but this
observation alone does not support the conclusion of one recent paper that
such computerization puts "a substantial share of employment, across a wide
range of occupations, at risk in the near future."[13]

The number of teller jobs is not likely to grow much in the future and
might well decline. Banks have stopped adding new branch offices and online banking is growing rapidly; not surprisingly, the number of teller jobs
has declined slightly since 2009. But the more important impact of technology on bank tellers may be on their wages, which have been stagnant
despite the change in skills. Since the late 1980s, the median hourly pay of
bank tellers has risen about 6 percent. To date, bank teller turnover has remained high and labor markets do not compensate tellers well for their experience. The next case study illustrates why average wages can remain
stagnant, even while employment grows and skills increase.

*Skills in Flux*

Consider typesetting and publishing technology, where wages have
been stagnant and technological change dramatic. Printing with movable
type was invented in China during the eleventh century, and separately in
Germany by Johannes Gutenberg in the fifteenth century. At that time,
individual casts of metal letters were assembled by hand in a holder for each
line of type. This work was automated by the Linotype machine, first used
in 1886. The operator typed on a keyboard and the machine cast individual

lines of type in hot metal. Although the Linotype machine was heralded as a way of replacing skilled hand compositors with unskilled workers, the Linotype operator actually needed substantial skills. For many decades these skills began with a five-year apprenticeship program run by the International Typographical Union. The ITU was a powerful union, and typographers and compositors earned above-average wages.[14]

But technology began changing things, very slowly at first. Metal type worked with letterpress printing, where the metal type was inked and impressed on the paper. Offset lithography, another printing technology, used a plate that was photographically etched. To prepare type for this printing process, it was advantageous to have a photographic print of the type rather than cast metal. In the 1940s, phototypesetting was developed. With this technology, the operator also worked on a keyboard, but the effect was to expose photographic paper with masks of the letters, producing a print that could be etched onto a printing plate. This technology did little to alter the skills of a typographer, but it opened the door to further changes.

Computers were first applied to composition and typesetting in the early 1960s. The first great advantage was that a file saved in the computer's memory eliminated the need for re-keyboarding of typewritten text to correct errors. This development was accompanied by editorial systems that also eliminated much re-keyboarding. Experiments with WYSIWYG (what-you-see-is-what-you-get) page makeup on graphic computer screens also began during the 1960s. This technology would eventually allow designers to create and then change a layout on a computer screen without having to make a physical dummy of each page.

Although the technological advances of the 1960s did not greatly affect jobs, the typographers saw what was coming. New York newspaper workers went on strike in 1962, shutting down the city's newspapers for over three months, in part over issues of automation. To settle the strike, the publishers agreed that they would not introduce technological changes without the unions' consent. This agreement eventually led to a 1974 contract giving the newspapers a free hand to automate in exchange for lifetime job guarantees for the union members, which set the pattern for buyouts of typographers at newspapers throughout the country.[15]

When computer composition came along, the effect on jobs and wages was drastic. The number of jobs for typesetters and compositors in all industries fell from 170,000 in 1979 to about 74,000 in 1989. During the same interval, their median wages fell 16 percent after adjusting for inflation. Membership in the International Typographical Union fell sharply, and in 1986, much weakened, it merged with another union.

But computer publishing technology also created jobs. Much typography is now done by desktop publishers and graphic designers, whose numbers grew rapidly, more than offsetting the loss of typographers' jobs. The number of designers of all types more than quadrupled from 1979 to 2007, to over 800,000, more than making up for the loss of typesetting jobs.[16] While computer publishing technology eliminated tasks such as the need to rekeyboard text, it also made typesetting more accessible and less costly, and far more versatile. Consequently, the demand for graphic design and desktop publishing has soared. Publications that were once produced with a typewriter are now laid out on computers with high-quality type. Many of the words we read today are much more highly designed than those of thirty or forty years ago.

This transition required that graphic designers learn new skills related to using computers and page layout programs—a considerable change that involved significant investments in learning. Yet these new skills are not reflected in designers' wages and salaries. After accounting for inflation, the average hourly pay of graphic designers has been stagnant in recent years; the average pay of all types of designers has actually fallen since the 1970s. While designers are paid, on average, a bit more than typographers, the median designer of 2007 earns only about a dollar more per hour than the median typographer of 1976. Designers seem to have shared little in the benefits of this technology.

Why don't average designers earn more, now that they have acquired substantial new skills and job responsibilities? Because the technology and organization of work for designers seem to be in constant flux. The print designers who replaced the typographers have been partly replaced by web designers, who are partly being replaced by mobile designers. Technology is continually redefining what publishing is and how it is done. Each of these changes requires new, specialized skills—skills learned largely through experience or by sharing knowledge, rather than in school. Each year, designers have to learn new software and new standards in order to keep up. A few years ago they learned Flash; now it is HTML5. Next year, perhaps something else.

These technological changes have come with equally radical organizational changes. Work formerly done at printing facilities or typesetting job shops is now done by customers, ad agencies, or design studios. The portion of designers working freelance has grown from 18 percent in 1979 to 26 percent in 2007. Occupations are being redefined and new ones are emerging, such as "desktop publisher" and "information architect." Business models are in flux. Newspapers that were flush with profits in the 1980s after automating their production are in financial trouble today. Book publishers are making profits from e-books, but the dwindling of their sales channels threatens their long-run prospects. And these changes are far from over.

The Linotype operators are long obsolete, but they have not yet been replaced by a new, stable occupation with well-developed institutions to train and hire skilled workers. Many graphic arts schools cannot keep up with the latest technologies, and even educational programs that emphasize web design often have difficulty keeping up with the latest standards and software. The people who have this knowledge can earn far more using their skills than by teaching others.

And because technical knowledge becomes obsolete faster, the value of experience has declined. During the late 1970s, a designer with fifteen years' experience earned 65 percent more, on average, than a designer working less than five years; that experience premium has declined to about 52 percent.[17] Many experienced print designers still earn good pay, but increasingly, designers today have the wrong experience on an obsolete technology.

The most able designers teach themselves and thus earn high pay, often as freelancers. Freelancers in some cities earn $90 or $100 per hour or more. The pay of the top 10 percent of designers has substantially outpaced the median wage.[18] But the pay of the average designer has stagnated. With all of the churn in technologies and organizations, the average designer cannot easily acquire new skills because those skills are not sufficiently standardized. While there is a reputation-based market for elite designers with advanced skills, the average designer is not able to benefit.

Publishing illustrates the current predicament: until technology, skills, and organizations stabilize, the benefits of the new technology will not flow to many workers. Instead, they flow to highly able workers who can learn new skills on their own, and to employers, just as during the early decades of the Industrial Revolution.

### Standardized Knowledge and Higher Pay

But the story of licensed practical nurses (LPNs, also called licensed vocational nurses in some states) offers some hope. The pay of LPNs has risen 10 percent over the last decade, after adjusting for inflation. Over the last three decades, LPN employment rose 37 percent and real median hourly wages increased 24 percent.[19] LPNs comprise one of the largest middle-income occupations where both wages and employment are growing robustly.

Of course, the health sector has been experiencing strong growth generally, partly because the elderly are a growing share of the population. But while employment in most health occupations has been increasing, not all occupations have experienced wage growth, especially those that pay below the median wage. For example, the median wage for home health aides declined 8 percent between 1999 and 2010. The difference can be explained by technology and the standardization of technology-specific skills. LPNs mainly work at jobs where there is significant new technology; home health aides do not. Moreover, LPNs have acquired major new knowledge and skills on the job, which might seem surprising because most LPNs are not highly educated.

Yet for over forty years, people have been predicting the demise of the LPN because, they claim, these nurses lack sufficient education to deal with new technology.[20] Qualifying for an LPN license requires nine to eighteen months of training at junior college or vocational school (sometimes hospital based), depending on the state. Given the growing role of technology and scientific knowledge in health care, this requirement has been seen as inadequate since at least the 1960s. The American Nurses Association (ANA) saw the growing burden of new technology in 1965 and predicted the extension of some existing training programs to eighteen months. The ANA proposed eliminating LPN licensure in favor of an associate degree nurse, requiring a two-year program at a junior college, and lobbied state regulators to implement this program, with little success.[21] Still, the employment of LPNs did not grow much, and some hospitals, concerned about the quality of care, stopped hiring them.

But a strange thing happened on the way to obsolescence. From the 1970s through the 1990s, the number of LPNs remained flat or fell slightly, depending on which statistics you look at. Since 1999, however, the number of LPNs has risen nearly 50 percent, and wages have grown substantially.

This might seem puzzling. On one hand, it is true that the technology of health care has changed dramatically, which has surely affected the work of LPNs. They are now required, for example, to monitor patients with all sorts of biometric instruments. On the other hand, the formal training period for LPNs has not changed since 1965, with only a few states requiring eighteen months of training. LPNs are in greater demand, they command higher pay, and they do more technically advanced work, yet they get no additional formal training.

This paradox is resolved if we consider that licensed practical nurses learn on the job. Some evidence suggests that for LPNs, learning by doing has become much more economically important. In the late 1970s, an LPN with fifteen years' experience earned only 11 percent more than an LPN with less than five years on the job. Experience did not earn a substantial premium; LPNs apparently learned little that was valuable on the job. But today, the average LPN with fifteen years' experience earns 37 percent more than one with less than five years. Experience has become quite valuable, suggesting that LPNs are making substantial human capital investments on the job. They now have a valuable learning curve.

What changed to make learning on the job more important? A combination of technological and organizational factors allowed the skills required of nurses in specialized settings to become standardized. One major change was the widespread adoption of techniques for minimally invasive surgery. Advances in electronics, fiber optics, and robotics now allow surgical patients to recover quickly enough to return home the same day, avoiding an expensive hospital stay. Endoscopy allows a wide range of surgeries to be performed through only a small incision. Lasers permit minimally invasive eye surgery. Advances in anesthetics and pain medications allow patients to regain consciousness more quickly and to manage their pain at home. Although endoscopy has been used since the nineteenth century, improvements in endoscopy and other advances in medical technology make it much more useful today.

In addition, organizational changes, along with changes in medical insurance and government payment programs, allowed for a new business model, the "ambulatory surgery center." Centers specializing in just one type of surgery—knee surgery or eye surgery, for instance—grew much more proficient by learning through experience. Recall that surgeons have learning curves, too. This meant that medical outcomes could be improved while avoiding the extra cost of a hospital stay and the complications that tend to arise from more invasive procedures. Better quality at lower cost opened up a profitable opportunity, which was met with explosive growth. In 1983, there were 239 freestanding ambulatory surgery centers in the United States; by 1996 there were 3,300. In 1983, 380,000 ambulatory surgical procedures were performed at freestanding centers and at hospitals. In 2006, there were 53 million procedures.

Ambulatory surgery centers hired lots of LPNs. Most of the growth in LPN employment has been at doctors' offices and outpatient clinics. About 60,000 more LPNs worked in doctors' offices and outpatient clinics in 2009 than in 1979. Much of this shift can be attributed to the growth of ambulatory surgical services.

This new business model also demanded different sorts of skills. Health management experts Clayton Christensen, Jerome Grossman, and Jason Hwang identify the transition from the hospital to outpatient surgery as an instance of a more general transition from "intuitive medicine" to "precision medicine."[22] Hospitals treat all sorts of patients with all sorts of symptoms. Many diseases, however, are difficult to diagnose with certainty, and once a diagnosis is made, not all therapies work for all patients. Medical professionals often have to make a tentative initial diagnosis, start a therapy, and then possibly modify both the therapy and the diagnosis depending on how the patient responds. This is "intuitive" medicine, and it requires highly trained professionals to make complex judgments about the patient's condition. In this situation, LPNs can assist highly skilled medical professionals by performing the routine tasks of monitoring and caring for patients, but because patients differ so much from one to the next, there is little the LPN can learn from one patient that applies to many others.

The ambulatory surgery centers, by contrast, work in specialized areas where diagnoses are well identified, patients are screened for complications, therapies are well known, and medical outcomes are predictable, if not always successful. Physicians can reliably diagnose nearsightedness or carpal tunnel syndrome and treat these ailments with laser eye surgery or endoscopic hand surgery, respectively. The procedures are standardized and the outcomes are predictable.

This is precision medicine, and LPNs play a different role. Because the procedures are standardized, an LPN learns valuable skills on the job. Because specialization limits the range of circumstances they encounter, repetition allows LPNs to learn faster and better, acquiring skills that, though narrow, are more valuable. Through experience, an LPN can better anticipate the needs of medical professionals, can monitor and care for patients more effectively, and can identify signs of impending problems and alert other medical professionals. Moreover, because the procedures are standardized, skills are transferable. A nurse who acquires experience at one knee surgery clinic can be hired at another. The standardization of precision medicine facilitates the emergence of a labor market for experienced LPNs. And so their wages have been rising. Also, with nursing skills sufficiently standardized, the labor markets for LPNs are able to quickly adapt to changes in technology, as happened with weavers in the past.

## The Big Picture

In these case studies, technology displaced workers; it did not replace them. Typography jobs were displaced to graphic designer jobs; typist jobs became secretarial jobs. Bank tellers, graphic designers, secretaries, and LPNs all have new skills to learn, thanks to technology. But in these cases new technology did not lead to a total drop in employment. Some jobs migrated to different occupations, but they did not disappear. And the transition to new roles and new skills has been slow and, so far, not always successful.

*Aggregate Jobs*

How representative are these case studies? A look at aggregate data reinforces the finding that stagnant wages are not primarily the result of technological unemployment. In the aggregate, too, the picture is mainly one of displacement not replacement.

One statistic that economists use to judge the health of the labor market is the share of the population that has a job. If automation were causing systemic unemployment that stalled wage growth, we should see a drop in the share of working-age Americans who have jobs since 1980. Figure 7.2 shows the portion of the working-age population (the civilian noninstitutional population aged 25 through 54) that is employed. This line graph

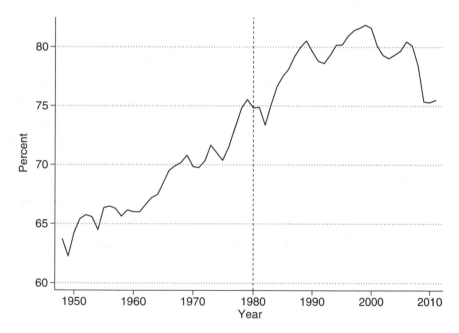

Figure 7.2. More Americans have jobs, not fewer: Share of the civilian, noninstitutional population aged 25–54 that is employed. Note the large dip caused by the latest recession. (Bureau of Labor Statistics, Labor Force Statistics from the Current Population Survey, Series LNU02000060Q and LNU00000060Q, obtained from http://www.bls.gov/data/.)

reflects the number of jobs available and filled by working-age Americans. We see a long-term rise in this percentage as more and more women entered the workforce and a recent sharp decline related to the recession.

The failure of employment to rebound after the most recent recession is worrisome. Economists debate the causes for persistent unemployment and they have identified a variety of factors that might explain recent poor performance. Some blame government policy for failing to provide sufficient economic stimulus; others note the aging of the population and changing gender roles. Some other economists note that more young workers are choosing to go to school, and some also think technology has an effect.

Regardless of the cause behind the recent poor performance, however, the graph clearly shows that endemic unemployment *cannot* explain the wage stagnation that has been occurring since 1980. From 1980 until the 2008 recession, the employment share rose substantially. Even since the recession, a higher percentage of working-age Americans are employed than in 1980. The economy has been able to create enough jobs to employ a rising share of working-age Americans, despite all the new technology. Technology might be a factor in the poor performance of the labor market over the last several years, and perhaps the slow recovery is a sign of things to come. But technological unemployment does not explain the wage stagnation of the last three decades; it cannot be a simple story of machines replacing workers.

### Occupational Changes in Jobs

Nor is wage stagnation explained by a simple story of new information technology replacing workers. If this were the case, then those occupations most affected by information technology should see the greatest declines in the number of jobs. Table 7.2 shows how different technologies affected jobs and wages across five broad groups of occupations, and the share of workers who use computers at work.

The occupational groups are listed in order of declining computer use. They are:

1. Scientific, engineering, and computer occupations. Many of the workers in these occupations create technology.

**Table 7.2** Technology and Occupational Change

| | Share of Workers Using Computers (2001) | Annual Job Growth Rate (1982–2012) | Employment 2012 (millions) |
|---|---|---|---|
| Scientific, engineering, and computer occupations | 85% | 2.1% | 8.0 |
| Occupations affected by office computing and the Internet | 69% | 1.2% | 55.5 |
| Health care occupations | 55% | 2.5% | 11.3 |
| Occupations less directly affected by technology | 31% | 1.4% | 52.6 |
| Occupations affected by manufacturing automation and offshoring | 30% | -1.1% | 13.3 |
| ALL OCCUPATIONS | 51% | 1.1% | 140.7 |

*Source:* Bureau of Labor Statistics, March Current Population Survey, http://www.bls.gov/cps/.

*Note:* The major occupational groups included in each of the five categories are as follows: (1) Computer and mathematical occupations; architecture and engineering occupations; life, physical, and social science occupations; (2) Office and administrative support; sales and related occupations; management; business and financial operations occupations; arts, design, entertainment, sports, and media occupations; (3) Health care practitioners and technical occupations, and health care support occupations; (4) Transportation and material moving occupations; food preparation and serving occupations; education, training, and library occupations; construction and extraction occupations; building and grounds cleaning and maintenance occupations; personal care and service occupations; protective service occupations; community and social service occupations; legal occupations; farming, fishing, and forestry occupations; and (5) Production occupations; installation, maintenance, and repair occupations. These groupings are rough, to be sure, but the general conclusions I draw from the table do not change significantly if the exercise is repeated with different occupational groupings.

2. Occupations affected by office computing and the Internet. This group includes management, administrative, sales, and media occupations. These occupations have been affected by a wide range of office computing technologies, including accounting software, word processing, enterprise management systems, and e-commerce. Typesetting, desktop publishing, and graphic design fall into this category, as well as bank tellers and the other occupations listed in Table 7.1.

3. Health care occupations. These occupations, which include doctors, dentists, mid-skill providers such as LPNs, and health service workers, are affected by a combination of new technologies combined with new business models and other organizational changes. Some of the mid-wage occupations in this group are closely related to specific technologies, such as radiological technicians who operate MRI and CT scanning machines, or sonographers. Many mid-skill occupations have expanded roles thanks to new diagnostic and preventative technologies, allowing mid-skill workers to perform more important tasks independently of doctors.

4. Occupations less directly affected by technology. The diverse occupations in this group include restaurant workers, teachers, transportation jobs, and construction workers. Although most of these occupations have been affected by technology in some ways, arguably the effects have been less direct than in the occupational groups listed above.

5. Occupations affected by manufacturing automation and offshoring. This group includes manufacturing jobs and installation, maintenance, and repair occupations. Like weaving, which is included in this group, many of these occupations employ mature technologies, where technological change tends to eliminate jobs.

Table 7.2 shows that computer use is not associated with job replacement and technological unemployment. While the workforce as a whole grew 1.1 percent per year from 1982 to 2012, the occupational groups that used more computers grew faster, not slower. In particular, administrative and sales occupations—the group that includes bank tellers, typists, and bookkeepers—grew a bit faster than the workforce despite the effect of technology on many jobs within this group. Jobs also grew faster in the other computer-intensive occupations, including health care and scientific/engineering jobs. It is possible that other factors increased employment even while computers were eliminating jobs in these categories, but that seems unlikely over such broad occupational groups.

Only manufacturing-related occupations grew slower than the labor force, exhibiting a major loss of jobs. These losses surely put downward pressure on wages. However, even these job losses are not entirely due to computers, new information technology, and robots. First, manufacturing jobs have also been hurt by import competition, especially from China, and are more sensitive than many other jobs to the business cycle.[23] This means that the loss of manufacturing jobs is only partly due to technology.

Furthermore, the loss of manufacturing jobs is nothing new, and not specific to the period since 1980. Like weaving, many of these manufacturing occupations employ mature technologies where technology has been eliminating jobs for much of the past century. Figure 7.3 shows manufacturing employment as a share of all nonfarm jobs. Manufacturing jobs have been declining steadily compared to total employment at least since the 1940s. Yet overall wage stagnation is a much more recent phenomenon. Moreover, there are no signs that the manufacturing decline has accelerated recently in response to new technology.

While computer numerical control systems and robotics surely contributed to recent job losses, much of the technological replacement comes from other technologies. As Table 7.2 shows, relatively few manufacturing jobs use computers. A 2014 MIT study finds that manufacturing industries that use computers intensively did not experience job-reducing productivity growth during the last decade.[24]

To summarize, the evidence in Table 7.2 provides little support for the idea that smart machines are permanently replacing humans in the workforce overall, at present. There is some technology-related job loss in the manufacturing sector, but jobs appear to be growing in other sectors sufficiently to offset these losses. The recovery from the recession is slow, to be sure,

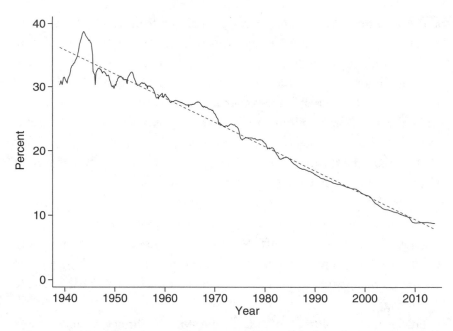

Figure 7.3. Manufacturing employment as a share of total nonfarm employment. (Bureau of Labor Statistics, Employment Situation, http://www.bls.gov/ces/.)

but that might have much to do with other factors such as, perhaps, the largest downsizing of government employment in recent history.

## Wages, Skills, and Displacement

Although information technology does not seem to be replacing workers overall, it has had a dramatic effect on some specific occupations. While the total number of administrative and office workers grew, the numbers of switchboard operators and typists dropped sharply, thanks to information technology. Economists have concluded that computers reduce the need for routine tasks, not only those performed by manufacturing workers, but also many tasks performed by clerks, typists, and other white-collar workers.[25] But the reduced need for routine tasks was matched by an increased demand for workers performing nonroutine tasks. Sometimes this occurred within an occupation, as with bank tellers who now perform relatively more tasks that are nonroutine. In other cases, jobs were displaced from one occupation to another, as secretaries displaced typists. Moreover, secretarial work has shifted from routine tasks, such as typing, taking shorthand, and answering the phone, to more complex tasks that involve significant learning, such as researching on the Internet or arranging travel.

Thus, although the broad occupational groups most affected by computer technology did not suffer technological unemployment, jobs were displaced to new occupations or new skill sets within these groups. If this interpretation is right, then we should see increased demand for skilled workers in these groups.

Data on relative wages do, in fact, show evidence of increased demand for skilled workers in these occupations. Skilled workers generally earn higher wages than less skilled workers because they earn a return on their investments in training. We can measure that difference as a wage premium, the difference between the wage paid to a skilled worker and the wage paid to a less skilled worker. All else being equal, an increase in demand for skilled labor relative to the supply should bid up the wage premium. And if the skills associated with specific computer applications become more valuable, then we should see wage premiums rise faster in those occupations that use computers more.[26]

The data in Table 7.3 show that those occupational groups most affected by computers—the top three rows—experienced the greatest increase in the relative wages paid to educated and experienced workers. The first two columns show changes in wage premiums for two groups of educated workers relative to the wage earned by workers with only a high school education. The third column shows the change in the wage premium paid to workers with fifteen years of experience relative to workers who have fewer than five years' experience.[27]

The wage premiums paid to educated workers rose overall, suggesting an overall increase in demand relative to supply for these workers. But the increase in wage premiums was especially strong in those occupations that use computers more. The increase was strong both for those workers with four years of college and also for those with fewer than four years of schooling after high school.

These differences across occupations suggest that workers in computer-intensive jobs acquired particular skills related to the technologies they use. Many of these workers acquired specific technical training, including courses

**Table 7.3** Changes in Hourly Wage Premiums and Wages by Occupational Group

| | Change in Wage Premiums, 1982–2012 | | | | Annual Growth in Median Wage, 1982–2012 | Median Years in School, 2012 | Median Years of Experience, 2012 |
|---|---|---|---|---|---|---|---|
| | Some Postsecondary Education | College or More | Experience | 90/50 Spread | | | |
| Scientific, engineering, and computer occupations | 15% | 18% | 10% | 13% | 0.4% | 16 | 20 |
| Occupations affected by office computing and the Internet | 10% | 18% | 4% | 27% | 0.5% | 13 | 21 |
| Health care occupations | 12% | 33% | 27% | 49% | 0.9% | 14 | 20 |
| Occupations less directly affected by technology | 4% | 11% | -8% | 15% | 0.0% | 12 | 19 |
| Occupations affected by manufacturing automation and offshoring | -1% | 7% | -11% | 2% | -0.2% | 12 | 24 |
| ALL OCCUPATIONS | 6% | 18% | 1% | 18% | 0.3% | 13 | 20 |

*Source:* Bureau of Labor Statistics, March Current Population Survey, http://www.bls.gov/cps/.

*Note:* Workers with some postsecondary education report more than 12 but fewer than 16 years of schooling; workers with college or more report 16 or more years of schooling; experienced workers have 15 potential years in the labor force (calculated as age minus the number of years of school completed minus 7). The first four columns report the change in geometric means from 1982 to 2012. Wage premia are calculated relative to the wage of workers with 12 years of schooling in the first two columns and relative to workers with fewer than 5 years of potential labor force experience, as indicated in the third column. The fourth column shows the change in the premium of workers in the 90th percentile to the median wage earner. Hourly wages are deflated using the Consumer Price Index.

at community colleges and vocational four-year degrees in fields such as nursing. Many of the technology-specific skills were likely acquired on the job. Indeed, Chapter 8 argues that there is an important link between education and learning on the job; the combination of education and experience matters most.

The table also shows increased demand for experienced workers. The wage premium paid to experienced workers also rose faster in the computer-intensive occupations than in the less intensive occupations. This increase was especially strong in health care. In contrast, manufacturing-related occupations saw a substantial decline in their experience premium, suggesting that many manufacturing skills learned through experience have become obsolete.

Finally, Table 7.3 shows a sharply widening gap between the wages of workers in the 90th percentile in each group and the median wage (the 90/50 spread) in health care and in occupations affected by office computing. This evidence, too, is consistent with the notion that some workers are able to learn valuable new skills in these technology areas on their own, to establish their reputations, and to earn high pay. Without well-established training institutions, standards, and robust labor markets, however, the median worker has not been able to benefit much by comparison. The widening of the gap between the most highly paid and the median workers in these technology areas reflects the increased value of technology-specific skills. The implication is that with the emergence of institutions, standards, and markets, the median worker could fare much better as well.

### The "Talent Shortage"

The wage data support the notion that workers in occupations affected by computers have been displaced and are required to learn new skills and new technical knowledge. The increased demand for workers with new specialized skills increases wage premiums, especially if the supply of such workers is limited. And the supply of workers having such skills might be limited if, as in the past, training institutions and labor markets lag.

This is the case with the supply chain workers mentioned at the beginning of the chapter. It also appears to be true in many other fields. The

Manpower Group, a human resources consultancy, conducts an annual "Talent Shortage Survey" of some 38,000 employers.[28] In 2013, 35 percent of employers worldwide experienced difficulty filling jobs due to lack of available talent; in the United States, 39 percent of employers faced difficulty hiring. Of these, the largest proportion cited a lack of specific technical competencies (or hard skills) required for a particular role. Employers reported having the most difficulty filling these five jobs: skilled trade workers, engineers, sales representatives, technicians, and accounting and finance staff. Several of these jobs are specifically occupations affected by information technology. The effect of, say, accounting software has not been to eliminate accounting staff overall, but, instead, to require new and specific skills that not enough workers possess at this time.

And, according to the Manpower survey, one in four employers report that lack of experience is at the root of the talent shortages they face. Management professor Peter Cappelli cites survey results highlighting the difficulties seen both by employers and prospective employees.[29] Employers provide little training—as little as eleven hours per year per employee in one survey. A major reason they did not provide training (other than cost) was that they did not want to risk investing in employees who might leave the company soon thereafter. On the other hand, according to one survey, 81 percent of employees were willing to get training even outside the workplace, presumably on their own time. However, like employers, 41 percent reported that they were uncertain as to the payoff. Why? Because they did not know what skills would be relevant in their future. Cappelli highlights the catch-22 nature of this problem:

> If job experience is a major requirement for vacancies, then employers are not looking to fill those jobs by hiring entry-level applicants right out of school. Employers want new hires to be able to start contributing, with no further training or start-up time. That's certainly understandable, but the only people who can do that are those who have done virtually the same job before, and that often requires a skill set that, in a rapidly changing world, may be dying out even as it is perfected.[30]

This catch-22 is a symptom of poorly developed training institutions and labor markets for new skills. Employers limit their investment in training because employees leave; workers limit their investment in training because without standardized skills they lack a clear career path that will provide them a secure return on that investment. And the lack of institutions that can train and certify new skills makes these investments cost more.

This "talent shortage" is not a source of unemployment. Some commentators have sought to blame persistent unemployment on a "skills gap."[31] This view is based on a particular notion of mismatch where workers have the skills that employers want, but they are just in the wrong place (e.g., skilled welders are in Texas but the jobs are in California). The situation highlighted in the occupational data here is different: few prospective employees have the desired skills in the first place, and the greatest mismatch between supply and demand occurs in occupational groups that have been growing, not those suffering from unemployment.[32]

Indeed, the groups that appear to be suffering a talent shortage have seen median wages rise more than average, as shown in Table 7.3. Much of the rise in median wages can be attributed to the rising wage premiums of educated and experienced workers. The median worker in occupations affected by office computing and health care technology has some postsecondary training and more than fifteen years of workforce experience; the median worker in engineering and computer occupations has a college degree and more than fifteen years' experience. The increase in the wage premiums can account for much of the increase in the median wage of these occupational groups over the last three decades. Of course, increases in skill premiums are not the only factor driving wage trends. Old skills have become obsolete, depressing wages, as does poor macroeconomic performance; in some occupations global competition has also undercut wages. Nevertheless, rising wage premiums are an important driver of the increased median wage in computer-intensive occupations.

Yet only in health care has the rise been more than anemic. The talent shortage in occupations using new technology may limit the number of workers who see rising wages. If labor markets can resolve the talent shortage in these occupations, even more workers will acquire newly valuable skills, markets will compensate them more for their skills, and the median wage will grow more rapidly in these large occupational groups. As we shall see, however, current policy is tilted against these developments.

### General Purpose Technology

Still, an important question remains: why does technology's effect on wages seem to be different today as compared with much of the twentieth century, when new technologies were accompanied by a growing median wage? We are now seeing widespread *synchronous* technological change. A large group of interrelated technologies, involving semiconductors, computers, and software, have transformed most industries at the same time. In 1997, 50 percent of workers used computers at work, up from 25 percent in 1984, and the number has grown since then. More than 80 percent of us now have computers at home, up from 8 percent in 1984.[33] And digital technology includes much more than computers. Digital electronics are now used in all sorts of manufactured items, from automobiles to cell phones to medical imaging and hearing aids. And information technology is beginning to play a key role in the analysis of genetic information. The result of these very widespread and rapid changes is that many industries are going through transitions at the same time. This is evident in Table 7.2. Although one might quibble with my categorization, over half of all jobs are in occupations directly affected by information technology.

Past technologies have affected only narrower segments of the workforce at any one time. For example, the advances in organic chemistry following the development of the periodic table dramatically affected the chemical industry and a few others, but they did not require the development of substantial new knowledge and skills in most other industries, which saw their own changes at different times. Asynchronous changes meant that while some industries were undergoing a transition with little wage growth, others saw technologies and labor markets mature. The combined outcome was a rise in median wages.

Information technology has been called a "general purpose technology," meaning that it is a building block for a wide range of applications.[34] Because general purpose technologies are so widely used, they create a need for new knowledge in many industries at once. Other general purpose technologies include electrification, which affected almost all manufacturing industries as well as households during the early decades of the twentieth century, and mechanization, which dramatically affected most manufacturing industries and agriculture during the nineteenth century. Mechanization allowed many tasks to be performed by machines driven by inanimate power, initially water power and steam. Electrification replaced water and steam power and provided a large number of new applications for electric motors at work and in the home.

Both mechanization and electrification caused manufacturing wages to remain stagnant for decades while these technologies were first being deployed. We have seen that weavers' wages grew very little in the decades before the Civil War. During the British Industrial Revolution, wages were stagnant for decades as well. The same was true for manufacturing wages during the early twentieth century when factories were being electrified. In 1899, electricity provided 5 percent of the power used in manufacturing establishments, and 53 percent by 1919. Over the same interval, the average weekly wage in manufacturing, adjusted for inflation, fell by 6 percent.[35] Then, during the 1920s, wages grew rapidly. This pattern suggests that changes in technology and organization, including the assembly line, required new skills and knowledge and that labor markets took time before they compensated workers for these skills and knowledge.

In this account, wages are stagnant because knowledge institutions lag technology. Despite the need for new skills, technology develops faster than either the institutions needed to train workers or the labor markets needed to provide them with strong incentives to develop new skills. The transition from obsolete technical knowledge to new knowledge lags because new institutions and labor markets require widely accepted standards. A variety of factors can delay the emergence of dominant standards, including technological uncertainty and competition between different standards.

The reasons knowledge lags technology today are different from past episodes. In the nineteenth century, for example, labor markets for skilled factory weavers did not develop until there was a permanent urban workforce in the mill towns. That is hardly an obstacle today. Nevertheless, as the example of desktop publishing shows, new technologies today involve organizational changes, competing standards, and a high level of churn. The details differ, but the underlying problem—the difficulty of developing the knowledge and skills to implement new technologies—is the same.

# Is This Time Different?

The evidence shows that over the last three decades, technology has mainly displaced workers to jobs requiring new skills rather than eliminating jobs overall. This was especially true with information technology. But perhaps things are now changing. Perhaps in the near future, technology really will begin replacing workers.

This could be the case because the pace of technological change might be accelerating. Erik Brynjolfsson and Andrew McAfee make a convincing argument that we are about to see a whole new wave of disruptive information technologies.[36] Major new advances in artificial intelligence are challenging common assumptions about what computers can and can't do. Not long ago, experts thought that tasks such as driving a car, understanding speech, and translating languages were in the distant future. But Google and other companies now have driverless cars on the road. Cell phones do a passable job understanding speech (Siri) and translating language (Google Translate).

But does a faster pace of change mean that technology will begin to permanently replace workers? If the mass replacement of workers by machines is imminent, then policy should focus on that problem, even if replacement does not explain the wage stagnation of the last three decades. Perhaps we are at a sharp turning point in history.

## The Hazards of Prediction

But predicting a turning point in history is a risky business. Past predictions have been off the mark. Although it is difficult to know the future, we should at least understand why past predictions failed and make sure that today's conditions really are different, so we don't repeat those errors.

Indeed, there is a long history of predictions that machines were about to cause massive unemployment. In his 1995 book *The End of Work*, Jeremy Rifkin observed high levels of unemployment worldwide and warned, "Now, for the first time, human labor is being systematically eliminated from the production process. . . . Intelligent machines are replacing human beings in countless tasks, forcing millions of blue and white collar workers into unemployment lines, or worse still, breadlines."[37]

In 1962, when technological automation was also seen as a major threat, President Kennedy declared that "the major domestic challenge of the Sixties" was to "maintain full employment at a time when automation is replacing men."[38] Before that, in 1930, John Maynard Keynes declared that the world was suffering from "technological unemployment," meaning "unemployment due to our discovery of means of economizing the use of labor outrunning the pace at which we can find new uses for labor."[39] The grandfather of these doomsayers was of course Karl Marx, who claimed that the elimination of labor by technology in the Industrial Revolution would lead to the progressive immiseration of the working classes. He predicted that a new machine for spinning yarn, the "self-acting mule," would allow the mills to replace adult spinners with children and adolescents.[40]

None of these predictions were accurate. The 1960s and 1990s both turned out to be decades of strong employment growth. Keynes abandoned technology as the main explanation for unemployment in *The General Theory of Employment, Interest and Money*, published in 1936. And at the time of Marx's death, in 1883, there were more adult spinners in England than when the self-acting mule was invented.

What did these forecasters not see? The dynamic nature of technological change. What the examples of weaving technology and the ATM and many other cases show is that while technology took over tasks from humans, the remaining tasks became more valuable. The power loom did not automate all of the weaver's tasks and the lower cost of production increased demand. The result was that the number of weaving jobs grew for at least a century. The ATM machines did not take over all of the tasks of bank tellers, especially those tasks involving human interaction; the lower cost of operating a bank branch increased the number of branches, offsetting any loss of teller jobs. Although technology might eventually eliminate bank tellers—just as textile technology now tends to reduce the number of weaving jobs—economic dynamism postponed the replacement of work far into the future.

Two factors came into play so that automation did not lead to immediate job losses: (1) the technological change was sufficiently valuable that increased demand for the product or service offset potential job losses, and (2) significant tasks remained for human labor to perform. Past futurists underestimated the economic dynamism of new technologies and overestimated how much of work machines could perform.

Do these factors apply to major innovation today? Although some economists such as Robert J. Gordon think that today's technology generates little new value, they do not think that machines are replacing humans on a large scale, either. The view that technology is about to lead to massive unemployment seems to assume that technology is taking over work that is indeed valuable.

On the other hand, the new "smart machines" are taking over a whole new range of tasks from humans, perhaps to the point of leaving few significant tasks for humans to do. Routine tasks performed by white-collar workers have already been automated. If artificial intelligence technology can diagnose diseases, drive cars, and translate languages, then perhaps there will soon be little left for humans to do. Indeed, some people such as science fiction writer Vernor Vinge argue that we are approaching a "technological singularity" when machines will become more intelligent than humans; Vinge anticipates this happening within the next fifteen years.[41] If he is right, massive unemployment might well be imminent.

There is a certain seductiveness about the view that "science fiction is now here." Perhaps something similar seduced past futurists. But machine intelligence is not everything. Computers might diagnose better than the average doctor if they are given all the symptoms, but nurses and doctors can read body language and nonverbal cues to detect symptoms that might not be stated; they might also provide a more reassuring bedside manner. Computers can select financial portfolios and make investment recommendations, but they might not provide secure guidance to investors panicking because the market is down 30 percent. Computers can compare product prices and specifications, but sales representatives also help consumers reason through which features are most important to them, and they build trust that a supplier will respond well to unforeseen contingencies.

As technology journalist Timothy Lee writes, "This isn't because computers aren't 'smart enough.' It's because raw intelligence isn't the only qualification for these jobs. Human beings are social creatures. We care about our interactions with other people in ways that we'll never care about our interactions with machines, no matter how intelligent they might be.

Already, jobs with a social component account for a large fraction of the workforce."[42]

Humans perform major tasks today that that are not about to be taken over by machines, artificial intelligence notwithstanding. There is no evidence that machines are likely to replace humans in these areas anytime soon. For these reasons, it seems doubtful that the forecasts of imminent doom are likely to be accurate this time around, either.

### Today's Challenge

Nevertheless, there are important differences between what is happening with jobs today and what happened in the past. It appears that information technology is affecting a larger share of all jobs than the general purpose technologies of the past. Also, the pace of change might be faster today, as Brynjolfsson and McAfee argue. Faster change does not necessarily imply that machines are more likely to replace humans; it might just mean that displacement occurs more rapidly and, perhaps, causing more stress. In desktop publishing and in supply chain systems, there have been repeated waves of disruptive technologies, each eliminating some tasks and changing the nature of skills needed.

Because of these differences in scope and pace, today's transition may be more difficult than similar transitions in the past. That is all the more reason why good policies are needed now. Even with the best of policies, wage stagnation and growing economic inequality are likely to continue for some time. Today, across a wide swath of industries, technologies are changing the way people work. Broad advances in electronics and information technology are affecting jobs, skills, and wages for large numbers of workers. Most workers do not appear to be benefiting.

The problem is not that technology is eliminating jobs overall. The real problem is that new technology-related skills are difficult to acquire and most workers cannot yet gain much benefit from the new skills they do acquire. The institutions, organizations, and labor markets needed to train workers and to provide them incentives to learn these new skills are just emerging. Some technologies are still changing too rapidly; others lack the necessary organizations or widely accepted standards. Yet a number of important occupations are showing increasing wages associated with the acquisition of

new technology-related skills. This has been true for college-educated workers for some time; now these increases are coming to some occupations
where most workers are not highly educated—for example, in some health
care occupations.

Good policies can accelerate this process. They can ameliorate the problem of job displacement that has been affecting many workers for the last
three decades. But a focus on the supposedly imminent end of work from
the inexorable workings of technology is at best a distraction. Without strong
evidence that the nature of work will change sharply in the next few years,
it makes no sense to turn away from policies that might improve the lives
of many now. Yet, as we shall see, many key policies have taken a turn for
the worse during the last three decades.

# PART III

## TECHNOLOGY POLICY

THE FIRST TWO SECTIONS OF THIS BOOK offered a distinct vision of how technology affects society and, in particular, our current predicament, where technology is associated with stagnant wages. This section looks at implications of this analysis. I will propose policies to foster the development of institutions and labor markets that can help large numbers of ordinary workers acquire the skills needed for new technologies. Of course, there exist many policy prescriptions for developing new skills and knowledge, for instance, by subsidizing higher education. Yet the conventional analysis does not often consider the special nature of technical knowledge, especially for early-stage technologies. Chapters 8 through 12 look at the particular challenges involved in providing large numbers of people with new technical knowledge and what they mean for policy.

Unfortunately, in each of these areas, the trend in recent decades is not positive. Policies have changed in ways that make the acquisition of new technical knowledge on a large scale slower and more difficult.

## CHAPTER 8

# Does Technology Require More College Diplomas?

IN HIS FIRST STATE OF THE UNION ADDRESS in 2009, President Obama announced a new goal: "By 2020, America will once again have the highest proportion of college graduates in the world." He expanded on this theme in his 2011 address:

> The future is ours to win. But to get there, we can't just stand still. As Robert Kennedy told us, "The future is not a gift. It is an achievement." Sustaining the American Dream has never been about standing pat. It has required each generation to sacrifice, and struggle, and meet the demands of a new age.
>
> And now it's our turn. We know what it takes to compete for the jobs and industries of our time. We need to out-innovate, out-educate, and out-build the rest of the world. (Applause.)
>
> . . . This is our generation's Sputnik moment. . . . Think about it. Over the next ten years, nearly half of all new jobs will require education that goes beyond a high school education. And yet, as many as a quarter of our students aren't even finishing high school. The quality of our math and science education lags behind many other nations'. America has fallen to ninth place in the proportion of young people with a college degree. And so the question is whether all of us—as citizens, and as parents—are willing to do what's necessary to give every child a chance to succeed.

Boosting college graduation rates has long been high on the agenda of educational establishment organizations such as the College Board—so much so that Diane Ravitch, a leading historian of education, sees college for everyone as a matter of "political correctness."[1] Part of the rationale concerns international competitiveness. The United States has fallen slightly in international rankings of the proportion of young people with postsecondary degrees.[2] It now ranks behind South Korea, Canada, and Russia. While the share of young Americans with postsecondary degrees has been growing, in other countries it has been growing faster. Then there are countries, like Russia, that have long had high levels of postsecondary educational attainment. To meet Obama's goal, the portion of young Americans with postsecondary diplomas will have to increase by 50 percent by 2020, even assuming that Korea and others make no further progress. Currently 64 percent of South Koreans aged 25 to 34 have at least an associate's degree; only 43 percent of young Americans do.

Yet it is not obvious why meeting this goal is good for America. When other countries have increased their ranks of college graduates, they have sometimes suffered a "brain drain"—some of those graduates had to emigrate to other countries to put their skills to work. As management professor Peter Cappelli points out, just because individuals benefit from receiving higher education does not mean it is necessarily good for society as a whole to educate more people at the college level.[3] Increasing college graduation rates does not necessarily improve the economy. The flood of college graduates during the early 1970s was followed by a decade of economic malaise and large numbers of "overeducated Americans."[4] China increased college enrollments sixfold from 1998 to 2008, but Chinese college graduates today have a hard time finding appropriate work. On average, they earn little more than migrant workers, and they have much higher unemployment than less educated workers.[5]

President Obama's argument appears to be about technology: New technology requires new knowledge and skills. Therefore, many of the new jobs created over the next ten years will require higher education. Building a large workforce with these skills will allow firms to implement new technologies, boosting the economy in absolute terms and also relative to other countries, hence providing "international competitiveness."

This line of analysis fits squarely within the conventional wisdom about how technology affects workers. Many policymakers and economists argue that today's technology requires workers with a college education. College graduates are more likely to work at jobs that use computers, and these jobs pay higher wages. Because computer jobs "require" college diplomas, many economists argue, the rapid spread of computers at work is responsible for the growing gap in pay between college graduates and less educated workers. In this view, the supply of college graduates has not kept pace with the rising demand for skill required by new technology, and the solution is to support more investment in college education through scholarships, loans, and subsidies. Economists Claudia Goldin and Lawrence Katz call this a "race between education and technology."[6]

Yet this logic hinges on the assumption that technology "requires" workers with advanced degrees. Historically, much of the knowledge and the skills that workers needed to implement new technologies was learned on the job. Education was important as well, especially after technical knowledge had been somewhat standardized. The relationship between technology, education, and skill is more complex than a simple story of technology "requiring" a certain amount of schooling. It is helpful to look at how this relationship played out in the past.

## What Education Does Technology Require?

When Lucy Larcom was hired at the textile mills of Lowell, the mill owners made literacy an express requirement of employment. A look at the payroll records from one of the mills confirms that they meant it: during the 1830s, 97 percent of the weavers could sign their names in the payroll register to verify that they had received their monthly pay.

Now this might seem strange, because literacy was in no way necessary to perform a weaver's tasks. English textile workers of that time had much lower levels of literacy. Nevertheless, the U.S. mill owners argued that their workers were superior to the British because of their education. An examination of the payroll records from the mills shows that the illiterate weavers were indeed less productive. Literate new hires learned the required skills faster and better. Overall, literate weavers produced 12 to 18 percent more cloth per hour than illiterate weavers, all else equal.[7] Although this difference was modest, it was enough to spell the difference between commercial success and failure.

It appears that some primary-school education was beneficial, even if literacy was not required by the technology. Literate weavers had apparently "learned how to learn" in the classroom; they had acquired skills and discipline in school that were helpful to learning in a new environment. Other evidence suggests that schooling, even at a primary-school level, enhances workers' ability to learn from experience. For example, Mark Rosenzweig, studying Indian farmers during the Green Revolution, found that primary schooling accelerated the speed with which farmers benefited from new seed varieties.[8]

So the mill owners made literacy a condition of employment for sound economic reasons. But this was not permanently true. Beginning in the late 1840s, they began hiring significant numbers of illiterate weavers, and by 1855, half of the new hires could not sign their own names. From then on, literacy was no longer a job requirement for weavers. Two things changed the economic calculus. First, while literate weavers learned faster, they did not stay in the mills as long as illiterate workers because they had more opportunities elsewhere, for example, teaching school. As the mills made deeper human capital investments in their workers, this greater turnover made it harder for them to recoup their investments. Literate weavers were "overeducated." And as a local labor market for skilled weavers developed, many weavers made their own investments in acquiring these new skills. They stayed in the mills longer and formed a pool of local skilled labor that could be rehired. But they were drawn from a local population that was increasingly immigrant and illiterate. As the economic value of technology-specific skills increased, the stability of this resident workforce became more important than the speed with which workers acquired new skills.

Second, the shift from more educated workers to less educated workers depended on standardization of skills. Educated workers had an advantage at acquiring technical skills during the early years, when the nature of these skills was uncertain and the institutions for acquiring and hiring skilled workers were not developed. Once these institutions emerged, and once labor markets compensated workers for their own investments in learning on the job, formal education was less important.

This shift from more educated to less educated workers is not unique to nineteenth-century weaving. According to a Rand Corporation study, "The early ranks of computer programmers included a high proportion of Ph.D. mathematicians; today, high school graduates are being hired. During the early stage of transistors, chemical engineers were required to constantly supervise the vats where crystals were grown. As processes were perfected, they were replaced by workers with less education."[9]

Similarly, highly educated graphic designers today have an advantage learning the newest technologies of websites and mobile apps. Most did not learn these technology-specific skills in school, yet education has given them the ability to teach themselves new skills, often on the job. Economists have found evidence over a range of industries that highly educated workers are more in demand for new technologies, but as technologies age, firms hire more workers with less education.[10]

This difference between skill and education arises because not all formal schooling is vocational. Some forms of education, such as apprenticeships, vocational programs, or college-level programs in nursing and engineering, do teach technology-specific skills. Other programs, such as the typical four-year college liberal arts program, mainly provide students with general skills and knowledge. General education might nevertheless help workers acquire skills on the job, just as a primary-school education helped the early weavers. New technology can raise the demand for educated workers, especially during the years before the technology-specific skills have become standardized enough to be taught in schools.

But there are two very different senses in which technology "requires" a certain level of education: in one, a true technical requirement, students learn specific vocational skills directly related to the technology; in the other, students acquire a general ability to learn that is helpful in gaining new skills on the job. The latter might be called a screening requirement because it helps employers select employees who will better learn on the job. Screening requirements will be important for new, uncertain technologies where little knowledge is standardized; true technical requirements will be important when technical knowledge is sufficiently standardized so that it can be taught in a classroom. This distinction critically influences which policies will be effective. If vocational training is becoming feasible in many new technology areas, then policy should promote technology-specific training. A major push to increase the number of college graduates with general degrees might be ineffective and possibly even detrimental.

## Technology and the Demand for College Today

In which sense does technology today require college-educated workers, and does this requirement support policies to sharply increase college attainment? President Obama justified his goal by noting that "over the next ten years, nearly half of all new jobs will require education that goes beyond a high school education." This statistic comes from the Bureau of Labor Statistics, which projects the growth in different occupations over the next ten years and classifies occupations by the level of education typically required for entry.

Government data do not really support Obama's policy. The Bureau of Labor Statistics asks industry experts to rate the education required for several hundred detailed occupational classifications. Table 8.1 shows these ratings tallied up for all occupations. The first column shows the educational requirements based on actual employment in 2012; the second column shows these estimates applied to the employment projected for each occupation for 2022. These estimates show only what the experts believe to be the typical education required to obtain entry into the occupation. Advanced education might still be valuable beyond what is strictly necessary in order to perform the job, but that is exactly the point of distinguishing between the two senses of the term "required."[11]

Two things stand out. First, the strict educational requirements of jobs are not projected to change very much over the next decade. Although these estimates might not fully capture the extent to which new technology could change the minimum technical requirements for each occupation, they nevertheless do not provide support for a radical increase in college graduation rates. Second, schools already produce enough graduates to meet the strict requirements of jobs today and in 2022, based on the numbers of graduates. The right columns of the table show the actual education of the cur-

**Table 8.1** Education Required to Meet Occupational Needs

| | Technically Required Education Level | | Current Population | |
|---|---|---|---|---|
| | 2012 | 2022 (Projected) | Labor Force | Aged 25–34 |
| High school or less | 66% | 65% | 35% | 33% |
| Some postsecondary | 11% | 12% | 30% | 29% |
| Bachelor's degree | 18% | 18% | 23% | 27% |
| Master's or higher | 4% | 5% | 13% | 11% |

*Source*: Bureau of Labor Statistics Economic and Employment Projections, 2012–2022, and March Current Population Survey, http://www.bls.gov/cps/.

rent workforce (column three) and of the population aged 25 to 34 (column four). Judging by the sheer numbers of workers at each educational level, there are clearly more workers with postsecondary education than are strictly needed to meet occupational entry requirements. Again, education beyond the minimum is often quite valuable.

Also, these aggregate figures are based on the number of years of schooling and not on the specific vocational or technical content of the education received. A certified licensed practical nurse with a year of postsecondary education might be much more employable than someone with a year in a liberal arts bachelor's degree program. The type of postsecondary education provided may be much more important for policy than the sheer numbers graduated.

Much of the concern over college graduation rates has specifically been about the number of science and engineering graduates, especially as other countries, such as China, are rapidly increasing their numbers of engineers. But the number of science, technology, and engineering graduates has grown strongly in the United States as well; about 50 percent more computer science majors graduate each year than in 1998.[12] There are few signs of a labor shortage. Our colleges and universities graduate twice as many scientists and engineers each year as the number actually hired, and many graduates report that IT jobs are not available. Moreover, wages for computer and IT jobs have remained flat over the last decade, hardly suggesting a labor shortage in information technology. While software developers with specific technology skills are in high demand, many of these skills are learned on the job, just as with the highly skilled graphic designers.[13]

Nor do all the jobs that use new technologies specifically require college degrees, as is often claimed.[14] Auto mechanics may use computer diagnostics, but they do not necessarily need a degree in computer science. Even many programmers lack degrees from four-year colleges. During the 1970s, the majority of computer programmers had less than four years of college (54 percent in 1979); in 2007, the number was 34 percent.[15] And only about one-third of the IT workforce has an IT-related college degree.[16] So it is hardly clear that the occupations that do require specific college degrees are growing so fast as to justify a radical expansion of college education.

Nevertheless, there is strong evidence that with the adoption of new technologies, the demand for college graduates, as reflected in the relative wages paid to college-educated workers, has grown robustly over the last three decades. In 1979, the mean hourly earnings of a college-educated worker were 34 percent more than the earnings of a worker with just a high school diploma; in 2009, the college-educated worker earned 65 percent more (see Figure 8.1).[17] This finding implies that the demand for college-educated workers increased substantially relative to the demand for workers with only a high school education. Moreover, these wage increases are associated with information technology—occupations that use computers had greater wage gains, as we saw in Chapter 7.[18]

Some economists, such as Claudia Goldin and Lawrence Katz, see this increase in demand as a sign that new technology requires more college diplomas.[19] In their view, new technology increasingly requires more education. When the needs of technology pull ahead of the education level of the workforce, the demand for workers with more education surges. The policy response should be to produce more workers with college diplomas.

Yet a closer look at the evidence suggests that what is wanted from college graduates is mainly not technology-specific skills. First, the increase in wages over the last three decades for college-educated workers has largely been for *experienced* workers. Entry-level wages for college graduates have gone up only modestly compared to those with high school diplomas.[20]

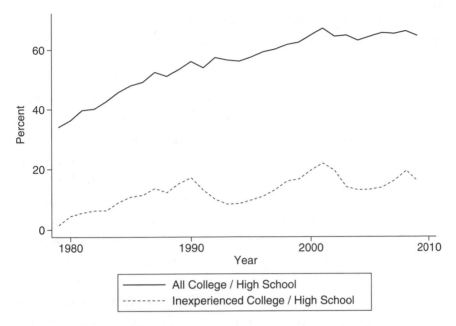

Figure 8.1. Relative pay has risen for experienced college grads until recently: Premium of mean hourly wages of college-educated workers to wages of high school–educated workers. (Bureau of Labor Statistics, Current Population Survey, Merged Outgoing Rotation Group surveys, http://www.bls.gov/cps/.)

The wage premium for college-educated workers with less than five years' job experience is shown by the dashed line in Figure 8.1. The growth in the wage premium is mainly for workers who have college *and* experience. The demand for college-educated workers is mainly for those who can learn on the job, not for specific vocational skills that they learned in college.

Second, four in ten college graduates work in jobs that do not require a college degree.[21] A study by the New York Federal Reserve Bank finds that unemployment and underemployment for recent college graduates has been growing since 2001.[22] It has also become common for underemployed college graduates to end up in poorly paid or part-time jobs. This suggests that employers use a college diploma as a screen to find applicants who can learn on the job effectively. But many college graduates might not be good learners on the job, so they end up in jobs that do not require a diploma.[23]

Thus, while demand for college graduates has grown in relative terms, it appears to be mainly because college-educated workers are better at learning new, unstandardized skills on the job, not because their college educations conferred specific technical skills. The current high demand for college-educated workers stems from the large number of occupations affected by early-stage information technologies today. If this is right, then the greater demand for college-educated workers will not continue indefinitely. As technical knowledge in these occupations becomes increasingly standardized, more and more workers will be able to acquire the needed skills without a college education, in formal training provided by employers or vocational and technical schools. They will still learn on the job, but a college diploma will no longer be such an asset. Like the weavers and those in hundreds of other occupations, the more educated workers will be gradually replaced by those with less general education, but who have technology-specific vocational training. And, unless there is another wave of general purpose technology affecting large numbers of occupations at once, the relative demand for college workers will level off and decline.

There is evidence that this is already happening. The wages of college-educated workers have pretty much stopped increasing relative to the pay of high school graduates, despite continued growth in the use of new technology. Over the last decade, the wage premium has stopped growing while investment in information technology continued.

The health care industry stands as a clear counterexample to the notion that technology uniformly increases the demand for workers with more education and decreases demand for the less educated. Health care technology is maturing and becoming standardized, as demonstrated by the role of ambulatory surgery centers. As this has happened, the sector has undergone a broad restructuring where work formerly done by top-level providers such as physicians and dentists has been displaced to specialized mid-skill providers and technicians. There are many more dental hygienists per dentist, and many more nurses, nurse practitioners, and physician assistants per physician. This shift has created about two million well-paying mid-skill jobs over the past two decades.[24] Many of these new jobs require four years of college or more, but still *less schooling* than the top-level providers. And very many of the new jobs, such as those for LPNs, require less than four years of college. As we saw in Chapter 7, the health care industry has a rising median wage, growing employment, and rising wage premiums for education and experience.

## Education for Today's Knowledge Gap

If this analysis is correct, is it really such a good idea to increase college attainment by 50 percent over the next decade? Boosting college graduation rates in the 1980s, at the start of the information technology boom, was probably beneficial. Perhaps modest increases today in the proportion of young people getting college diplomas will reduce the cost to employers of hiring people to work with new technologies in their early stages. But a drastic increase in college graduation rates probably cannot be achieved without diverting resources from vocational and technical education. The Obama administration's fiscal 2012 budget cut spending on career and technical education by 21 percent while increasing total spending for education by 11 percent.[25] This is a step in the wrong direction.

More generally, the policy trend over the last decade has been to starve community colleges in order to feed four-year colleges, especially private research universities. After adjusting for inflation, these universities increased spending per student by $14,000; at community colleges, spending per student remained unchanged.[26] Moreover, this trend is occurring in an environment that already highly favors universities. Private universities spend over three times as much per student as do community colleges, yet community colleges arguably have the students who need the most remedial help. This inequality is substantially the result of policy. Public research universities receive about twice as much government funding per pupil as do community colleges. Private universities benefit from tax subsidies on donations and on endowment funds. Taking these incentives into account, economist Richard Vedder estimates that the state and federal subsidies amount to $54,000 per student at Princeton; state and federal subsidies at the nearby College of New Jersey, a four-year public institution, come to only $2,000 per student.[27]

Moreover, community colleges overall are left to educate the least prepared students. They need extra resources to provide remedial education and, even then, they experience high dropout rates. In the words of one study, "two-year colleges are asked to educate those students with the greatest needs, using the least funds, and in increasingly separate and unequal institutions. Our higher education system, like the larger society, is growing more and more unequal."[28]

If past employment patterns are being repeated, then now is the time to expand community colleges and vocational/technical education for those without college diplomas, especially as technical knowledge becomes more standardized. The demand for LPNs and bookkeepers and EMTs will not be met by four-year colleges, but by technical education at community colleges and elsewhere. A massive increase in bachelor's degrees may lead to a lot of college graduates working in jobs that no longer require so much general education.

Today, job opportunities for less educated workers are growing in health care, construction, and retail trade. Many of the new jobs in these sectors require new skills or specialized training. A report published by the Russell Sage Foundation summarized where the well-paying jobs for the less educated are emerging:

> In health care, many of these are jobs as nurses, technicians, and therapy assistants that require certificates or degrees. In construction, these jobs include workers in the skilled crafts, such as plumbers, electricians, and the like. In manufacturing, the remaining jobs often require sophisticated numeric and computing skills, as in machinist jobs, or other specific skills (such as welding). And even in retail trade, an individual seems to need a range of communication and arithmetic skills to obtain one of the better-paying jobs.[29]

These are the kinds of skills that might benefit from something other than increasing the number of college diplomas. To the extent that these skills can be learned in a classroom, policy can promote the availability of technical education at community colleges, job retraining programs for laid-off workers, and financial support for workers while they are being retrained. Training programs are often more effective when coordinated with employers, targeted to sectors with growing opportunity for further learning, and incorporating a work-study component to promote learning on the job. Employers can be given tax incentives to encourage on-the-job training. Also, employers will invest more in training if workers have a stronger foundation of literacy and numeracy; improved K through 12 education can facilitate on-the-job training for young workers.[30] Appropriate policies might include subsidies for adopting new technologies or hiring new workers.

Unfortunately, it seems that the kind of training programs that might be most beneficial have been underfunded, and recent policy has gone in the wrong direction. This trend seems likely to slow the benefits from new technology, especially the benefits going to less educated workers.

But this policy direction also encourages those who choose to go to college to make a large and risky bet on future earnings. It is well known that the cost of attending a four-year college has soared, and that the volume of student loan debt now exceeds the amount of debt on auto loans or credit cards.[31] Not to worry, a number of researchers have counseled: although the required investment has increased, the return on that investment will still be high.[32] But these predicted returns are based on some questionable assumptions. One is that college graduates' future earnings will still exceed those of high school graduates as much as they do today.[33] But the college/ high school wage gap changes over time, and it can go down as well as up—it did, in fact, decline during the 1970s. More to the point, if today's technologies mature as technologies have in the past, then valuable experience will be acquired not just by college graduates but also by workers with less education. Then the wage gap will decline, and today's heavy investments in college will not pay well. Workers with postsecondary training will earn more than those with only a high school diploma and those with bachelor's degrees will earn relatively less than they do today. If historical patterns hold, investing in four-year college today is a risky bet for many prospective students.

## CHAPTER 9

# Whose Knowledge Economy?

CHAPTER 8 SHOWED THAT OCCUPATIONAL CHANGES are not substantially raising the years of school technically required to perform most jobs, even
though higher education is still often valuable beyond the minimum requirements. Yet many people fervently believe that technology increasingly requires workers with advanced degrees. This belief rests on the view that the
manufacturing economy is transforming into a knowledge economy. While
manufacturing workers could learn on the job, knowledge economy workers need formal education and therefore must meet rising educational requirements in order to work in the new economy.

Yet this notion misunderstands how technology affects learning. Worse,
it is a dangerous guide to policy. Some people use the knowledge economy
to justify raising the educational requirements for occupational licensure.
Indeed, the last three decades have seen a dramatic increase in the number
of workers subject to such educational licensing requirements. Others see
the knowledge economy destroying good jobs for less educated workers; they
argue for trade protections and other subsidies to preserve manufacturing
jobs. Both of these policies actually work against the development of broad-
based new knowledge that can create well-paying jobs.

Knowledge is what allows most people to benefit from technology. Workers with valuable knowledge earn high wages; firms with knowledgeable
employees earn high profits. From this perspective, the Industrial Revolution launched an era in which society developed new institutions and orga-

nizations to create and share technical knowledge on a large scale, and these advancements were central to the tremendous growth in living standards over the last two centuries. Economic historian Joel Mokyr describes the Industrial Revolution ushering in a new "knowledge economy."[1]

But people usually use the term to describe a recent development. Consider Peter Drucker's formulation:

> This new knowledge economy will rely heavily on knowledge workers. At present, this term is widely used to describe people with considerable theoretical knowledge and learning: doctors, lawyers, teachers, accountants, chemical engineers. But the most striking growth will be in "knowledge technologists": computer technicians, software designers, analysts in clinical labs, manufacturing technologists, paralegals. These people are as much manual workers as they are knowledge workers; in fact, they usually spend far more time working with their hands than with their brains. But their manual work is based on a substantial amount of theoretical knowledge which can be acquired only through formal education, not through an apprenticeship. They are not, as a rule, much better paid than traditional skilled workers, but they see themselves as "professionals." Just as unskilled manual workers in manufacturing were the dominant social and political force in the 20th century, knowledge technologists are likely to become the dominant social—and perhaps also political—force over the next decades.[2]

Drucker's knowledge workers are professionals whose work is "based on a substantial amount of theoretical knowledge which can be acquired only through formal education, not through an apprenticeship." Nor, apparently, do these people acquire their knowledge on the job. In Drucker's view, the evidence for this new economy is seen in the manufacturing sector's declining share of jobs. Moreover, he predicts, the decline of the old industrial economy will bring increasing calls for trade protection for manufacturing.

This notion of a new knowledge economy is a popular way to frame policy discussions, but knowledge economy policies are sometimes neither as neutral nor as purely beneficial as they are typically described. For example, people in many occupations want the professional status and economic benefits conferred by high educational requirements for occupational licensing, but these restrictions typically limit, rather than promote, the number of people who acquire new knowledge. Such policies implicitly favor certain groups at the expense of others, and these biases are often obscured by grand rhetoric. The knowledge economy too often represents a meritocratic ideology with a damaging influence on private and public decision making. It is fine for society to reward people who invest in acquiring critical knowledge. But not all such knowledge comes via a professional diploma.

## We Are All Knowledge Workers

This notion that sectoral shifts in employment were giving rise to a new, knowledge-based economy was first formally stated in 1962 by Fritz Machlup.[3] In his book *The Production and Distribution of Knowledge in the United States*, he did a sectoral accounting and estimated that the "knowledge industry" accounted for 32 percent of U.S. employee compensation in 1958. The knowledge industry share of employment has grown since then, as has the popularity of the concept. With the addition of the Internet, widespread information technology, and globalization, the concept broadened, with many commentators using the term "new economy." But these terms, not always well defined, share common elements: the economy is seen as shifting from making physical things to making ideas, and manual workers are being replaced by highly educated professionals.

The shift of employment out of manufacturing is a significant trend, but it is important to understand precisely how it is related to knowledge. Manufacturing does indeed claim a smaller share of jobs, and this decline has been steady for over fifty years.[4] In 1950, about one-third of all jobs were in the manufacturing sector; in 1980, about 20 percent were; today the figure is under 10 percent (see Figure 7.3). The absolute number of U.S. manufacturing jobs peaked in 1979 at over 19 million; now there are about 12 million. Most new jobs since then have been created in the service sector, including health care, finance, and retail.

### Why Is Manufacturing Employment Declining?

Surely this is a profound shift. Moreover, it is seen in developed countries worldwide. Is it caused by the changing role of knowledge, perhaps as science plays a greater role? In fact, manufacturing industries tend to employ a relatively larger proportion of engineers and scientists. Something else is responsible.

One major cause of the shift is that manufacturing industries have tended to increase output per worker faster than service industries.[5] Thanks to technology, many manufacturing industries experience the kind of rapid growth in output per worker that we saw in the textile industry. In textiles, this growth in output initially led to increasing employment, but, as the technology matured, further technological advances led to a declining share of employment in the industry. This pattern appears to be more general, with young industries increasing their share, older industries declining.[6] Manufacturing industries today are shedding jobs because output per worker is increasing, but demand increases little. Globalization has also reduced manufacturing employment recently.[7]

On the other hand, many service industries do not experience such rapidly growing output per worker. Some service industries suffer from "Baumol's cost disease": output per worker increases slowly if at all. For example, performance of a quartet always requires four musicians.[8] Yet, thanks to information technology, output per worker is now increasing in many service industries as fast as in most manufacturing industries.[9] Nevertheless, these industries tend to adopt more early-stage technologies and employment does not decrease with growing output per worker. We saw in Chapter 7 that the occupational groups affected most by computers were growing faster than the labor force, increasing their share of employment.

In other words, a key difference between manufacturing and the service sector is that more manufacturing technologies are mature. Yet maturity affects the relative demand for educated workers: newer technologies increase demand for more highly educated workers. This suggests that at least part of the difference in the education of the workforce between manufacturing and other sectors is not inherent to the technology, but is instead a result of differences in maturity.

*Education and Manufacturing*

In any case, the educational characteristics of the manufacturing sector differ only modestly from other sectors. Manufacturing workers are not, on average, quite as highly educated as those in other sectors: 53 percent of them have education beyond a high school diploma, while 63 percent of workers in other sectors do.[10] On the other hand, educational attainment in manufacturing is higher in the "hard" subjects of science, technology, engineering, and math. More important, manufacturing workers with a given education will earn more than comparable nonmanufacturing workers, all else equal: their pay is 7 percent higher, and total compensation, including benefits, that is 15 percent higher.

But this finding does not imply that the shift out of manufacturing is a shift out of occupations that use hands instead of minds. Even the supposedly unskilled factory workers of the Industrial Revolution used their hands *and* their minds. They acquired their knowledge through experience on the job. And the higher pay that manufacturing workers earn today suggests that they too have valuable knowledge learned on the job rather than in the classroom.[11] Moreover, the number of years of schooling of manufacturing workers has been increasing just as fast as that of workers in other sectors.

It is true that the decline in manufacturing has diminished apprenticeship programs like those that once trained typographers. Today, only 1.6 percent of all jobs require apprenticeships, and this percentage has been small for a long time. But manufacturing employers have long relied on less formal means of learning on the job. Today, 65 percent of jobs require some other form of on-the-job training.[12]

Nor is technology decreasing the importance of learning on the job, replacing it with theoretical knowledge learned in the classroom. The data in Chapter 7 show, to the contrary, that the wage premiums of experienced workers are rising in computer-intensive occupations; experience is becoming more valuable in these occupations. On the other hand, experience premiums are falling in manufacturing as old skills become obsolete.

Some service-sector occupations, such as teaching, inherently require a certain level of schooling. But the differences in the demand for highly educated workers between sectors have much more to do with differences in the maturity of technologies used. Moreover, there are many important exceptions. There are new technologies in manufacturing and mature technologies in the service sector. Advanced robotics, nanomaterials, and 3-D printing offer manufacturing opportunities for more educated workers.[13] On the other hand, legacy computer systems, where the computer programming is outsourced overseas, are a mature service-sector technology. We are seeing growing globalization of services, including well-known services such as those provided by call centers, and many more service jobs are "off-shorable."[14] The economy is not shifting from making things to making ideas; it is shifting from old technologies to new ones, and these changes are found in both sectors. Sectoral shifts in employment do not by themselves justify major shifts in the schooling required to perform many occupations.

## What Professionals Require

It is true that many manufacturing jobs allowed less educated workers to learn skills on the job that brought them good pay. But it is also true that many service-sector jobs also allow less educated workers to acquire skills and good pay, especially as new technologies become standardized. This was the case with licensed practical nurses explored in Chapter 7. But knowledge economy arguments are increasingly being marshaled to *limit* the opportunities for these less educated workers.

Indeed, the American Nurses Association has been lobbying to raise the educational requirements needed to obtain a nursing license since 1965. The ANA has been seeking to require "technical nurses" to receive a two-year college degree (up from nine to eighteen months for LPNs, depending on the state) and to require a bachelor's degree for registered nurses. And the association justifies this effort with a knowledge economy argument: "The constant explosion of scientific knowledge makes education preparation for occupations based on applied sciences both more important and more difficult. . . . When scientific knowledge is used effectively as a basis for practice by an occupational group, no practical way of acquiring training can exist except through organized programs within the education system."[15]

Yet, as we have seen, LPNs with limited schooling are quite economically valuable today despite fifty years of "exploding" scientific knowledge. The motivation of the American Nurses Association might have less to do with the supposed demands of scientific knowledge and more to do with pecuniary advantages of limiting access to the profession. By limiting the number of people permitted to practice an occupation, professional associations reduce competition and raise pay. But these benefits come at the expense of consumers and of prospective workers who might otherwise enter the occupation.

Drucker notes that the new knowledge workers want to be seen as professionals. And professionals frequently want to raise educational requirements in order to restrict access. These demands arise not from the technical needs of the knowledge economy, but from the political influence of professional associations. Although the American Nurses Association has largely not been successful at raising the education required for occupational licensure, many other occupations have been more successful. In fact, occupational licensing has dramatically changed the labor market. In 1950, 70 occupations had licensing requirements, accounting for 5 percent of all jobs; in 2008, more than 800 occupations were licensed in the various states and they accounted for 29 percent of all jobs.[16] This increase was very much driven by political lobbying.[17] In 1995 alone, 850 health professions licensure bills were introduced in state legislatures and more than 300 were enacted into law.[18]

Lobbyists not only argue that the knowledge economy raises the need for higher educational requirements; they also cite the importance of licensure for guaranteeing public safety and quality of service. Safety and quality are important issues because consumers often have difficulty obtaining information about service providers. How can I tell if my doctor knows what she is doing or not? Her medical license tells me that she at least has a minimum level of competence and knowledge.

However, occupational licensing regulations often far exceed the function of providing a baseline level of safety and quality.[19] For one thing, occupational licensing regulations now cover many occupations where there is little plausible need to regulate safety and quality, such as flower arrangers and interior decorators. Also, much of the regulation is oriented to limiting entry into the occupation in ways that have little to do with quality and safety. Professional associations control the exam pass rate, the fees to enter the profession, and sometimes waiting periods. They often prevent professionals licensed in one state (or country) from practicing in another. Professional associations also limit the availability of schooling by controlling accreditation. For example, the American Dental Association limits the availability of training for dental hygienists so that many programs receive twice as many applicants as available openings.[20] Professional associations affect the division of labor between occupations, too. The American Dental Association influences the scope of tasks that dental hygienists are permitted to perform, what services must be performed under the direct supervision of a dentist, and whether services provided by hygienists will be reimbursed.[21]

There is little evidence that these extra restrictions beyond the basic certification of quality do anything to enhance the service provided. Kleiner and Kudrle compare oral health outcomes of Air Force recruits and find that tougher state licensing requirements for dentists are not correlated with oral health.[22] Nor are insurance premiums lower in states with licensing restrictions.[23]

However, these restrictions do have well-documented effects on the pay of existing members of the profession and the cost to consumers. Occupational licensing restrictions increase wages by 18 percent on average.[24] A Federal Trade Commission study found that state restrictions on the scope of tasks performed by dental hygienists and assistants increased the cost of a dental visit by 7 to 11 percent;[25] restrictions on nurse practitioners increased some costs by 3 to 16 percent.[26] And dental licensing restrictions reduce access to care.[27]

The economic impact of licensing restrictions is, perhaps, greatest in health care, where 76 percent of nonphysician health workers are subject to occupational licensing. Humphris et al. estimate that the extra annual cost to consumers of these licensing restrictions was $102 billion in 2008.[28] Performing a similar thumbnail calculation suggests that licensing restrictions implied a loss of nearly half a million jobs for nonphysician health care workers.[29]

The health care sector has had both growing employment and a growing median wage as technology has facilitated the reallocation of work away from physicians and dentists toward mid-skill providers. This sector has been a major source of good jobs for workers who do not have bachelor's degrees or higher. Yet without significant and excessive licensing restrictions for mid-skill occupations, employment would be even higher and the adoption of new technologies and new business models would be even greater. Under the progressive-sounding guise of boosting the knowledge economy, educational restrictions actually limit the spread of new knowledge.

## Manufacturing Policy

Some people advocate very different policies in response to the supposed shift to a knowledge economy. They see this shift destroying well-paid manufacturing jobs and want to preserve these jobs with subsidies or trade protections.

But manufacturing jobs are not well paid because they are in manufacturing; they are well paid because workers in manufacturing today possess valuable technical knowledge. This is not always true. The manufacturing workers of the early Industrial Revolution were certainly not well paid, and their wages increased only after their skills and labor markets developed over many decades. Also, valuable manufacturing knowledge, once acquired, can become obsolete as new technologies emerge; we saw evidence that this is happening today as experience premiums decline in manufacturing. Then workers must acquire new knowledge in order to maintain high pay. Trade protection tends to benefit politically influential established interests and preserve jobs with obsolete knowledge. It would be better to facilitate the retraining of workers and the transition of firms to new technologies.

The case of the steel industry illustrates how trade protection—ostensibly to protect workers—hurt consumers, delayed the transition to new technology, and delayed the development of a workforce with new skills that could sustainably earn good wages. Perhaps no American industry has been better at winning trade protection in recent decades than steel. Import quotas were first put into place in 1969, with variations of protectionist measures made by the Carter, Reagan, and George W. Bush administrations, until commitments to the World Trade Organization forced Bush to lift steel tariffs in 2003.

The industry first ran into trouble during the 1950s and 1960s when it failed to keep up with new technologies—the basic oxygen furnace and continuous casting—that were being widely adopted in Japan and Europe. American steel at the time was dominated by a few large, integrated producers.[30] Because of their complacency, the United States became a net importer of steel in 1959, and imports increased during the 1960s. This motivated the steel producers to lobby repeatedly for various forms of trade protection that served to keep prices high so that their outmoded mills could stay in operation. The larger, older, and less competitive firms tended to lobby the most aggressively.[31]

Some of the newer, smaller firms that were pursuing a new, more efficient technology actually opposed trade protection. It turned out that the real threat to the large steel producers came not from foreign competition but from American "minimills" that used electric arc furnaces to melt recycled steel. The older integrated steel makers began production by smelting iron ore into pig iron and then converting that into steel. Minimills could operate at a much smaller scale, they could be located closer to consumers, and they required substantially less labor and energy per ton of steel.[32] They accounted for only 7 percent of U.S. steel shipments in 1979; today they account for 70 percent.[33] With the growth of the minimills, and the subsequent shakeout of outdated mills, the amount of labor needed to produce a ton of steel fell from ten hours in 1980 to around two hours today.[34]

This new sector was not interested in trade protection.[35] Kenneth Iverson, CEO of Nucor, the leading minimill company, told a congressional committee in 1984, "We believe that tariff or nontariff trade barriers will delay modernization of our steel industry, will cost the consumer billions of dollars, and could seriously injure both our economy and smaller steel producers."[36] Instead, he urged policymakers to employ programs to retrain workers and to provide incentives to encourage modernization. Trade barriers might have boosted Nucor's profits in the short run, but they would diminish incentives to modernize.

Three decades of steel protection are estimated to have cost consumers and taxpayers over $100 billion.[37] In addition, the higher prices likely encouraged other industries to move production overseas, where, among other things, steel would have been cheaper. Perhaps most significantly, these policies delayed the transition of workers into new *sustainable* jobs with high wages. Today, steelworkers still earn high wages, but there are only a quarter as many jobs as there were in 1980. When the political economy was tilted to preserve the producers using old technology, little was done to transition steelworkers into new jobs requiring new skills.

The political influence of Old Steel did not last. The competing interests of other industries, which benefited from more open trade, finally came to bear when the World Trade Organization required that special steel tariffs be abandoned. And the growth of minimills and the substantial improvement of their technology forced many of the obsolete mills into bankruptcy.

Steelworkers in U.S. minimills earn high wages, thanks to their specialized knowledge and skills, just as steelworkers have done for over a hundred years. And the United States is now the world leader in minimill technology—Europe and Japan, where integrated steelmakers hold greater power, have been slow to adopt this technology.[38] There are fewer steelworkers today, to be sure, but their jobs were not preserved by thirty years of preferential trade policy. The development of the minimills was, if anything, delayed by that policy. In some cases, temporary trade protection might, arguably, create extra time to retrain the workforce; the example of the steel industry shows that with political influence, a short transition can easily grow into a long, damaging delay.

The role and nature of knowledge in today's economy is not so different from its role in the past. For 200 years, manufacturing technologies have critically depended on workers' acquiring new technical knowledge and skills. Much of this learning, however, happened on the job rather than in the classroom. For this reason, it is a mistake to pursue policies that disregard experience-based knowledge and encourage a shift to exclusively "professional" occupations.

On the other hand, we must recognize that as manufacturing technologies mature, some of this knowledge becomes obsolete, and ongoing change will continue to reduce manufacturing jobs in these industries. That is no reason to try to preserve these jobs. Better policy is to provide retraining to transition these workers to new skills and knowledge. New jobs are emerging, in both the manufacturing and service sectors, that require new skills but do not necessarily demand years of formal schooling.

Technology needs knowledge acquired in the classroom as well as on the job. Although these sorts of knowledge correspond to the interests of different groups—professionals seeking to preserve the exclusivity of their knowledge, and manufacturing workers seeking to preserve their well-paid jobs—promoting one sort of knowledge at the expense of the other is ultimately harmful. Historically, manufacturing industries have permitted large numbers of less educated people to earn middle-class pay. While jobs in mature manufacturing industries will continue to decline, it is important to grasp the opportunities for less educated people to acquire skills in emerging new technologies, wherever they are.

## CHAPTER 10

# Procuring New Knowledge

ALL OVER THE WORLD, GOVERNMENTS ARE trying to spur economic growth by becoming "public venture capitalists," providing loans, grants, tax credits, and other subsidies to companies, especially start-ups, that are working with new technologies. The goal is to encourage start-up firms that will develop new knowledge and skills.[1] Everyone wants to emulate the technology clusters around Boston and Silicon Valley.

Yet overall, the results of these efforts are mixed at best. A few have succeeded, most have not, and many are little more than corrupt boondoggles. The reasons for failure vary. Some administrators are inept or lack fundamental knowledge of the technology and markets; they have difficulty "picking winners." In other cases, decisions are based on political influence rather than economic merits.[2]

A different kind of government policy appears to have more success at spurring the development and commercialization of new technologies. Programs of this sort facilitated the development of computers, semiconductors, the Internet, global positioning satellites, and digital wireless communications. One such program was responsible for the "American System of Manufactures" that allowed the United States to become an international leader in manufacturing technologies during the late nineteenth and early twentieth centuries.

What were these programs? They were government procurement programs, including procurement-related R&D and programs supporting research conducted at government labs. The technology clusters around Boston and in Silicon Valley were aided not so much by government venture capitalists as by government agencies purchasing technologies to aid their own missions. Ironically, this policy did not have economic growth as its main objective.

Procurement can play an important role in the development and spread of technical knowledge because of the way it promotes learning through experience. Procurement programs demand a level of performance, rather than just subsidizing promising entrepreneurs, and achieving performance goals with new technologies requires large numbers of people to develop specific new skills. Sometimes, that broad base of people can then turn those skills to commercial applications, to powerful effect. Because costly learning by doing is so critical to new technologies, procurement can be a powerful engine of innovation.

Defense Department and space program procurement spurred many new technologies, but government contracting spurred innovation in many other fields as well.[3] Thomson finds that the majority of nineteenth-century innovators in all fields had experience as government contractors or employees.[4] State governments and the Agriculture Department were influential in biological innovation, the U.S. Geological Service played a key role in mining knowledge, and a wide variety of other federal, state, and local agencies promoted the spread of new knowledge especially regarding infrastructure, health, and sanitation.[5]

Some people question whether government can play a positive role commercializing technology beyond the support that the National Institutes of Health (NIH), the National Science Foundation (NSF), and other agencies provide for basic research. But procurement programs largely involve spending money that the government needs to spend in order to meet its other missions anyway.

Procurement programs *can* play this role, but they do not always do so—the specific design matters. As we shall see, important programs today are prevented from playing such a beneficial role. It is helpful to look at how procurement programs worked to foster early-stage technologies in the past, and why they no longer do so.

## Interchangeable Parts

The first major industrial procurement program in the United States was for firearms. After having difficulty arming the troops during the Revolutionary War, the newly founded government realized that it needed to be able to produce large numbers of firearms, especially ones that could be easily repaired in the field.

The federal government set up two armories, one in Springfield, Massachusetts, and one in Harpers Ferry, Virginia. The armories produced firearms and also contracted with machine shops to build rifles made of interchangeable parts. If the parts for every rifle were made to the same specifications within close tolerances, then when one failed, the parts could be cannibalized and combined with parts from other rifles. In this way, working guns could be reassembled in the field from used parts. In addition to facilitating battlefield repair, this program promised to free the new republic from dependence on foreign arms—interchangeable parts did not require a large number of artisan gunsmiths, which the new nation did not have.

But manufacturing truly interchangeable parts proved harder than advocates realized. Slowly, over decades, machine shops, working with the two public armories, developed new machine tools and gauges, specialized machines and jigs, new types of work organization, and a newly skilled workforce. Key to the success of this system were the learned skills of the "artificers" who machined and hand-filed the parts to fit within tolerances. By the 1850s, specialized machines and workers with specialized skills were producing large numbers of firearms with truly replaceable parts.[6]

This became the foundation of the American System of Manufactures, and it had ramifications far beyond arms production.[7] With interchangeable parts built to high tolerances, any complex mechanical product could be broken into components, each produced by specialized workers using specialized tools, and separately assembled by other workers. The high degree of specialization meant that each worker had a steep learning curve and could achieve a high level of efficiency. Historian David Hounshell documents how firms used interchangeability to establish efficient mass production of everything from sewing machines to automobiles. This technology established American prowess in a range of mechanical industries during the late nineteenth century, and it facilitated assembly-line production during the early twentieth century.[8]

## Building a Knowledge Base

Why was procurement of interchangeable parts so successful at spurring subsequent innovation? Partly luck, but also because it created a broad base of skilled workers who could use their skills in civilian applications. Interchangeable parts turned out to be a general purpose technology. The U.S. War Department was not trying to spur broad change when it initiated the program. Its goal was just to produce weapons that were easy to repair. Fortuitously, the technique that was used happened to be broadly applicable. A similarly happy result followed from the development of digital wireless communications for deep space satellites, and from the use of computers for code-breaking and artillery calculations. Of course, many technologies developed for the special needs of the government had little outside application.

But we are interested in the ones that did have broad application. Government procurement of interchangeable parts was especially effective at spurring broad technological changes because it fostered the acquisition of new knowledge and skills among a large number of artificers and mechanics. Several activities contributed to the development of this broad knowledge base. First, rather than rely on the existing supply of artisan gunsmiths, the War Department effectively paid for the training of new workers. The government established two public armories, but it also gave work to a significant number of private contractors—twenty-seven in 1798 and 1799, and an additional eighteen in 1808.[9] Moreover, the government was willing to pay higher prices for interchangeability, thus subsidizing the development of new skills. It obtained agreements from its private contractors not to poach trained employees from other contractors, thus securing the private investments made in worker skills.

Second, it encouraged knowledge sharing. As economic historian Ross Thomson writes in *Structures of Change in the Mechanical Age: Technological Innovation in the United States, 1790–1865*,

The government organized a communications system through which units learned from each other. The federal armories became the system's centers, especially the Springfield Armory. Inspection by Springfield Armory personnel, though a source of disagreement, did enforce standards, and it became more cooperative when armory staff worked with contractors to minimize rejects. Springfield was a center of technology sharing. It loaned out tools, patterns, and skilled pattern makers and toolmakers, and performed services such as rolling iron. It shared knowledge of machine design, manufacturing techniques, gauging, and inspection methods. It learned from private firms, and firms learned from each other. Knowledge sharing was entailed by the contract system, which required contractors to open their shops to the armory and other contractors. The Ordnance Department made clear that future contracts depended on technological progress and knowledge sharing.[10]

Finally, the government promoted standards that facilitated the development of markets for both labor and specialized machine tools. The Ordnance Department defined the product, set quality standards, and established inspection systems. The parts had to meet specific tolerances, and the firearms had to meet performance and repair standards. The contractors were pushed to work to tolerances not required by other customers. Initially the standards were embodied in pattern weapons that the government supplied to contractors, which had to be matched. Later, new methods of measurement were developed that made the standards more generally applicable.

Thus the procurement program for interchangeable parts developed a broad base of knowledge because of three characteristics. It subsidized on-the-job training for workers with new skills; it promoted knowledge sharing; and it established open standards. With a corps of trained workers and common standards, these new methods were ready to be applied to other types of production. Machine tool technology to create interchangeable mechanical parts was not the only technology to benefit from procurement during the nineteenth century. Ross Thomson finds that 54 percent of leading innovators in fields ranging from mining, construction, and agriculture learned from government contracting or employment.[11]

There are more recent examples of influential government procurement programs that also established broad bases of knowledge among significant numbers of people. For example, Claude Shannon founded information theory while working at AT&T in 1948. This mathematical theory promised to improve digital communications, but it did not find practical application until the 1960s, when NASA sought better methods of communicating with deep space satellites. These satellites faced special problems because they could only send weak signals over a high level of background noise. After NASA funded individual consultants and small companies to apply information theory to this problem, researchers began to share important developments, such as a decoding algorithm that is now widely used in cell phones.[12] These specialized technologies began to find civilian uses. Engineers with experience in space and military applications eventually applied their knowledge to create digital wireless communications technology.

## How Procurement Can Promote Learning

Well-designed government procurement programs can foster the creation of broad bases of knowledge in ways that private firms might not. Because private firms do not always capture all of the benefit from training employees, sharing knowledge, and establishing common standards, their incentives to do these things are not as great as they are for government agencies. Government agencies, contracting with multiple firms, suffer no loss of benefit when trained employees change firms, when knowledge is shared between firms, or when the firms agree on a common standard. For example, we saw how Time Warner did not have a strong incentive to establish open standards in the development of interactive TV. The Defense Department and other government funders created the early Internet with open standards that contributed to creating a broad base of people with the skills and knowledge to implement applications. Procurement contracts can encourage firms to make investments they might otherwise not make in developing employee skills, sharing knowledge, and coordinating on common standards.

Economic analysis of innovation has typically focused on the entrepreneur's incentives to invest. But developing new skills and knowledge is also important, and usually requires more than just motivating entrepreneurs.

The rationale for subsidizing entrepreneurs is that in competitive markets, firms tend to underinvest in innovation. But they also underinvest in commonly shared skills, knowledge, and standards. A well-designed procurement program can play a distinctive role in fostering these things. This is why some of the most effective government contributions to technological development stem from procurement programs whose main objective was not economic growth.

Of course, not all procurement programs have such beneficial effects. Military procurement and the "military-industrial complex" are famous for their inefficiencies. David Mowery and Timothy Simcoe look at why the Internet and World Wide Web were largely developed in the United States even though some of the initial inventions—such as the Web—were made elsewhere.[13] They found that key aspects of government policy made the difference. Most U.S. research on computer networking during the 1960s was funded by the military with the goal of facilitating efficient shared use of scarce computing resources.[14] Although the Defense Department sought to develop specific applications for its own use, Mowery and Simcoe write, it "supported 'generic' research and the development of a substantial infrastructure in academia and industry for this research, in the expectation that a viable computer industry capable of supplying defense needs would require civilian markets."[15] Consequently, the funding of research and development in network computing for the military had several characteristics that enhanced the creation of a broad base of technical knowledge.

First, the Pentagon funded many different entities, including academic researchers and startup companies, and trained a broad base of people: "Federal R&D investments strengthened US universities' research capabilities in computer science, facilitated the formation of university 'spinoffs' such as BBN and Sun Microsystems, and trained a large cohort of technical experts who aided in the development, adoption, and commercialization of the Internet."[16] The government did not attempt to "pick winners" but instead backed diverse approaches, architectures, and suppliers. The Internet's basic design, as a packet-switched network, was actually competitive to the telephone monopoly, which used a circuit-switched network. Other countries did not take such a catholic approach. Britain had a policy of supporting national champions in the computer industry; France backed

Minitel, a precursor to the Web produced by its government-owned telephone company.

Second, the Department of Defense widely shared emerging technical knowledge. Defense contracts often required "second sourcing" so that the military did not have to rely on a single supplier. This practice often forced firms to license their technology to rivals, encouraging the diffusion of practical knowledge gained from using the technology. More generally, the Defense Department sought to create a broad research infrastructure accessible to academics and civilian firms as well as defense firms and the military. In the United Kingdom and the USSR, security concerns isolated military researchers and engineers from their civilian counterparts.

Third, consistent with the objective of broad and diverse participation, the Internet was developed with open standards. Key standards such as TCP/IP (for the plumbing of the Internet) and HTTP (for the World Wide Web) were developed with open public participation and placed in the public domain. The government did not itself promulgate these standards, but instead encouraged the formation of public standard-setting organizations.[17]

These characteristics suggest that the development of the Internet and the development of interchangeable parts succeeded for similar reasons. Yet other procurement programs, including many recent ones, do not share the same characteristics and have not succeeded in developing broad-based technical knowledge.

## Procurement Today

Some people argue that defense R&D should be spared from the budget cuts hitting other government agencies today. Because defense R&D plays a special role in fostering commercially valuable technologies, they argue, any budget cuts will hurt the economy as well as U.S. defense supremacy.[18] In making this case they cite such technologies as electronic computers, integrated circuits, global positioning systems, and the Internet, including e-mail.

Yet the key early stages of these technologies all came before the mid-1970s. More recent defense R&D does not seem to have produced similar results. Part of the reason may be because some military needs do not have commercial applications, or because some technologies already have well-developed commercial markets.[19] Nevertheless, several major defense investments have failed to spur broad commercial development, even when commercial versions of these technologies were later developed independently. They include numerically controlled machine tools, very high speed integrated circuits, and "strategic computing," including parallel computers and artificial intelligence.[20] Even military investments in "dual use" technologies saw the military benefiting more from commercial innovation than the other way around.[21] Moreover, these failures occurred despite a doubling of defense R&D spending since the 1960s.[22]

Economist Jay Stowsky identifies the failures as resulting from what he calls "shielded innovation": The R&D was targeted at specific needs of defense rather than generic development of the technology; traditional defense contractors were put in charge to guarantee fealty to the military's needs; and these contractors restricted the flow of information to other potential technology users.[23] Thus, for example, when the Air Force wanted to use computers to control machine tools for cutting complex metal airplane parts, it worked only with a few large aerospace and automobile companies to develop and use these tools. Those companies were required to use a specialized computer language for programming, and programmers had to keep the technology secret. This was a far cry from the earlier programs for interchangeable parts or the Internet, where a broad array of private parties were involved in development, knowledge was freely shared, and open standards were used. Not surprisingly, the Air Force's program did not spur significant commercial development of numerically controlled machine tools. Instead, inexpensive, widely used computer-controlled machine tools were developed with little help from the military, much of the technology coming from Germany and Japan. This failure permitted Japanese imports to dominate the market and to replace U.S. toolmakers in global trade.[24]

Why has the military shifted to a model of innovation that seems designed to choke off commercial growth? One reason is a greater emphasis on security. Especially since 9/11, much more information is classified or restricted. Another possible factor is the growing influence of the military-industrial complex. Defense R&D is a well-known target for Washington influence peddlers. Shielded innovation meets the needs of the influence peddlers—information about projects is hidden from public scrutiny, the projects avoid accountability, and well-established defense contractors run them.[25] But these priorities mean that defense R&D and procurement fails to develop skills and knowledge among civilians.

By requiring that purchases of new technology meet high-quality standards, government procurement and related R&D can facilitate the development of new skills that are often key to commercializing early-stage technologies. Yet influential industry lobbies have prevented military procurement from playing this role. "Capture" of military R&D reached a peak under Secretary of Defense Donald Rumsfeld, when bidding on many research projects was restricted to major defense contractors, funding to university researchers was slashed in half, foreign graduate students were prevented from participating in research, and much research was classified and focused on short-term results.[26] That direction appears to have been reversed recently. The Defense Advanced Research Projects Agency (DARPA) has relaxed restrictions on foreign students and classified information, funding to universities has increased, and more dollars now go to longer-range projects, including a major university-based consortium to develop the next generation of semiconductors. DARPA has also sought to broaden participation among young university researchers and hackers.[27] It remains to be seen whether these initiatives can reverse several decades of misdirected policy.

## Other Sectors

Government procurement holds promise as a way of developing skills among people working with new technologies in other, less recognized sectors. For example, municipal procurement policies favoring green buildings have been shown to increase private investments in the skills of engineers and builders. A careful study found that when municipalities required new government buildings to meet the U.S. Green Building Council's standards for energy efficiency, the adoption of standard-compliant building within those municipalities doubled overall, and green building in neighboring towns increased as well.[28]

Perhaps more important is government's role in health care, which appears to be in the early stages of major technological and organizational change. The federal government is the largest direct and indirect consumer of health care services. The Veterans Health Administration alone is the largest integrated health care system in the United States, with over 1,700 sites. Yet during the early 1990s, the VHA had a terrible reputation for the quality of its care and the safety of its patients. Then, in 1994, Dr. Kenneth Kizer took over as Under Secretary for Health of the Department of Veterans Affairs, and by the early 2000s, surveys showed a dramatic turnaround. The VHA was ranked first in quality, above many well-known hospital systems and Medicare fee-for-service providers.[29] Moreover, the quality improvement was achieved while keeping cost per patient level, at a time when the cost of health care for Americans overall increased 60 percent.[30] Although the recent scandal over scheduling at VHA facilities has brought attention to problems with access to care, the evidence indicates that the quality of care provided by the VHA is still quite high.[31]

Central to Kizer's reforms was a new technology: the electronic health record, or EHR. By centralizing and computerizing medical notes, instructions, charts, and other data and images, including patient X-rays, the VHA realized several advantages. First, it reduced medical errors, such as giving patients the wrong treatments or medicines. Studies have found that medical errors are responsible for as many as 98,000 preventable deaths each year and over a million injuries.[32] Second, EHR technology facilitated coordinated care. A large share of health care costs come from a small percentage of patients with complex problems. Typically, these patients receive different and often conflicting or unnecessary treatment from different providers. When providers can provide consistent, coordinated treatment—which electronic health records facilitate—they can give better care at significantly lower cost.[33] The EHR system also reduced administrative work. In the long run, EHR systems may be vital to collecting data on health outcomes to provide far more meaningful measures of health quality and to determine which medical procedures work well and which do not.

Clearly, this technology can play a part in changing health care outside the VHA. One study estimates that EHR systems might save $81 billion a year while improving the quality of health care.[34] Large numbers of commercial vendors now offer EHR systems, and large numbers of hospitals and other providers are installing them. The VHA system is also freely available. Moreover, the federal government is encouraging the process through its procurement of health care for the elderly and poor. As part of the 2009 economic stimulus package, the Obama administration included the Health Information Technology for Economic and Clinical Health (HITECH) Act. The HITECH Act provides as much as $36 billion in incentives for Medicare and Medicaid providers to adopt electronic health records.

Yet as with other technologies, large-scale change will take time. It will be costly and will involve major organizational and institutional changes. Many early implementations increased costs rather than reducing them.[35] As with other computer systems, the effectiveness of the technology depends on having a core of people with specialized skills to use and adapt it. One study shows that hospitals with access to skilled IT professionals save money; those with limited access do not.[36] Building a broad core of people with these skills is clearly critical.

A related obstacle is the lack of standardization. Even within leading hospital systems such as the Mayo Clinic, different parts of an organization often have incompatible EHR systems, so they don't fully share patient data.[37] The lack of standardization not only hampers the technology's effectiveness, it also prevents the emergence of robust labor markets. Here, too, the federal government is taking steps to encourage standardization, encouraging the formation of private-public health information exchanges under the Office of the National Coordinator for Health Information Technology in the Department of Health and Human Services.

Deeper obstacles may also limit this technology. As long as most health care providers are compensated based on the number of procedures they perform rather than on the health of their patients, they may have little incentive to use the new technology. Worse, entrenched interests may derail well-intentioned government programs and government efforts to establish standards. The experience of the VHA shows that EHR technology can be implemented to great benefit on a large scale, but this is no guarantee that it will.

Overall, it does seem that government procurement no longer promotes the development of broad-based knowledge of new technologies as it once did. Perhaps that will change. Perhaps military research in robotics or drones will foster civilian applications, or procurement in the health care or energy sectors will play the role military procurement once did. But the trend of the last three decades has been in the wrong direction.

# CHAPTER 11

# The Forgotten History of
# Knowledge Sharing

WILLIAM GILMOUR EMIGRATED FROM GLASGOW, Scotland, to Boston, arriving in September 1815.[1] A skilled machinist, he had become acquainted with the British power loom and thought he might be able to build looms in the United States. He first proposed building weaving and dressing machinery for the Slaters, owners of a pioneering cotton spinning mill in Providence, Rhode Island. Because the market was depressed, the Slaters did not want to make a risky investment at that time, but they gave him work in their machine shop. A few months later, he pitched his services to Judge Lyman, owner of the Lyman Cotton Manufacturing Company, who immediately contracted with him to construct a power loom and related machinery.

Gilmour drew the plans for the loom on the floor of a vacant room in Lyman's mill. As he proceeded, machinists took measurements from the floor and built twelve looms of wrought iron. They went into operation in the spring of 1817.

A half dozen other power looms had already been patented in the United States, and some of them were being used to produce cloth. Gilmour's design proved to be superior, however, and eventually replaced the other models. Yet Gilmour did not patent his loom at that time or even try to monopolize its use. Instead, he shared the design, charging another mechanic, David Wilkinson, $10 for the drawings. Wilkinson and Gilmour began building textile equipment for other manufacturers, with Judge Lyman's blessing.

Later, these manufacturers raised a $1,500 reward for Gilmour to thank him for his contribution.

Gilmour and Lyman were not utopian dreamers. Why did they freely share their design with other machinists and other textile manufacturers? They made no attempt to protect their invention from imitators but willingly assisted them. It is often asserted that patents are the *only* way that start-up firms can profit from their ideas. Otherwise, large firms will swoop in, copy their innovations, and drive them out of business. Yet these pioneers of weaving technology in the United States succeeded by acting contrary to the conventional wisdom.

The notion that patents are critical for the survival of technology start-ups seems at odds with other, more recent examples. Many of today's big technology companies—Google, Microsoft, Apple, Amazon—did not depend on patents for their funding, nor did patents seem to play a significant role restraining their rivals. Moreover, many early-stage developers seemed willing to freely share technology with potential rivals. The Internet was based on patent-free open standards and freely shared software. Many of the early personal computer companies, including Apple, began at the Homebrew Computer Club, where designs were freely shared. Open source software powers everything from web servers to smartphone operating systems. Some have described our time as the Age of Open Innovation.

There are sound economic reasons for this behavior. Learning by doing is essential to understanding much of it.

## A Forgotten Story: Innovators Sharing Knowledge

"Open innovation" has been described as a "new paradigm," a break from the past when firms maintained complete proprietary control of their innovations.[2] Open source and free software are, of course, recent developments. But knowledge sharing among innovators, especially during the early stages of a technology, is nothing new. It was going on during the twentieth century, during the Industrial Revolution, and long before that.

This is a largely forgotten history. Textbooks and museums often depict inventors as jealously guarding their secrets against imitators. The Wright brothers, for example, kept news of their first flight secret for several years so as to buy time to patent their invention. Yet significant evidence shows that inventors often shared their knowledge. Before their successful flight, the Wright brothers themselves actively shared knowledge in a vibrant international community of inventors and scientists who openly reported and discussed the merits and limitations of different designs for flying machines.[3]

Despite the difficulty of obtaining documentary evidence on early practices, economic historians are beginning to develop a more complete picture of knowledge sharing.[4] Economic historian Robert Allen speculates that one form of knowledge sharing, "collective invention," was "probably the most important source of inventions" during the nineteenth century.[5]

Before the Industrial Revolution, a strong tradition of innovation was supported by the guilds, which actively promoted the sharing of technical knowledge through person-to-person communication among their members in a period when other means of transmission were limited.[6] In nineteenth-century Britain, knowledge sharing has been documented in many key technologies, including blast furnaces for making iron, the high-pressure steam engine in the Cornish mining district, textile equipment, the development of coal-burning houses in London, and in civil engineering.[7] During the nineteenth century in the United States, knowledge sharing has been documented in the cotton textile industry, in the development of the high-pressure steam engine for western steamboats, in papermaking, in the Bessemer process for making steel, and among mechanics generally, including the ones who developed the techniques for interchangeable parts.[8] In addition, knowledge sharing was practiced widely in both American and British agriculture, leading to methods of crop rotation and extensive biological innovation in wheat, cotton, tobacco, alfalfa, corn, and livestock.[9]

More recently, researchers have found knowledge sharing among steel minimills and in other industries: early work on digital wireless communications, the early personal computer, surgical procedures, a wide range of user innovations from sports gear to laboratory equipment, and, of course, free and open source software have all benefited from knowledge sharing.[10]

While many of the innovators involved in sharing technology explicitly disavowed patents, much of this sharing occurred alongside some patenting.

Many of the early mechanics in the United States got patents but enforced them only against downstream manufacturers, not against fellow mechanics with whom they shared knowledge.[11] The engineers using the Bessemer steelmaking process actively exchanged knowledge, meeting regularly with engineers from rival mills and publishing technical bulletins. The chief engineer from the Bethlehem Iron Works called this group a "band of loving brothers."[12] But all of the mills were licensees of the Bessemer patents and members of a patent pool. Often, patents were simply not very profitable or useful to innovators during the early stages of technologies.

That changed as technologies matured. Many technologies seem to have followed a common pattern: a regime with knowledge sharing and little patenting is followed by a regime with aggressive patent acquisition and enforcement. Apple Computer shared its designs and features for the Apple I and Apple II with the Homebrew Computer Club every two weeks or so, receiving valuable feedback.[13] During its first decade the company obtained just 14 patents. In 2012, Apple obtained 1,236 patents and is involved in over 100 lawsuits enforcing its smartphone patents in venues around the world. Steve Jobs famously said, "We have always been shameless about stealing great ideas." These included the idea of the graphical user interface, the MP3 player, and the tablet, which Apple borrowed and improved. Some cynics accuse Apple of pulling the ladders up behind it, using patents to prevent others from doing what it once did. The pattern is evident with other tech leaders. Microsoft did not obtain its first patent until 1986, when it was eleven years old. Today it has over 20,000 patents and actively enforces them. Qualcomm is known today for its large patent portfolio, which it aggressively enforces. But the founders of Qualcomm freely shared their technology during the early years of digital wireless technology, including a decoding algorithm widely used in cell phones today.[14]

The same pattern can be observed in the past. Aviation technology was widely shared among an international community of innovators until successful flight was realized in 1903. In the United States, the period of sharing was followed by a period of aggressive litigation, resulting in a highly destructive patent war where no one could produce an airplane without violating someone else's patent. These blocking patents stalled aviation development for a decade in the United States, until the government, desperate to have airplanes as it was entering World War I, forced the warring parties to form a patent pool.

Most episodes of knowledge sharing were limited. Often they lasted just a decade or two, in one region of the world, sometimes only within a community of mechanics or engineers. A variety of factors caused these periods of sharing to end. In some, markets collapsed or industry structure changed, causing the community to break down. Perhaps it is the temporary nature of these episodes that has allowed historians to overlook the importance of knowledge sharing. The winners write history.

Nevertheless, despite lasting only a decade or two, these episodes have resulted in major improvements in key technologies. They brought about a fivefold increase in the amount of cloth a weaver could produce in an hour in the United States during the first half of the nineteenth century, an 80 percent reduction in the cost of producing steel rails using the Bessemer process in the United States, and a tripling of the efficiency of high-pressure steam engines in Cornwall. It is not an overstatement to say that innovations made during these sharing episodes were responsible for the successes of these technologies.

## The Puzzle of Knowledge Sharing

From the perspective of the traditional economic analysis of innovation, the frequency of knowledge sharing is puzzling. In the standard analysis, if rivals replicate inventions, then they will enter the market, increase competition, drive down prices, and eliminate profits.[15] Innovators will not be willing to invest in R&D, the argument goes, unless they can either prevent rivals from copying them or they are provided some other incentive such as a prize. Patents are seen as a key means to prevent copying of inventions, although firms use other methods as well.[16]

Why, then, would innovators actually *encourage* rivals to imitate by sharing knowledge with them? This seems to be a puzzle.

It is not hard to find possible benefits from sharing. Sharing knowledge is key to creating common standards or best practices, which, as we have seen, have significant economic benefits. Also, some knowledge sharing might really be an exchange or innovators might share in the expectation that other innovators will reciprocate: I share my innovations with you, you share yours with me, and we are both better off. Such benefits are well understood. Nevertheless, people apparently assume that the damage done by competition will normally outweigh these benefits.

The frequent occurrence of knowledge sharing in the past suggests that this assumption is not always correct. Knowledge sharing might occur under special conditions, but these conditions are not rare. To understand what the enabling conditions were in the past, how common they are today, and what that means for policy, it helps to look more closely at one of these knowledge-sharing episodes.[17] Specifically, we want to see whether sharing did dissipate profits and, to the extent that innovators did obtain patents, whether patents increased profits significantly, as in the standard analysis.

## Sharing Weaving Inventions

William Gilmour freely shared his design for a patent loom. Other important weaving inventions of the 1820s and 1830s were also shared, but not all of them. The Boston Manufacturing Company in Waltham, Massachusetts, initially patented several inventions but soon abandoned this practice. Key advances in power transmission technology developed during the 1820s by the company's chief mechanic, Paul Moody, were widely shared throughout the industry. The most important weaving invention of the 1830s was the weft fork, which detected when the weft thread was broken and stopped the loom. Clinton Gilroy claimed to have invented the weft fork in 1831 but did not patent it.[18] On the other hand, designs for the loom temple, an important attachment to the looms, were patented; these parts did not, however, generate much profit.

More generally, the mechanics of this era, who formed a tightly networked community, actively shared their knowledge.[19] Many had trained with others in the network, sometimes job-hopping as journeymen to gain different types of experience; some were related by marriage or birth. Exchanging knowledge had well understood benefits. Textile technology was highly complex; there were many ways to build the equipment, and for each step in the process there were many different ways of proceeding. No one machine shop on its own could expect to develop the best equipment in all areas and build it using the best techniques. So mechanics shared knowledge. Anthony Wallace describes this "International Fraternity of Mechanicians":

> They visited each other's shop constantly to exchange information, to stand silently watching a new machine or a new process, to speculate about the future of the mechanism. By and large, they knew each other's business and did not hesitate to show each other inventions in embryo, trusting their peers to honor their priority and the economic advantage it might mean. Their patents were often not taken out until years after the invention had become widely known in the fraternity; patents once taken were sometimes not announced or enforced, the patentee trusting his customers to honor his interest without reminder.[20]

### The Profits of Sharing

In the conventional story, start-up firms need patents to prevent others from copying. But William Gilmour shared his design with other mechanics and Judge Lyman allowed it to be shared with other prospective manufacturers. Did this decision drive down prices and profits?

Not for at least two decades. Both the machine shops and the textile manufacturers made very high profits that competition only gradually diminished. The first textile manufacturer using power looms, the Boston Manufacturing Company, paid annual dividends of 12.5 to 27.5 percent during its first seven years. Other mills in the 1820s did not do as well, but they still paid dividends of 5 to 14 percent. The machine shops were also profitable, earning markups of 50 percent above cost during the early years. By 1830 this rate had declined somewhat, but they still earned 30 to 35 percent markups above cost. Only around the end of the 1830s did conditions become competitive for both textile manufacturers and machine shops making textile equipment.

The textile mills made high profits because their costs were well below the market price. Early on, this market price was effectively determined by weavers working on handlooms, mainly at home, because power loom manufacturers accounted for only a small share of the total market. By the end of the 1820s, however, the home weavers had been largely replaced, but some cloth was still being imported from Britain, subject to a healthy tariff. Only when domestic power loom manufacturers dominated the market, in the mid-1830s, did things finally become competitive.

Competition between users of the new technology was "soft" for two decades because the new technology coexisted with more costly alternatives. Additional power loom manufacturers did not significantly affect prices as long as most of the market was still being supplied by handloom weavers or by expensive imports. In this situation, it did not hurt to share technology with prospective rivals. Sharing only expanded the new technology's market share. It took two decades for competition between power loom manufacturers to grow intense.

But if textile manufacturers were making large profits, why did not more firms quickly enter the market? An important reason was learning by doing. Acquiring the requisite knowledge took time and was costly. Few people initially knew how to build, install, operate, and maintain the new machinery.[21] Mechanics not only needed general skills as mechanics, but they also had to learn the intricacies of textile manufacturing equipment. As late as 1845, skilled labor shortages caused production delays, thanks to a scarcity of mechanics and the long training requirements and experience needed. Managers too needed intimate knowledge of the technology. No mill survived during the early years without its own machine shop or a close relationship with an outside shop. Workers' skills mattered as well. Mills failed if they could not attract and keep workers who could learn skills on the job.

### The Limited Value of Patents for Early Technologies

When new technology coexists with inferior alternatives, patents have limited value. The main value of patents to their owners is to exclude others from a new technology, thus limiting competition.[22] But if the patent owner's profits are not hurt by competition from a few rivals using the technology—as was the case with early loom technology—there is little value in excluding others from the market. Patents might still have some value, for instance, if they cover an incremental improvement that others might pay for. But if the purpose of patents is to protect an innovator from imitators, there is little purpose in spending money to obtain and enforce patents when the effect of imitation is benign.

The Boston Manufacturing Company began by patenting its inventions, but later reversed course. Francis Cabot Lowell of the BMC introduced the first commercially successful power loom in the United States two years before Gilmour. Gilmour's design proved superior, but for a brief period, the BMC loom was the leading technology. Unlike Gilmour, Lowell and his agent, Patrick Tracy Jackson, patented their loom in 1815. The company's talented mechanic, Paul Moody, also acquired eight additional patents on related equipment. In 1817, the BMC began offering to license its equipment designs, and it began manufacturing patent looms and other cotton textile equipment then as well.

After a few years, however, the BMC reversed course. Moody did not obtain any patents after 1821, despite making key innovations in such areas as power transmission within the mill. These innovations were not patented but instead diffused rapidly through the industry, quickly becoming standard in all new mill construction. In 1823, the BMC ceased sales of equipment and patent licenses except to closely related companies, and for the next two decades the machine shop operation sold to outsiders only occasionally.

Why the change in direction? Because patents did not generate much profit. BMC sold patent rights to a loom for a one-time fee of $15. If BMC built a patented loom, it earned a one-time profit of $35. But if it put that loom into production, it earned *annual* profits of over $200! The one-time patent royalty on a loom was less than 1 percent of the present value of expected profits from the operation of a loom. It made no sense for BMC to tie up its mechanics building looms for others or supporting customers who had purchased patent rights; those mechanics were much more valuable building looms for BMC or its sister companies. So BMC redirected its efforts away from patents.

This disparity did not reflect a failure of the patent system. The $15 royalty per loom compares reasonably well with royalties earned by patent pools later in the century.[23] Even if patent royalties had been two or three times larger, they still would have been dwarfed by the profits BMC could gain from using the looms.

The reason for this disparity between profits from patents and profits from use is the same as the reason competition was soft: a shortage of skilled and knowledgeable mechanics, managers, and workers. Another mill might buy the rights to a loom from BMC, but those rights were valuable only if that mill had access to mechanics who could build, install, and maintain the loom, managers who could organize production, and workers who could learn to operate the equipment efficiently. There was not so much a scarcity of ideas as a scarcity of knowledge and skills.

Independent inventors could earn profits on their patents, but these profits were limited for similar reasons. Ira Draper developed a successful "loom temple," patented this device, and sold it to manufacturers. But Draper captured only a small part of the value of his invention because the textile manufacturers were in a strong bargaining position relative to independent inventors.[24]

Because patents had limited value, most of the important innovations during the first two decades of power loom weaving were not patented. Nevertheless, innovators made dramatic improvements in the technology. From 1814 to 1835, the amount of time it took a weaver to produce a yard of coarse cloth fell from forty minutes to eight. Of this reduction, only three minutes—about 10 percent—can be attributed to patented inventions.[25]

## Regime Change

By the mid-1830s, the cotton textile industry had become much more competitive. No longer could firms freely share knowledge with rivals at little risk. Beginning in the 1830s, patenting rates on loom inventions jumped sharply higher and stayed high for the rest of the century. Almost all of the important advances during the 1840s and 1850s were patented.

Independent inventors also began playing a more important role. Bargaining power relative to the textile manufacturers shifted in their favor. Also, with the growth of a market for patents, they could employ a new strategy: building large portfolios of patents to fence off possible alternatives. They could buy up all the patents covering different ways of achieving a result, gaining a monopoly over a general technological function. For example, Draper's successors created a pool of key patents on high-speed spindles in the 1870s and later acquired over 400 additional patents. In 1895, when Draper's company (George Draper and Son) introduced the Northrop automatic loom, a major new weaving technology, it acquired a large portfolio of over 2,000 patents that gave it a dominant market position for decades. Thus, by the end of the century, loom patents had become valuable to their owners, helping the owners establish dominant, if not monopoly, positions in the market for advanced power looms.

This is the opposite of the pattern implied by the conventional story about start-ups and patents. In the heroic story, patents are crucial to independent inventors and their start-up firms in order to prevent others from copying their ideas and thus undermining their profits. Patents are supposedly less valuable to large firms, which have other ways of protecting their markets. But with loom technology, the early inventors had little to gain from patents. Only later on, when the technology had matured, markets had become competitive, and knowledge became more standardized did patents became valuable in helping one firm become a large, dominant player in the loom equipment market.

## Why Sharing Is Common

This pattern—patents not being very valuable at first, then becoming more valuable to firms later—appears to be more common than the standard story. Mark Lemley argues that the heroic portrayal of the sole inventor is a myth.[26] He documents a large number of major and minor inventions where different people developed the same idea independently at more or less the same time. Sociologist Robert K. Merton argues that in science, such "multiples" are the rule rather than the exception.[27] Economic historian Joel Mokyr argues that multiples are the result of many people having access to a common base of shared knowledge.[28] Knowledge sharing gives rise to simultaneous invention.

Extensive knowledge sharing occurs frequently in the early stages of major technologies because the conditions that give rise to it are common. In the loom example, the key condition that permitted knowledge to be freely shared was the coexistence of the new power loom technology with inferior alternatives for a period of two decades. This is not unusual. Economists studying the diffusion of new technologies find that it typically takes one, two, or even several decades before a new technology dominates the market.[29] During this time, the new technology coexists with inferior alternatives and often producers using the new technology earn high profits.

But if producers using the new technology earn high profits, then why don't competitors adopt the new technology, replacing the inferior alternative? Some constraint must be at work. With the power loom the constraint was the limited supply of technical knowledge needed by managers, mechanics, and ordinary workers to implement the new technology. Sometimes other constraints came into play, such as a limited supply of necessary inputs such as special mineral ores.[30] But it appears that some scarce input, often technical knowledge, can give rise to conditions that allow start-ups to earn profits even while sharing knowledge with rivals.

Technical knowledge is often scarce today, especially during the early stages of a technology. Even with science-based technologies coming out of university labs, leading scientists acquire a great degree of tacit knowledge that is often critical. A series of studies show that in biotechnology and semiconductors, the personal involvement of the "star scientists" significantly improves the prospects for successful commercialization.[31] And universities generate much more licensing revenue when faculty members participate and share in the proceeds.[32]

But when technical knowledge is scarce, start-up innovators can make profits even when they share knowledge, so patents may be of little value to them. This is as true of free and open source software today as it was for a wide range of new technologies during the nineteenth century. Later in the technology life cycle, patents may help owners consolidate market power in one or a few firms. This happened with loom equipment, in steelmaking, and in digital wireless communication. It appears to be happening now in smartphones.

The conditions giving rise to sharing regimes also create opportunities for diverse business models. The start-ups in power weaving did not make money mainly by licensing patents or selling exclusive patent-protected products. They made their money as users of the technology (textile mills) or by contracting to build and install it (machine shops).

Today, innovators in emerging technologies frequently earn returns on their knowledge as users or consultants or contractors, rather than as owners of an exclusionary patent right. Sometimes they contract on government procurement projects. More generally, most business spending on software is not on prepackaged software products but on contracting or internal development.[33] Firms providing free and open source software, such as the billion-dollar Red Hat Inc., make profits based on their complementary knowledge even when they give the software away for free. And because the main benefits of a new technology often come from using it rather than selling it to others, many innovators are users rather than manufacturers.[34]

The technology life cycle might help explain a puzzle about the role of patents during the Industrial Revolution. Institutional economists such as Douglass North have argued that stronger property rights, including patents, were an essential precondition to the Industrial Revolution. Yet scholars studying the role of patents during that period have had difficulty finding a central role for patent incentives. Many of the era's major inventors did not benefit from patents.[35] Economic historian Petra Moser finds that of the inventions shown at the 1851 Crystal Palace exhibition, only 11 percent were patented in the United Kingdom and 15 percent in the United States.[36] Most patents in the United Kingdom appear to have been obtained in fields with relatively little technological innovation.[37]

This paradox is resolved once we realize that technical knowledge was in short supply. Knowledge scarcity meant that patents were often insufficient to generate profits, and that innovators such as Richard Arkwright, who built one of the first spinning mills and realized great profits from it, could benefit even without enforceable patents. Arkwright obtained patents on his spinning technology, but they were invalidated in court.

## Policy to Promote Sharing

Given the particular conditions facing start-ups, what sort of incentives would encourage them to innovate? Often, patents provide their owners only limited value. The oft-repeated assertion that small innovators can only profit with patent protection is plainly false. Of course, patents do not necessarily hurt technology start-ups, although they sometimes do, as we shall see in Chapter 12. But aside from patents, policies that encourage knowledge sharing can promote innovation.

Individual innovators and firms exchange technical knowledge in a variety of ways: through trade associations, technical publications, meetings and conferences, informal exchanges, contracting, consulting, licensing, hiring, and personnel exchange.[38] Government policy can significantly impact the nature and extent of some of these activities, and empirical evidence finds it can make a major difference to innovation.

In the 1990s, political scientist AnnaLee Saxenian began exploring the divergent fates of Silicon Valley technology firms and those along the Route 128 corridor around Boston.[39] During the 1970s, both regions hosted substantial numbers of new technology companies in computers, electronics, and semiconductors. Both regions were anchored by leading engineering universities, both were coastal, both benefited from government procurement–related R&D programs. Yet during the 1980s and 1990s, their fates diverged. The leading computer technology firms of Route 128—Digital Equipment, Data General, Wang, and Prime—went into decline, while those in Silicon Valley blossomed, including Hewlett-Packard, Intel, Sun Microsystems, and Cypress Semiconductor. Between 1975 and 1990, Silicon Valley generated 150,000 new tech jobs; Route 128 created a third as many.

Based on extensive interviews, Saxenian located a crucial difference in how firms exchanged knowledge:

> Silicon Valley has a regional network-based industrial system that promotes collective learning and flexible adjustment among specialist producers of a complex of related technologies. The region's dense social networks and open labor markets encourage experimentation and entrepreneurship. Companies compete intensely while at the same time learning from one another about changing markets and technologies through informal communication and collaborative practices.[40]

This pattern is, of course, reminiscent of the networks of mechanics 200 years ago. Route 128, meanwhile, was dominated by a few large companies that relied little on outside suppliers and whose cultures of secrecy and corporate loyalty limited exchange of knowledge with other firms. Knowledge sharing was restricted, which made a critical difference in the ability to adapt to rapidly changing technology.

This difference was partly the result of legal differences between the two states. Legal scholars Ronald Gilson and Alan Hyde identified important differences in the treatment of employment agreements.[41] Under California law, agreements that prevented an employee from working in the same industry after leaving a job could not be enforced. In Massachusetts, these agreements could be enforced and often were. This legal difference meant that one important channel of knowledge sharing, namely job-hopping, was effectively shut down or at least limited in Massachusetts. Since the guilds encouraged journeymen to learn by working at different workshops, job-hopping has been an important way for workers to exchange knowledge, especially tacit knowledge gained through experience. Subsequent research has confirmed that differences in the enforcement of noncompete agreements do affect employee mobility and, in turn, affect a variety of measures of innovation.[42]

At first glance, one might think that noncompete agreements would encourage the development of new knowledge—firms might be more willing to invest in employees' knowledge because employees would be less likely to take it to a competitor. But by the same token, a strong noncompete agreement reduces the employee's *own* incentive to invest in new knowledge. Overly broad noncompete agreements effectively undermine the labor market by preventing employees from using their skills elsewhere in the same industry. Just as with the weavers discussed in Chapter 6, a robust labor market allows workers to earn the greatest benefit from their own investments in skill and knowledge, and noncompete agreements additionally restrict the creation of new knowledge in early stage technologies by limiting knowledge sharing.[43]

It turns out that knowledge sharing and employee incentives tend to be more important than employer incentives.[44] Studies show that in states that do not enforce noncompete agreements, key employees are paid more and are more likely to receive bonuses and other incentive pay. That is, employees have stronger incentives to invest in new knowledge. And in these states, firms invest more capital and R&D per worker, and venture capital investments generate more start-ups, more patents, and more employment. Because nonenforcement results in greater investment in workers' knowledge, it also stimulates greater investment in complementary capital and R&D by employers. While noncompete enforcement may be beneficial to established firms, it inhibits the development of early-stage technologies.

Other laws also affect the ability of employees to job-hop and otherwise exchange knowledge. For example, employees are discouraged from job-hopping if trade secret law is applied too broadly.[45] Trade secrecy is important to protect employers' investments in specific secrets such as the formula for Coca-Cola or the code of a software program. But during the last two decades, trade secret law has been expanded in many states to include much more, such as employee know-how and information not used in the business.[46] And in some states, former employees are presumed guilty of trade secret misappropriation without evidence—former employees can be prevented from working at a rival firm just on the presumption that they would "inevitably" disclose secret information to their new employers. These laws act like employee noncompete agreements even for employees who have not signed such agreements. As with noncompete agreements, there is some evidence that expanded trade secret laws undermine the labor market and limit knowledge exchange. When states have expanded trade secret laws in the ways mentioned, technical employees change jobs less frequently, their pay is reduced, and firms reduce in-state R&D spending.[47]

The recent expansion of trade secret law represents a broader policy tilt favoring employer incentives at the expense of employee incentives.[48] Employers are using noncompete agreements and trade secret law to limit employee rights on a widening scale. About half of all technical personnel in the United States are now asked to sign noncompete agreements.[49] And while noncompete agreements were once used almost exclusively for key executives and technical personnel, now a broad range of ordinary workers are required to sign them, including even yoga instructors and camp counselors.[50] Moreover, employers are much more willing to sue former employees. The number of lawsuits involving noncompete agreements and trade secrecy has nearly tripled since 2000.[51]

This tilt represents a departure from a long-established historical balance. In the early nineteenth century, employees maintained ownership of their inventions unless they signed a specific contract granting patent rights to their employer. By the early twentieth century, the law took the assignment of patent rights to the employer as a default without a contract. This proved important in motivating employer investments in R&D.[52] Yet while employees were restricted from taking protected trade secrets to other firms, they were free to seek other work that might use skills learned on the job. But during the last two decades, policy has dramatically expanded employer control over employee knowledge.

These policy changes may be having a significant effect on overall employee mobility. Historically, the U.S. population has relocated and changed jobs more frequently than the rest of the world. But job mobility has declined substantially during the last two decades. Both the rate at which employees switch to new employers and the rate at which they switch to new occupations are down.[53] When laws limit job mobility, they undermine labor markets and the economic incentives to create and spread new knowledge. Knowledge that workers learn on the job—both on their own and by exchanging with others—is critical to new technologies. The policy tilt against employees' rights to their own knowledge impedes the flow of benefits from new technology.

## CHAPTER 12

# Patents and Early-Stage Knowledge

IN THE YEARS BEFORE THE CIVIL WAR, Rufus W. Porter pursued a variety of trades, working most often as an itinerant painter. He traveled across New England painting portraits and murals on the walls of inns and houses, some of which can be seen today at a museum in Bridgton, Maine. Porter was also a prolific inventor. He patented an improved life preserver, an automatic grain-weighing machine, a blower fan, churns, a punch press, clocks, and steam engines. He invented, but did not patent, the first percussion cap revolving rifle, which he sold to Samuel Colt. Other than that small success—Colt paid Porter $100 to protect his own patents—Porter did little to make money from his inventions.[1] That did not matter much to him because he was devoted to "the great work of saving human manual labor—which is the real end of all truly American progress, and the main object of American civilization." Porter was seen as an exemplar of the American obsession with invention. As one English obituary writer saw it, his example showed "that the true genius of the American people is inventive and mechanical . . . and it would appear as though invention, relatively speaking, has flourished more in the United States than in all the rest of the world, making due allowance for time."[2]

This obsession was the reason for Porter's most lasting success. In 1845, he founded a weekly publication for mechanics and manufacturers that claimed to be "the only paper in America devoted to the interest of those classes." Each issue was to include

New Inventions, Scientific Principles, and Curious Works; and will contain, in addition to the most interesting news of passing events, general notices of progress of Mechanical and other Scientific Improvements; American and Foreign. Improvements and Inventions; Catalogues of American Patents; Scientific Essays, illustrative of the principles of the sciences of Mechanics, Chemistry, and Architecture: useful information and instruction in various Arts and Trades; Curious Philosophical Experiments; Miscellaneous Intelligence, Music and Poetry.[3]

Porter named the newspaper *Scientific American*. Although he quickly sold the publication, it was successful because America was mad over inventions. Mechanics, manufacturers, and farmers wanted to keep abreast of the latest technical improvements and scientific developments. Many, like Porter, were also inventors themselves.

Patents played an important part in the popular culture of invention. As the knowledge and skills needed to work with mechanical devices became standardized and widespread, large numbers of people could make technical improvements. They could readily obtain patents because patent filing fees were relatively low and the process was not difficult. Economic historian Zorina Khan argues that the U.S. patent system was uniquely accessible to common people, helping to foster inventive activity by small inventors.[4] During the latter part of the nineteenth century, a robust market for inventions developed, allowing individual mechanics and farmers to sell their patents as well as allowing individual inventors to start new firms.[5] The patent system provided incentives to these inventors, and it also played an important role in standardizing and spreading technical knowledge by documenting inventions in standard language and disseminating these descriptions to the public. These inventors and their start-up firms were responsible for many of the inventions that implemented new technologies such as weaving. A unique strength of American innovation was the way small inventors advanced early-stage technologies; although not all inventors used patents, patents were a part of that strength; and small inventors like Rufus Porter placed high value on patents.

So it seems surprising that today's software developers—the analogs of yesterday's mechanics—have a very different attitude. Surveys show that strong majorities are opposed to allowing patents on software inventions.[6] Software developers in Silicon Valley have vocally opposed recent patent litigation on their inventions by their own employers.[7] One company has even begun signing an agreement with its engineers to use their patents only "defensively." In this major new technology area, the very class of people who are the putative inventors now opposes patents. It appears that in information technology, patents no longer foster early-stage technology. While patents once served to aid large numbers of small inventors, they now seem mainly to benefit large companies and harm small ones. How have patents, the friend of the start-up innovator, become an enemy in this key technology?

## Patent Trolls and Small Firms

Consider Webtech, founded in the late 1990s to provide web-based business solutions for its customers in a particular industry niche (I changed the name of the company to preserve its anonymity). Webtech's business was based on applying generally available tools and methods commonly known to web programmers to this niche's needs. It sought to "build what the customer wants," developing the detailed sort of applications knowledge that is the subject of this book.

The approach met with success: the company grew to nearly 200 employees over the last decade. That success is now threatened by patents—more specifically, by misuse of the patent system. Over the last two and a half years, Webtech has had seven patents asserted against it or against its customers by non-practicing entities (NPEs), also known popularly as "patent trolls," firms that obtain patents for the sole purpose of extracting licensing fees from operating companies. These patents cover commonly used features of websites, such as topic-related geographic maps—even though publicly available geographic information systems have had similar features since the late 1970s. The patent trolls assert these patents against many other companies as well, in some cases against hundreds of other companies. It might seem that these patents represent weak threats, but challenging weak patents in court can often involve millions of dollars in legal fees.

Webtech has experienced significant costs already. The patent assertions have consumed a large amount of management time, much of it psychologically draining. Webtech has lost two million-dollar-plus contracts—each representing seven to nine new, well-paying jobs—because it could not indemnify its customers against similar suits from patent trolls. And Webtech is preparing for the possibility that it may have to drop an entire product line and lay off employees if troll claims hold up. It seems that rather than encouraging this start-up, patents have slowed its growth.

## Stopping Start-Ups from Growing

Webtech's experience is not unusual. Legal scholar Colleen Chien surveyed tech start-ups and found the following:

> Although [patent troll] suits are often called "nuisance" suits, one of the most significant findings of this study is that, among small company respondents to the survey, many reported one or more significant operational impacts. Receiving a demand was described as potentially representing a "death knell" for a prefunded company: no one wants to invest [in] a company where founder time and investor money is going to be "bled to patent trolls," as one interviewee put it.
>
> Among respondents to the survey that had received an NPE demand, 40 percent reported that the demand had a significant operational impact, which I define as resulting in: a business strategy pivot, business/business line exit, delay in hiring or meeting operational milestone, and/or a reduction in the value of the company.[8]

Some start-ups reported abandoning the U.S. market in favor of other nations; others reported significant financial distress from patent troll assertions. Nor are these losses merely subjective. Catherine Tucker, an MIT economist, did a careful study of the effects of lawsuits over one patent against medical imaging technology companies.[9] After controlling for a wide range of factors, Tucker found that the medical imaging business units of the companies that were sued lost 30 percent of their revenues during the two-year period the suit went on. In addition, they delayed the introduction of new product updates and innovative improvements.

These examples are not isolated. Lawsuits filed by patent trolls have grown exponentially over the last decade. In 2011, 2,150 unique companies were forced to mount 5,842 defenses in lawsuits initiated by the actions of patent trolls. Based on survey evidence, those defendants accrued direct costs—that is, legal fees and settlement payments—of $29 billion.[10] This amount does not include the costs of lost business, delayed innovation and delayed product introductions, management diversion, and other indirect costs. It is possible to get a rough measure of these other costs by estimating the amount of wealth a publicly listed company loses when its stock price declines after a patent lawsuit is filed. Several estimates suggest that the total cost of patent troll litigation is at least twice as high as the direct costs and possibly much more.[11]

To put these estimates in perspective, the direct costs come to about 12 percent of the total amount that businesses spend on R&D—businesses in the United States spent $247 billion on R&D in 2009. Including indirect costs, the total comes to 20 percent or more. Moreover, these are costs that cannot easily be avoided. Very few of the defendants actually copied the plaintiff's invention; to the extent that they did infringe the patents, they infringed inadvertently because the boundaries of these patents are often unclear (see the section on software patents).[12] This effectively means that patent trolls impose a 10 to 20 percent tax on R&D; firms looking to invest in innovation, unable to avoid the trolls, have to count on spending that much more on R&D. Accordingly, they will not invest as much in R&D and might not invest at all in projects that promise marginal returns. A tax of this magnitude places a large burden on innovators. The result is less investment, less growth, and fewer jobs.

Moreover, this tax falls disproportionately on small start-ups. While large established firms account for the majority of the $29 billion cost, small firms bear a larger burden relative to their size. Most firms targeted by patent trolls are small—the median defendant has revenues of only $10.3 million per year. Yet the legal fees and settlement costs paid by small firms is larger compared to their revenues than it is for large firms. And empirical analysis shows a dramatic effect of litigation on the R&D spending of small firms. Small firms subject to extended patent litigation sharply reduced their R&D spending relative to sales.[13]

Moreover, evidence is emerging that this litigation reduces venture capitalist investment and decreases the formation of new firms. A survey of venture capitalists found that 74 percent reported significant impacts of litigation on their portfolio companies, and 100 percent reported that patent demand letters affected their decisions to invest.[14] The majority of venture capitalists also reported that it cost their portfolio companies over $100,000 to defend or settle each demand letter. An econometric analysis concludes that frequent patent litigators (largely patent trolls) were responsible for a loss of $22 billion in venture capital investment over a five-year period.[15] Moreover, this analysis estimates that 12,600 fewer new firms were created during these five years because of excessive patent litigation from trolls and others.

## How Much Do Patents Benefit Start-Ups Today?

Rather than encouraging investment in start-ups and subsequent job growth, patents today do a lot to inhibit innovation by new companies. But what of the benefits that patents bring? Surely, some tech start-ups use patents to secure commercialization agreements or financing. Patents are valuable and perhaps even crucial for some start-ups.

In key information technologies, most start-ups do not benefit from patents. We know this for a very simple reason: they do not obtain patents. Only 12 percent of new, publicly listed software firms (listed less than five years) had any patents in 2006.[16] In a 2008 survey of a broader sample, 61 percent of tech start-up firms had never applied for a patent; in software, 76 percent had never applied.[17]

There are important exceptions to this rule. In some industries, such as biotechnology and pharmaceuticals, many more start-ups obtain patents.[18] Patents tend to be more effective in these technologies because they are more clearly defined (see the discussion of "fuzzy boundaries" below), they produce much less litigation, and they correspond more directly to the actual products a company makes. Tech start-ups that are funded by venture capitalists also tend to patent more, although they are also more likely to get sued by patent trolls.[19] A study of 12,000 venture-funded start-ups found that about one-third had filed patent applications.[20] Some people see this as evidence that patents help firms get financing. But patents do not, apparently, help software firms raise money from the stock market. And only 19 percent of the venture-financed firms in the large sample study had obtained patents *before* they received financing.[21] In any case, patents apparently provide help in securing funding, although that help may be marginal. Most software startups are not motivated to obtain patents.

One factor limiting the value of patents to small firms is the growing complexity of patent law. The strength of the U.S. patent system in Rufus Porter's age was its great accessibility. Fees were low, inventors could draft patents themselves, and enforcement was not expensive. Today, patent law is highly complex and few inventors can draft an effective patent without the help of an attorney. Rufus Porter could do it simply by describing what the invention did that was novel. Today's patent drafter specializes in the art of "peripheral claiming" and must know arcane rules from the case law, such as the critical distinction between "comprising" and "consisting of."[22] The complexity of patent law has doubled the average numbers of pages and of claims in patents over the last two decades. Patents today are simply much more expensive. While today's technologies are admittedly more complex, this is plainly not true of all inventions. Yet the patents have gotten more complex, perhaps because of a long history of aggressive lawyering, and the cost of enforcing a patent in litigation has soared to over $1 million for typical patents. Some suits cost much more. Not surprisingly, while most patents in the nineteenth century were awarded to individual inventors, today only about 10 percent go to individuals. The share going to "small entities"—individuals, small companies, and nonprofits—has also been declining, falling to under 20 percent.[23]

Some commentators argue that patent trolls aid small inventors in overcoming these problems by helping them enforce their patents. Trolls claim that they provide start-ups returns on their innovations by paying licensing fees or by purchasing their patents outright. So some portion of the $29 billion cost of patent trolls flows to the inventors who obtained the patents in the first place.

But the empirical evidence suggests that this benefit is more rhetorical than real. Only about half of the patents used by patent trolls were originally filed by small firms or individuals.[24] Furthermore, of the funds collected by publicly listed patent trolls, only a small part—no more than 5 percent—is paid to small start-ups or individuals in the form of royalties or acquisition fees.[25] Not surprisingly, respondents to the Berkeley survey listed licensing revenues as the least important reason for obtaining patents.

Moreover, the patents involved are not necessarily the kind that generate innovations, jobs, and economic growth. Some are exercises in creative patent drafting, using vague language that a jury might construe to cover a broad range of technology. For example, patent number 7,222,078, "Methods and systems for gathering information from units of a commodity across a network," is being used by a company called Lodsys to demand payment from hundreds or even thousands of smartphone app developers, even though no one quite knows what "units of a commodity on a network" are. Such egregious examples aside, most of the patents involved in patent troll lawsuits are very old—the mean age in one study was twelve years, a lifetime in many technologies—and often of dubious quality; in several studies, troll patents were more likely than other litigated patents to lose at trial or to be invalidated.[26] This means that payments to these patent holders are distantly related, at best, to the goal of encouraging innovations to spur economic growth. They might spur more creative patent drafting instead. Often, these patents were acquired for innovations that failed long ago, yet they can be interpreted to cover technologies that were subsequently developed. The sad irony is that it is the companies being sued that actually did the hard work to make the technology successful. The innovators are often the ones getting sued. And while the patents of the nineteenth century served to standardize and disseminate knowledge, too many of today's patents are just lawyerly concoctions that do nothing to promote technical knowledge.

Most of the patents in information technology go to large firms, not to start-ups. Among publicly listed software companies, for example, the ten largest firms acquire 81 percent of the patents.[27] These firms are likely to be the main beneficiaries of patents. Indeed, large firms in the smartphone business have scrambled to acquire new patents any way they can, in order to strengthen their bargaining position in future legal battles. As we saw in Chapter 11, large companies in mature technologies do typically realize value from their patents. That is why they get so many of them. What is less clear is whether patents granted to large firms spur innovation or benefit society in other ways. The historical examples suggest that patents may help large firms establish dominant market positions, but this may not be good for innovation. Michele Boldrin and David K. Levine argue that increasing monopoly is bad for innovation.[28] This issue is beyond the scope of the present discussion.

## Software Patents: Judges Create Disincentives

Why do patent trolls exact a heavier toll on start-up firms? Partly because start-ups are often more vulnerable than established firms and are therefore more willing to settle. Also, many start-ups use information technology, and the recent explosion of patent troll activity has focused very much on information technology. Depending on how one counts, information technology accounts for between 75 percent and 94 percent of patent troll lawsuits. The reason patent trolls focus on information technology is that many information technology patents have "fuzzy boundaries"—they use vague terminology, make abstract claims, or describe general functions rather than a detailed technique for making functions work. They can thus be stretched to claim much more technology than what their originator actually invented. Software patents are four times more likely to be in a lawsuit than patents on chemical compositions; patents on business methods are fourteen times more likely to be litigated than a chemical patent.[29] Judges are more likely to come up with different interpretations of the boundaries of software patents, and partly because of these fuzzy boundaries, patents on software are much more likely not to be truly novel.[30]

In *Patent Failure*, a book I wrote with Michael Meurer, we explore why information technology patents are so much more subject to fuzzy boundaries. The most important factor is a series of legal changes, beginning in the 1990s, that made it easier to obtain information technology patents. Before 1994 it was generally understood that one could not obtain a patent on most software algorithms or most methods of doing business. But the main appellate court for patent cases—the Court of Appeals for the Federal Circuit (CAFC)—was keen to expand the role of patents in these new technology areas.

The CAFC was created in 1982 to streamline patent appeals. It is a unique structure in American law: the only appellate court with exclusive jurisdiction over one area of law. According to some legal scholars, this institutional arrangement has made the court a booster of patents, wanting to expand the court's role in society.[31]

The court does seem to have behaved as a booster. During the 1990s, the CAFC removed obstacles to patenting software and business methods, removed requirements that software patents be tied to specific implementations, and allowed patents on mental processes. These changes led to a great increase in the patenting of software and business methods. They also led to a great increase in litigation. The number of patent lawsuits filed each year has increased sixfold since the CAFC was created, and this statistic understates the growth of the problem. Thanks to patent trolls, the number of companies sued in each lawsuit has also risen dramatically.

Figure 12.1 suggests that the patent litigation problem is getting worse.[32] This cannot go on much longer without creating a crisis in American innovation.

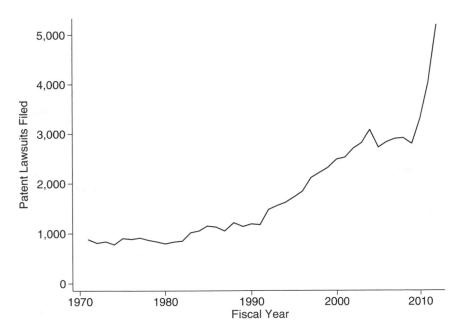

Figure 12.1. Number of patent lawsuits filed in federal district courts.
(Administrative Office of the U.S. Courts, Statistical Tables,
http://www.uscourts.gov/Statistics/JudicialFactsAndFigures.aspx.)

The policy changes that created this problem were many and, like much of patent law, complicated. The changes needed to reverse this trend will also be complicated. They might involve a variety of changes including, possibly:

- Restoring restrictions that bar patents on abstract ideas. In the past, these restrictions served to limit the number of patents issued on software, business methods, and mental concepts. Recently, a Supreme Court decision reversed the CAFC on this issue.[33] At this time, it remains to be seen how the lower courts will respond, potentially invalidating hundreds of thousands of patents.
- Doctrinal changes in patent law affecting how broadly a patent is interpreted and what concrete technology a patentee must demonstrate in order to obtain a patent.
- Stronger standards so that large numbers of patents are not granted on trivial improvements.
- Prohibiting patents from using vague language or from claiming general functions ("a system configured to . . . ") rather than actual technical solutions.
- Higher fees to keep a patent in force during the last ten or fifteen years of the patent life. This change will reduce the huge number of patents covering some technical fields by encouraging low-value patents to lapse.

Some combination of all of these measures might be required. But unless substantial reforms are put in place, the inevitable crisis might well create a backlash that seriously alters the present patent system.

This has happened in the past. During the late nineteenth century, railroads, farmers, and others were besieged by "patent sharks" who behaved much like today's patent trolls.[34] Eventually, a movement developed to counter the excesses of the patent system. In the United States, there was a push for legislation, but in the end, the Supreme Court reined in patent law and the U.S. Patent Office restricted problematic design patents. In other countries, the opposition to patents was more intense. In the United Kingdom,

Parliament debated ending the patent system, but settled for major reform instead. The Netherlands abolished patents entirely.[35]

We are not yet at such a crisis, but there are signs of an emerging backlash, as we shall see in Chapter 13. Nevertheless, the patent system that once fostered inventive activity among ordinary people has, in key technologies, become an impediment to innovators and start-ups. This, too, is a change in the wrong direction.

## CHAPTER 13

# The Political Economy of
# Technical Knowledge

IN EACH OF THE POLICY AREAS REVIEWED in the last five chapters, the trend has been in the wrong direction. Rather than encourage widespread development of new technical knowledge, we have made the transition to a new generation of technology more difficult:

- Funds have been shifted away from vocational education and community colleges at a time when large numbers of workers could acquire valuable skills at these institutions.
- The rapid growth of occupational licensing restricts training and jobs open to mid-skill workers and, in many cases, limits their use of new technology.
- Military procurement favors large defense contractors over university researchers and start-up firms, while heightened secrecy requirements limit the development of open standards and the broad sharing of knowledge.
- Job mobility has declined, limiting knowledge sharing and weakening labor markets, perhaps because of expanded trade secrecy and patent laws.
- Abusive patent litigation has exploded, making it harder for start-ups and small firms to develop new knowledge.

It might seem that policies that encourage these trends are simply misdirected. But such a judgment would be too simple, because the optimal policy for a particular technology depends on whether that technology is emerging or mature. Vocational education, for example, is particularly helpful for maturing technologies but less useful for early-stage technologies in which knowledge is not standardized; conversely, general education can be more valuable during the early phases.

Changes over the technology life cycle mean that policy affects different groups of people and firms unevenly. Technical knowledge is a source of wealth that helps some interest groups and harms others. Because various groups benefit differently from policies concerning knowledge, they act politically to bend policy to their interests. In other words, there is a political economy of knowledge.

Policy conflicts arise over the life cycle of technical knowledge, pitting interests using new technologies against interests using mature ones. Yet the political influence of groups using mature technologies often outweighs the interests of those developing new ones. The resulting policy bias can restrain the nation's economic growth. This bias might even help explain why some developing nations fall into a "middle income" trap that limits their ability to develop new technologies.

The two-sided nature of technical knowledge creates a problem for policymakers. The ideal policy is flexible and adaptable to all circumstances. A well-balanced economy includes mature technologies that operate on a large scale, creating jobs and profits. It includes developing technologies that provide opportunities for future jobs and profits. Yet crafting a balanced policy is difficult. It is hard enough for regulators and legislators to apply good policy when conditions are stable and uniform, but when conditions change over time and vary from industry to industry, surely the task becomes much more difficult. Maintaining a policy balance can be critical.

Through most of its history, the United States has been able to balance these competing interests reasonably well, achieving a highly innovative society. But as the analysis of Chapters 8 through 12 shows, policy seems to have shifted in the wrong direction in several areas over the last decades. While each of these changes has its own dynamic with specific issues at play, they share one common factor: the greater role of money in politics. If a flawed political system is uniformly pushing policy in a direction that harms the development of early-stage technologies, then the stagnant wages and slower growth of the past few decades may be with us for some time to come.

## The Uphill Battle of Japan's Software Start-Ups

Consider the difficulty some nations have had trying to develop a software industry. Even today, software firms can often be started with little investment. Many start-ups are begun by just one or a few developers with few resources, as Mark Zuckerberg did, for example, in starting Facebook. Given this supposed ease of entry, it might seem puzzling that the United States dominates the world software industry. There are bright developers everywhere, and the Internet allows them to communicate, learn, and even sell products at a distance. One might think that software firms can start anywhere. Yet eight of the ten largest software firms are in the United States; 116 of the top 250 ICT (information and communication technology) firms are U.S.-based; Japan is second with only 39 of the top ICT firms.[1]

The comparison with Japan is striking because Japan has such a large ICT industry, with so many engineers. It accounts for 22 percent of the R&D spending in ICT among the major developed countries (the United States accounts for 43 percent), and its computer firms have long operated at the technological frontier. Yet Japan's software industry is unproductive and uncompetitive in foreign trade.[2] Some economists attribute the recent decline in the performance of Japan's information technology industry to the growing importance of software innovation and the weakness of Japan's software industry.[3] Japan excels in mature technologies such as computers, where knowledge is highly standardized; it lags in emerging and fast-moving software technologies.

But this is no accident. In the view of one group of experts, the policy bias that created success in one area is responsible for weakness in the other: "National policies for the development of capabilities in computer hardware focused on mainframe development, and the very success of these policies contributed to the fragmentation of Japan's domestic software market and to the dominance of custom software."[4] These conditions make it difficult for start-ups to enter the market for packaged software products. While Japanese software engineers might develop innovative new products, they face significant barriers bringing them to market. Japan lags in an emerging technology because of the policies that propelled it to success in a mature technology.

How did this happen? The mainframe computer industry was one of the strategic industries that Japan's Ministry of International Trade and Industry (MITI) sought to promote. In the early 1960s, IBM Japan held about 70 percent of the computer market in Japan. IBM had been allowed to establish a local subsidiary only after it agreed to license its patents to Japanese firms. Beginning in the late 1960s, MITI sought to promote Japan's domestic computer manufacturers to challenge IBM Japan, with the ultimate goal of becoming successful exporters. MITI provided loans and subsidies to these firms, funded major cooperative R&D efforts, and restricted imports and levied tariffs on imported technology. In the early 1970s, to reduce competition and increase profits among the domestic computer manufacturers, MITI organized them into three groups, each limited to a specific market segment: Fujitsu and Hitachi focused on large computers; NEC and Toshiba on small and mid-level machines; and Mitsubishi and Oki on specialized scientific and industrial machines.[5] This extraordinary set of policies created a dynamic domestic computer industry consisting of a few large players that could challenge IBM at home and abroad.

But while these policies allowed Japan to catch up in computer technology, which had become highly standardized following the success of the IBM 360 mainframe in the 1960s, the firms and institutions created by these policies were a liability when it came to newly emerging software technology. First, there were relatively few truly independent software firms, because software vendors were tied closely to the computer vendors or to their major customers. Initially, the computer manufacturers considered software a "necessary evil" that was typically bundled with hardware.[6] At the same time, customers were expected to develop their own custom software. Some of these in-house software development organizations were spun off, but they remained closely tied to vendors or customers. Only about a third of Japanese software firms are independent.[7] In contrast, almost all U.S. software firms have only an arm's-length relationship with hardware firms, partly as a result of U.S. antitrust enforcement.[8]

Second, given this industry structure, computer firms had little incentive to coordinate on industry-wide standards, since they effectively controlled their own software and distribution channels, and common standards might weaken that control.[9] As a result, software developers must adapt their code to each manufacturer's hardware. This effectively fragmented the market for packaged software products; unsurprisingly, Japanese software is largely custom software written for individual user firms. Moreover, lack of standardization hampers the large-scale development of technical knowledge among software users and developers. MITI has funded programs to promote common standards, but these efforts have been unable to overcome the market fragmentation.[10]

Third, other characteristics of Japan's innovation system reinforced the bias against start-up firms. Venture capital in Japan is limited and has been more oriented toward debt than equity, which is more helpful to later-stage firms than to start-ups. The labor market for highly skilled technical professionals is also highly oriented to lifetime employment at large companies, making it harder for start-ups to recruit talent and harder for technical labor markets to develop.[11]

The net effect of these factors has been to limit the Japanese market for packaged software, delaying standardization and making it difficult for start-up firms to enter the market. Developing a market dominated by a few large hardware firms that were vertically integrated with software suppliers was an effective way to challenge IBM in the mainframe market. But this strategy made it difficult to establish common standards and a competitive market for packaged software. The policy tilt in favor of large incumbent firms appears difficult to undo, partly because of those incumbents' political power. For example, it seems unlikely that antitrust policy could be used to make software firms truly independent. The establishment of an industry organized around customized software and close vertical ties also makes it difficult to change behavior. Without a robust packaged software industry, for example, venture capitalists face limited investment opportunities. These institutions reinforce the policy tilt, as does Japan's business culture.

This policy tilt in favor of large computer firms does not affect all industries. In other technologies such as computer-controlled machine tools,

Japan has excelled at early-stage innovation while U.S. efforts faltered, partly because of restrictive Defense Department policies (see Chapter 10).

Japan's unbalanced policy in information technology is partly a product of history. Nations playing catch-up might naturally import mature technologies and bend policy to foster domestic industries to replace these imports. This was Alexander Hamilton's "infant industry" argument for tariffs in 1792. But mature technologies typically involve large-scale production and significant economies of scale. Fostering these industries might create a bias toward a few large firms. Such an unbalanced policy might limit a nation's future ability to develop early-stage technologies. Perhaps this is one reason why many developing nations experience a "middle-income trap": they are able to develop to a certain point on the basis of mature technologies, but face difficulty moving to the technological frontier.[12]

In any case, the example of the Japanese software industry shows how an unbalanced policy favoring established interests can inhibit the growth of newly emerging technologies.

## The Flexible U.S. Innovation System

Not all markets in all developing nations end up being dominated by a few large firms. The United States itself was the first major developing nation to play catch-up, in this case with British technology. Yet for most of the twentieth century, the United States was able to develop and maintain a balanced, flexible policy that supported the needs of both mature industries and start-ups. Recent developments seem to be undermining that balance.

The United States followed Hamilton's advice, providing trade protection for manufactured goods such as cotton textiles and steel. During the first half of the nineteenth century, tariffs increased the prices on imported goods by 25 percent—in some cases much more—and this policy spurred the development of domestic industries. Economic historians have found that tariffs likely promoted the domestic cotton textile industry initially, thanks to learning by doing, although the tariffs remained in force long after the industry outgrew its "infant" status.[13] Tariffs in steel and cotton textiles were critical to creating the conditions necessary to promote extensive knowledge sharing in these industries. Thanks to this protection, U.S. productivity in cotton textiles and steel caught up with, and then surpassed, British productivity.

And although U.S. policy did not seek to establish a select group of large companies to challenge British dominance—British firms themselves were not particularly large at this time—dominant firms emerged in industries where economies of scale created a significant advantage.[14] Mergers and acquisitions created U.S. Steel in 1901; this "steel trust" produced two-thirds of the steel made in the United States and was the largest steel producer in the world. Dominant firms in key industries formed cartels that could raise prices and limit production.

These large firms certainly had political clout. Chapter 9 showed the continued clout of Big Steel, despite the much diminished economic significance of the steel industry compared to a century ago. But their power was not inviolate, perhaps because of the diversity of political interests in the United States. Countervailing political movements, including the Progressive Movement and the rise of labor unions, emerged during the late nineteenth and early twentieth centuries to challenge the influence of large firms, leading, for instance, to antitrust legislation that forced the breakup of the Standard Oil monopoly in 1911.

The policy mix that emerged during the twentieth century was uniquely flexible. It encouraged both new emerging technologies, where small start-ups were important, as well as mature technologies, where standardized knowledge allowed efficient use of major scale economies by large established firms. The result was a policy balance and a set of supporting institutions that formed a highly effective "national innovation system."[15] Business management scholars David Mowery and Henry Chesbrough highlight some of the distinctive features of the U.S. system:[16]

- U.S. antitrust enforcement was uniquely stringent during the first part of the twentieth century and up to the 1980s. Moreover, the government did not promote selected large firms to play a privileged role, as Japan and many European nations did with the computer industry. The U.S. policies limited the ability of large established players to unfairly restrict entry by start-ups, but by and large did not prevent firms from operating at a large scale to realize productive efficiencies.

- In the United States, firms maintain arm's-length relationships with their suppliers, customers, and makers of complementary products. Elsewhere this is not always so. Japanese software firms, for example, often maintained close relationships, including co-ownership, with hardware firms and major customers. The United States was different, partly because of a business culture that often sought multiple sources of supply and partly because of antitrust enforcement. Antitrust authorities forced AT&T, which had invented semiconductor technology, to stay out of the commercial semiconductor market and instead to liberally license its technology at low royalties. IBM was forced to unbundle peripherals from its mainframes.[17] These actions permitted diverse players to enter these emerging markets[18] and encouraged the development of an independent market and common standards.

- The United States has encouraged relatively easy employee mobility between firms (in some states more than others). During the early nineteenth century, skilled immigrant labor was often important in emerging technologies, a guild system did not restrict entry into trades, and, as we have seen, mobility among early mechanics domestically contributed to knowledge exchange. Today, employee mobility is greater in technical professions in the United States than, say, in Japan.[19] Labor mobility facilitates knowledge sharing and is essential for a robust labor market.

- According to economic historian Zorina Khan, the U.S. patent system of the nineteenth century was uniquely democratic, allowing ordinary mechanics and farmers easy, affordable access to patent protection.[20] In other nations, patents were expensive to obtain and sometimes required significant lobbying, tilting their advantage to the wealthy and well-connected. The American system afforded an important tool to individuals and start-ups.

- Government procurement policies in the United States were uniquely effective at spurring new technologies during the nineteenth and twentieth centuries.

- Since the 1970s, U.S. venture capitalists have played a key role in funding early-stage companies in new technologies, and venture capital funds in the United States are more highly developed than elsewhere. The U.S. venture capital industry grew out of the Small Business Investment Act passed by Congress in 1958. In the late 1970s, regulatory changes fueled a boom by permitting pension funds to invest in venture capital partnerships.

Many of these factors reinforce each other. For example, venture capital investments require a market that independent start-ups can enter, which in turn depends on the availability of skilled personnel willing to leave their current employment to join start-ups. These practices are also reinforced by American cultural characteristics, such as a high value placed on individual autonomy and mobility, and a relaxed attitude toward hierarchy. Japanese culture might not reinforce these policies in quite the same way. Policies, culture, and past practices in the United States combine to foster both start-ups in emerging technologies and large firms in mature technologies.

These are not the only policies and institutions to promote the acquisition of technical knowledge on a large scale. Nor is this set of policies and institutions necessarily best for all technologies at all times. In industries where being first to market confers an advantage, such as software, it is essential to encourage start-ups and new entrants; being the first with a new technology might allow a nation's industry to claim and maintain a dominant position. But this advantage might not be as important in other technologies. For example, in mature industries where technology changes slowly, large firms that supply their own inputs might be better at coordinating and integrating new knowledge than independent suppliers working at arm's length. In the auto industry, for instance, the Japanese model of product development permitted engineers tied to large firms to acquire a broader range of skills and knowledge than the specialized automotive engineers in U.S. firms.[21]

Nevertheless, it appears that the American innovation system has achieved a balance between emerging and mature technologies that permitted U.S. firms to prosper in both automotives and software.

## "The Future Has No Lobbyists"

Now, many of the distinctive historical features of the U.S. innovation system are coming undone. The United States no longer has the most stringent antitrust enforcement; most observers consider Europe's to be stronger, although, to be sure, antitrust enforcement in the United States is now based on more rigorous economic analysis than in the past. Some of the policy shifts noted previously also represent a departure from history. Occupational licensure has grown to cover 29 percent of all jobs, restricting job growth, vocational training, and the use of new technologies. Military procurement has been restricted in ways that limit its ability to foster broad-based learning of new technologies. Stricter trade secrecy laws curtail knowledge sharing through job-hopping. Patent coverage has been extended to new areas, including software, methods of doing business, and mental processes; these changes also restrict the transfer of employee knowledge. And where patents were once beneficial to small firms, in some technologies they are now a significant burden.

These changes are not random. They benefit specific firms and interest groups. Changes in military procurement aid large defense contractors; changes in patent and trade secrecy law help large, established firms in mature industries as well as lawyers; greater emphasis on professional credentials for licensed practical nurses (LPNs) benefits college-educated nurses and professional associations; less funding for community colleges can mean more funding for research universities.

To the extent that special interests influence policy, they make setting good policy difficult. Of course, special interests and regulatory capture affect most areas of policymaking. Yet because of the two-sided nature of technical knowledge, political influence creates a systematic bias against some technologies in favor of others.

The reason for this bias is simple. Old technologies tend to support vested interests, such as Big Steel. Mature technologies, established on a large scale, provide jobs and profits for many people. Workers who have acquired skills in these technologies typically earn good wages; investors earn steady returns. But new technologies rarely have such established interests. Jobs, skills, and profits are all tentative. New technologies seldom operate at large scale until they have been standardized; they typically involve start-ups and small numbers of workers and investors. The parties benefiting most from new technologies are rarely well-established interests with substantial political influence. In the words of Tennessee congressman Jim Cooper, "The past, in general, is over-represented in Washington. The future has no lobbyists."[22]

In sector after sector, established groups working with mature technologies have been exerting an outsized role in policy conflicts since the 1980s. Established educational elites influence occupational licensing, established defense contractors influence procurement, large firms and patent lawyers influence patent and trade secrecy policy.[23] Similar lopsided conflicts are seen in telecommunications, where large phone and cable interests influence regulation, and in copyright, where the record industry and movie studios dominate legislative deliberation.

Political lobbying and interest groups are nothing new. But during the last few decades, the power of lobbyists seems to have grown while the interests of the public have been diminished. This change is illustrated by the way copyright law has adapted to new technologies. For much of the twentieth century, copyright law generally accommodated new technologies such as the player piano, the phonograph, radio broadcasting, jukeboxes, videotape players, and cable television.[24] New technologies were generally given a period in which they were not constrained by copyright law; later, Congress would mandate reasonable compulsory licensing fees to copyright holders. But today, facing powerful lobbies among existing broadcasters, more recent technologies such as satellite TV and Internet radio have been immediately hit with punitive licensing fees that were higher than the comparable fees paid by cable TV and broadcast radio. This is a marked change.

## The Best Patent Law Lobbyists Can Buy

Why, since 1980, are we seeing a tilt more toward the established players? The imbalance between established industries using mature technologies and start-ups using emerging technologies is an example of the standard collective action problem of public choice theory: a small group with much to gain often wields greater power than a much larger group with diffuse benefits.[25] Yet for most of the last century, vested interests have battled newcomers in politics without seriously hurting emerging technologies. A number of changes over the last few decades might help explain why that seems to have changed. Politics has grown more partisan; unions, which often represent broader consumer interests, have declined; the ideals of the Progressive Movement have lost much appeal; perhaps industry has become dominated by more powerful monopolies.[26] But one culprit stands out: the growing role of money in politics.

The timing of the policy tilt is particularly suspicious because it has more or less paralleled a dramatic growth of money in politics and of the political influence of large firms. Lawrence Lessig, in *Republic, Lost: How Money Corrupts Congress—and a Plan to Stop It*, describes how a dramatic increase in the role of money in politics is subverting the political process. The mean cost of winning a congressional seat has risen to over $1 million, a sixfold increase since 1974, after adjusting for inflation. As Lessig explains, the role of money in politics is mainly not illegal, nor does it involve acts of direct corruption such as bribery. Instead, it has created a system where politicians are dependent on donors and come to share their point of view. With the right views on a range of often highly industry-specific issues, a politician can look forward to continued campaign contributions and future employment after leaving Congress, and more.

This role of money is seen in the recent legislative battle over a patent reform bill. In 2011, as the patent troll epidemic was accelerating, Congress passed the America Invents Act. President Obama heralded it as the most significant attempt to reform the patent system since 1952.

The patent troll problem arose largely as a result of decisions made by the specialized court that hears patent appeals, the Court of Appeals for the Federal Circuit (CAFC). When that court was created, in 1982, patent law became the only area of law with a specialized court. Lobbying for the creation of the court emphasized that it would bring beneficial uniformity to patent law. But a number of observers have suggested that this specialization leads to undue influence of patent lawyers on the outlook of the court and hence on the nature of the decisions it makes.[27]

Many hoped that the America Invents Act would offer an opportunity to address some of the CAFC's excesses. This law was seven years in the making, and those seven years witnessed a pitched battle between competing interest groups. Over 1,000 lobbyists worked on this bill, including 10 former members of Congress, 280 former Congressional staffers, and over 50 former government officials.[28] Hundreds of millions of dollars were spent on lobbying and campaign contributions.[29] Patent lawyers and pharmaceutical companies argued that the patent system needs to provide strong incentives to develop new knowledge and that reforms should not weaken these incentives. Tech companies argued that patent trolls were inhibiting their ability to develop and share new knowledge. Mature tech companies like IBM and Microsoft argued for modest changes to the law; newer companies like Google, affected by patent lawsuits both from trolls and some of the older companies, sought more basic changes. These competing interests created a stalemate, resulting in a bill that made many technical changes but little substantive change. Many of the details of the bill were hammered out in closed-door negotiations between a representative of the pharmaceutical industry and a representative of a tech industry, mediated by the head of the Patent Office; small start-ups and the public did not have a place at the table. In the end, the new law did little to deter patent trolls or to eliminate the poor patents that allow the trolls to abuse the system.[30]

Except for one industry—the exception that proves the rule. Section 18 of the law provides a special procedure for challenging patents on the "practice, administration, or management of a financial product or service." In other words, the finance industry, one of the most powerful and high spending lobbies in Washington, obtained a special procedure to invalidate patents on its methods of doing business—the very patents that some patent trolls have used to win large settlements from major banks. Senator Charles Schumer of New York inserted section 18 into the legislation.[31] While this section had the support of the finance industry, it was opposed by a number of patent trolls and their law firms. Democrats Nancy Pelosi, Maxine Waters, and Dan Boren opposed section 18, apparently thanks to the activities of a Democratic "bundler" of campaign contributions from law firms; so did Republicans Jim Sensenbrenner, Dana Rohrabacher, Dan Lungren, and Charlie Dent, all recipients of funds from Intellectual Ventures, the largest patent troll. But they were no match for the big banks.

Established interests blocked meaningful patent reform that might have remedied the burden the patent system places on many small start-ups in emerging technologies. Only a very powerful lobby could extract a unique provision to deter patent trolls, and even it faced significant resistance.

Not surprisingly, patent trolls have continued to file more lawsuits, despite the America Invents Act. Patent troll lawsuits were up 18 percent in 2013 over the previous year.[32] Yet perhaps now the political calculus is changing as patent trolls have begun suing a broader range of defendants including retailers, nonprofit organizations, hotels, and restaurants as well as lots of small start-ups. Trade organizations representing these industries as well as the National Venture Capital Association and the Application Developers Alliance (software developers) have begun pushing for a new round of patent reform.[33] It appears that the patent trolls may have awakened small business, the sleeping giant of American politics.

So, just two years after passing a new patent law, the White House and Congress revisited patent reform in response to constituent complaints. In December 2013 the House passed a patent reform bill (H.R. 3309) that targeted trolls by a lopsided 325 to 91 vote. The White House supported this legislation and also made changes at the Patent Office to weed out some overreaching patents that should never have been granted.[34] Also, following the lead of Vermont, many states have passed legislation battling patent trolls who make fraudulent claims. These legislative efforts can limit the worst excesses, although none fully addresses the underlying problem of patent trolls. Nevertheless, they would be a step in the right direction. Yet the powerful lobbies of the pharmaceutical industry and the trial lawyers were able to stop reform in the Senate. In May 2014, just as a compromise bill was reached in the Senate Judiciary Committee, top Senate leaders, responding to lobbying by these groups, pulled the legislation from consideration. As of this writing, these established interests have been able to block reform.[35]

The patent troll problem is not so dire as to stop innovation altogether. Patent troll litigation reduces R&D spending and venture capital investment and appears tied to a decline in the entry of new firms. If patent trolls were contained, firms would invest more in new technologies and would make investments in innovation that they don't make today. The presence of trolls makes the transition to a new generation of technology longer and more painful.

## Buying the Future

Influential lobbies have helped patent law maintain a tilt that works against the interests of start-ups and early-stage technologies. The influence of money and lobbying is also seen in several of the other policy areas that have tilted the wrong way in recent years:

- Chapter 9 describes the dramatic growth in occupational licensure: from 70 occupations covering 5 percent of the workforce in the 1950s to over 800 occupations covering 29 percent of the workforce in 2008. This major change can only be understood as the outcome of massive lobbying.[36] In 1995 alone, state legislatures considered 850 licensing bills for health care occupations; over 300 of these were introduced into law.[37] This was the work primarily of lobbyists from professional associations. The public had no similar lobbies to represent the interests of consumers and prospective entrants to the occupations. Some licensing bills affected competing occupations—physicians vs. nurse practitioners, dentists vs. dental hygienists—with competing professional associations, but even these battles tended to favor the better-established occupation. The result has been reduced access to care, higher prices, fewer jobs for mid-skill workers, and delayed adoption of new technologies.
- Defense procurement has been the province of lobbyists since President Eisenhower warned of the "military-industrial complex" in his "Farewell Address to the Nation" in 1961. But as money and lobbying have become more important in politics, defense contractors became one of the most influential groups, supporting loyal

incumbents regardless of party or ideology.[38] Since 1990, this sector has contributed over $200 million to political campaigns and spent even more on lobbyists; in 2012 alone it spent $132 million on over 900 lobbyists.[39] And Congress has used the defense budget to promote vote-getting projects. The defense R&D budget regularly exceeds what the Pentagon requests in order to include pet projects for select congressional districts. A large portion of congressional earmarks have gone to the defense R&D budget.[40] It is hardly surprising that defense procurement rules have favored established defense contractors at the expense of university research and start-up technology firms.

• As with patents, changes in trade secret law were initially prompted by specialist lawyers seeking to provide "uniformity" to the law. In 1979, a lawyers' group, the Uniform Law Commission, published a draft Uniform Trade Secrets Act and promoted it in state legislatures. Over the last three decades, this language has been used to modify trade secret law in most states. After finance, insurance, and real estate, the law firms are the largest business contributors to political campaigns, responsible for $270 million in contributions to federal candidates in the 2008 election cycle.[41] Legislators are often happy to let this influential group draft its own bills. Now intellectual property lawyers and a group of large companies are attempting to make trade secret law even more uniform by passing a federal statute.[42] It seems, however, with both patents and trade secrets, that when lawyers make the law more "uniform" they also broaden its scope, creating more potential business for themselves.[43] A uniform federal law will almost certainly impose on California a regime that overrides the very policies that have made Silicon Valley so successful. To the extent that a broader interpretation of trade secrets tends to reduce employee mobility and the creation of spin-offs, then these efforts work against the interests of start-ups and firms developing emerging technologies.

• The contest between established interests and start-ups is seen in the battle in Massachusetts to repeal the state's strong enforcement of noncompete agreements. Recognizing the advantage that Silicon

Valley has over Route 128, Massachusetts governor Deval Patrick introduced legislation to change the state's law. Small-tech companies and venture capital firms supported this effort, but a few large-tech companies and well-established manufacturing firms opposed it. The latter group has so far successfully blocked reform.[44]

Although narrow interests lobbied for changes in these areas, some of the policy changes discussed do have broader support. Funding for four-year colleges has significant popular support, although the depth of support for actually diverting funds away from community colleges and technical education is less clear. Nevertheless, the policy shifts involving patents, trade secrets, occupational licensing, and defense procurement have the fingerprints of lobbyists and political spending all over them. And these forces have helped tilt policy in recent years toward mature technologies, established industries, elite occupational groups, and preserving the economic value of old knowledge, all to the benefit of vested interests.

The political process is not a competition among a plurality of interest groups on a level playing field; some groups have a built-in advantage. Moreover, an initial policy bias will often be strengthened because supporting institutions adapt to that bias and create a set of secondary players who have a stake in the status quo. However, the ability of a nation to keep the playing field less tilted toward mature technologies affects its ability to benefit from new technologies.

More generally, it does seem that the uniquely successful combination of policies and institutions that made the United States a world technology leader is being changed for the worse by, among other factors, the growing influence of moneyed interests. It is hard to know how much this change affects innovation in the United States today, but the real danger lies in the future, when the effects may be difficult to undo.

In any case, there are troubling signs that the U.S. innovation system has already been losing some of its dynamism. Researchers have found that business creation has been declining for the last three decades.[45] The rate at which new firms enter the marketplace has been declining and, with that, job creation has declined as well. Particularly important, the creation of new firms and new jobs has been declining in the high-tech sector over the last decade.[46] While there is not yet definitive evidence connecting these declines to the policy changes made over the last three decades, the declines provide a clear warning about the state of innovation in the United States.

## CHAPTER 14

# The Skills of the Many and
# the Prosperity of Nations

THE DIFFERENCES BETWEEN JAPAN AND the United States, and the recent changes in U.S. policy, are relatively minor. Both nations have well-developed institutions and laws to promote the development of new technical knowledge among large numbers of people, which allow both nations to take advantage of major new technologies and generate wealth for the majority of their citizens. This was not always so. Neither Japan a century ago nor the United States two centuries ago had these capabilities. The institutions and policies that enable learning on a large scale are an important part of economic development.

Some economists estimate that technology adoption explains 80 percent of the differences in income between rich and poor nations.[1] Societies differ crucially in their abilities to train ordinary workers in new technical skills and knowledge, and a growing body of research associates the ability to adopt new technologies with learning by doing.[2] National differences in the ability of ordinary workers to learn new skills may play a large, unrecognized role in explaining why some nations have much more wealth than others.

Scholars have long debated the sources of national wealth. In general, the explanations fall into three camps: geography, culture, and institutions. All three factors no doubt play a significant role. Yet interestingly, many of the specific explanations for how they affect wealth implicitly depend on an elite-driven view of history. Although the distinction is often glossed over, most of these explanations work only because geography, culture, and institutions affect the behavior of a narrow segment of technology entrepreneurs or inventors:

- Civilization is central to most geographical explanations of national differences in wealth, including the work of Jared Diamond.[3] Some regions were able to establish agriculture earlier and more sustainably than others. This allowed the creation of a hierarchical society whose elites could extract surplus wealth that could be invested. It also permitted a division of labor, allowing craftsmen to specialize in certain technologies. But the operative groups appear to represent a small slice of society.
- At least since Max Weber, culture has been seen as an important determinant of economic success. Weber attributed the productivity and high savings rate of the emergent capitalist classes to the Protestant ethic.[4] More recently, David Landes has described the ruthlessness and rationality of Western culture providing a critical edge: according to Landes, this is why the Industrial Revolution occurred in the West and not in China.[5] But the ruthlessness and rationality seem confined to entrepreneurs and inventors in Landes's account, and mainly to emergent capitalists in Weber's.
- Explanations based on a nation's institutions typically focus on how those institutions affect entrepreneurs. For example, economist Daron Acemoglu and political scientist James Robinson highlight the role of secure property rights in encouraging entrepreneurs to invest in new technologies.[6] This group is seen as driving the adoption of new technologies that increase wealth.

Capitalist societies that excel at generating wealth are indeed able to motivate capitalists to save, entrepreneurs to start new business, and inventors to invent. But that is not the whole story. For new technologies to be implemented, large numbers of ordinary workers also need to acquire technical skills and knowledge. That is a slow and difficult process, and history suggests that it often requires social changes supported by accommodating institutions and culture.

For example, the transition to the new technologies of the Industrial Revolution in the United States involved not only a transition to the highly disciplined workplace of the factory, but also the development of a large, permanent urban workforce in what had been a largely rural region. It is perhaps easy to forget that this rather radical social experiment required new institutions, including new forms of workplace organization and labor markets for new categories of skilled workers. These changes also required an accommodating culture. For instance, the U.S. textile industry of the 1820s through the 1850s recruited young, unmarried women to travel far from their families, live in boardinghouses, and work in mills with large numbers of other people. This was a bold social innovation.

The role of young women in industrialization might seem accidental, but, in fact, literate young women were an important part of the early mechanized cotton textile industry in Japan and, more recently, in China. They played a role as well in other early mechanized industries. Economic historians have suggested that young unmarried women were recruited for factory work because they had few other economic opportunities.[7] With few alternatives, they were willing to work in factories for relatively low wages. Because the early technology was often only marginally profitable at first, the low wages of women gave early manufacturers a crucial advantage.

But many cultures, even today, would not allow young women to participate in such experiments. What sort of culture and what sort of institutions allowed these experiments to take place? The culture that mattered was not just one that encouraged thrift, perseverance, rationality, and ruthlessness. The liberality to permit all sorts of people the opportunity to engage in independent economic activity was also critical, which included the willingness to let women work outside the household and to learn to read. The freedom of literate young women is everywhere a bellwether of social flexibility.[8]

But this sort of cultural flexibility, while lacking in many nations today, is not some immutable ancient inheritance. The same social freedoms would not have been permitted in China a century ago, when many young girls still had their feet bound,[9] or in Puritan New England a century before Lowell. What appears to matter in the long run is not just a particular set of cultural values but also a willingness to adapt to changing times.

Similarly, the institutions that matter are not just those that provide incentives to entrepreneurs and inventors but also those that encourage large numbers of ordinary workers to acquire new skills and knowledge. Here, too, flexibility matters. Strong incentives for the mass acquisition of new skills imply a willingness to extend economic power to large numbers of people. Entrenched elites—and not just economic elites—have not always been willing to share power, hence societies with a high degree of inequality have often failed to profit much from the benefits of technology. Slaves, for example, were not well motivated to acquire new technical knowledge and skills. Efforts to run textile mills using slave labor in the nineteenth century usually failed. More generally, societies may have difficulty adapting and implementing new technologies on a large scale unless they are willing to allow women, minorities, immigrants, and others to acquire significant economic power.

Beyond providing incentives for ordinary workers to acquire new knowledge, institutions can also mitigate the difficulty of the transition to new occupations and organizations. Although the power loom did not drive the handloom workers to starvation, as Marx claimed, it did force a transition on them. They often had to move to cities to find work, and their family members had to invest in new skills. Workers do not always go gently into such dislocations. Sometimes they smash machines, as the Luddites occasionally did. Social institutions provide support during such transitions. Indeed, economists Avner Greif and Murat Iyigun find that England experienced relatively little popular resistance to technology-related economic transformations; they attribute this peacefulness to England's welfare institutions that provided support to the poor.[10] They find a statistical association between the level of welfare spending and innovation. Counties in England that provided greater welfare payments had fewer food riots but also more patents; countries in Europe that provided more welfare also displayed more technological innovations at international exhibitions. This suggests that a nation's ability to implement new technologies depends on how the nation treats the many ordinary people who build and use that technology, and the freedoms, the incentives, and the protections it provides them.

The political powers in England were somewhat responsive to the needs of the workers facing economic dislocation, and this made a difference in their ability to implement new technology. In turn, the growing economic power of the workers may have had implications for political power. Economists have found that wealthier countries tend to be democracies, but there is an ongoing debate about what causes this correlation—whether democracies generate greater wealth or whether a wealthy middle class pushes for democracy, or whether both occur.[11] Acemoglu and Robinson, for example, believe that China will not be able to sustain its economic growth unless it provides greater political democracy.[12] They argue that while China broadly provides its citizens with economic incentives, the incentives are unlikely to be sustained unless those citizens also have greater political power. Whether it is correct or not, this argument is clearly much more significant if one views the relevant economic incentives as applying not just to entrepreneurs but to a large number of ordinary people working with new technology.

A major concern today is that growing economic inequality will diminish the responsiveness of the political system to common needs, leading to policies that lessen our ability to implement new technologies among other things. The growing share of wealth owned by the wealthiest 0.1 percent of the population threatens to set off what Ezra Klein calls the "Doom Loop of Oligarchy": concentrated wealth buys political power, which is used to further increase wealth by lowering taxes, and concentrating economic and political power even more among the wealthy.[13] Some others, such as Thomas Piketty, see this concentration of wealth undermining the legitimacy of democracy.[14] Piketty proposes a global tax on wealth to break the vicious cycle of the doom loop.

Yet the policies that inhibit the growth of wages for the median worker today are driven by a broader set of interests than the concerns of the top 0.1 percent. The professional associations that lobby to raise educational requirements for occupational licensing are not composed of billionaires. Nor are most of the shareholders of the defense contractors or electronic health system vendors who fight open standards. Nor are the lawyers who lobby against fixing the patent system. The members of these interest groups are well off, to be sure, but they are not billionaires. The relative wealth of the top 0.1 percent might not matter that much to the economic health of the average worker. The obstacles to restoring wage growth might have more to do with the broader dysfunction of our dollar-dominated political system than with the particular role of the extremely wealthy.

The role of political influence marks a difference from the past. The Luddites sought to put off the encroachments of new technology and the factory system. But they were impoverished workmen with little political clout. In the end, they achieved little. Today, patent lawyers, defense contractors, and professional associations gain from actions that delay the implementation of new technologies and restrict job growth. They don't aim to delay technology, but their lobbies have been more successful than the Luddites, to the detriment of the average worker and of society generally.

Yet even with the optimal policies in place, the transition to new knowledge and new institutions would be difficult because the technology life cycle turns slowly. Large numbers of ordinary workers as well as scientists, engineers, and managers have much to learn, and much of that knowledge can only be acquired through learning by doing at this time. Information technology seems to make this learning especially difficult because it affects so many different occupations and, in some industries, the rapid pace of change continually requires new knowledge and new standards. Acquiring the knowledge to implement information technologies is simply a difficult problem for society. The practical skills of ordinary people have been a wellspring of widely shared wealth for 200 years, and the economic power of mighty nations rests on the technical knowledge of the humble. Provide the means for ordinary workers to acquire the skills and knowledge to implement new technology today and the economic bounty will not only grow, it will be widely shared.

# NOTES

## Introduction

1. From 1979 to 2011, the hourly wage (Bureau of Labor Statistics usual weekly wage divided by average hours) adjusted for benefits (multiplying the wage by the ratio of total employee compensation to wage and salary accruals from the NIPA accounts of the Bureau of Economic Analysis) and for the cost of living (Consumer Price Index), grew only 0.2 percent per annum. Some economists contend that the CPI overstates inflation, in which case hourly wages would have risen by more. Also, note that because hours worked per household have increased, household income has not stagnated as much as the hourly wage.
2. Brynjolfsson and McAfee, *Second Machine Age.*
3. Clark, *Farewell to Alms.*
4. Piketty, *Capital.*
5. Cowen, *Average Is Over.*
6. Allen, "Engels' Pause."
7. Piketty, *Capital.*
8. I build on the work of other scholars who have pioneered the subject of technical knowledge. Three of the most important economic historians to do so are Nathan Rosenberg, Joel Mokyr, and Paul David. See David, *Technical Choice*; Mokyr, *Gifts of Athena*; Mokyr, *Enlightened Economy*; and Rosenberg, *Black Box*. Management literature studies the role of knowledge in the firm; see Foray, *Economics of Knowledge*. Learning by doing has been seen to play a role in the economic theory of growth; see Arrow, "Economic Implications," and Jovanovic, "Learning and Growth." David Warsh tells the story of knowledge in economic growth theory; see Warsh, *Knowledge.*
9. Some economists use the term "learning by doing" in a narrow sense to connote a very specific situation where a new plant will reduce its cost of production as its cumulative output grows. As I will discuss, this plant-level effect

often involves workers and managers learning through experience, but it might involve other things as well. When I use the term "learning by doing," I connote the much broader and original notion of the term, which includes "learning by using" (Rosenberg) and a significant swath of "user innovation" (von Hippel).

## Chapter 1. More Than Inventions

1. Larcom, *New England Girlhood*.
2. Appleton, *Introduction of the Power Loom*.
3. Dublin, *Women at Work*.
4. Montgomery, *Practical Detail*.
5. Zevin, "Growth of Cotton Textile Production."
6. This is not true of all technologies. For example, penicillin and small molecule pharmaceuticals often deliver most of their benefit soon after the initial commercialization. Delayed benefits are a feature of technologies where sequential innovation is important, as discussed in Chapter 3.
7. Rosenberg, "Technological Interdependence"; Hollander, *Sources of Increased Efficiency*; Nuvolari, "Collective Invention."
8. This quip is from Gavin Wright, "Foundations," paraphrasing the line in the 1954 film version of *The Caine Mutiny*: "The first thing you've got to learn about this ship is that she was designed by geniuses to be run by idiots."
9. Mokyr, *Gifts of Athena*.
10. Mokyr, *Enlightened Economy*; Landes, *Unbound Prometheus*; Allen, *British Industrial Revolution*.
11. Mokyr, *Enlightened Economy*, p. 110.
12. Meisenzahl and Mokyr, "Rate and Direction."
13. Wadsworth and Mann, *Cotton Trade and Industrial Lancashire*.
14. MacLeod, *Inventing the Industrial Revolution*, pp. 202–204.
15. MacLeod, "James Watt."
16. Von Tunzelmann, *Steam Power*.
17. To cite two instances, the Smithsonian Institution celebrates heroic inventors at the Lemelson Hall of Invention, commemorating the leading patent troll of the twentieth century who donated the funding; the National Inventors Hall of Fame is hosted by the U.S. Patent and Trademark Office and only includes inventors who secured patents, excluding, for example, Tim Berners-Lee, inventor of the World Wide Web.
18. Cringely, "Steve Jobs."
19. Lyman, "Transaction of the Rhode Island Society."
20. Clark, "Why Isn't the Whole World Developed?"
21. Thus to the extent that theory contemplates technology implementation, much of it only appears to consider investment in R&D and not the development of worker skills and knowledge. In economics, this problem is framed as one of

cumulative innovation, as in Scotchmer, "Standing on the Shoulders." In legal scholarship, the problem is framed as one of commercialization. See Kieff, "Property Rights and Property Rules"; Sichelman, "Commercializing Patents"; and Abramowicz and Duffy, "Intellectual Property for Market Experimentation." But again, the question, as framed, is only about the investments that firms need to make in order to bring inventions to market, not about the broader development of skills and knowledge.

22. This is a very old intuition about patents, expressed in a formal model by Kenneth Arrow, "Economic Welfare."

23. Other justifications for patents include the arguments that they facilitate trade and that they promote disclosure of knowledge. Economic analysis of patents has focused largely on R&D incentives. See, for example, the innovation theory textbook by Scotchmer, *Innovation and Incentives*. Notably, this text does not discuss implementation at all.

24. In many cases, theoretical economists simply ignore the difference between ideas and knowledge. In other cases, they recognize a potential difference but dismiss it. For example, Scotchmer's text mentions Mokyr's distinction between propositional and technological knowledge, but declares that this difference is not relevant to the economic analysis of innovation (Scotchmer, *Innovation and Incentives*, p. 3, fn. 2).

25. In human capital theory, workers invest optimally in their training when their skills are "general human capital." In order to be general, technology-specific skills must be widely accepted, requiring standardization. Without a widely accepted standard, the skills might be specific to a particular firm or small group of firms. A standard theoretical result is that worker investments in their own skills may be less than optimal when those skills are firm specific (see Acemoglu and Autor, "Lectures," chapter 9). If firms could coordinate on a widely accepted standard, labor markets would provide stronger incentives to workers to invest in training. However, firms often fail to coordinate on widely accepted standards for decades (see Chapter 4). This coordination problem can arise because of network externalities in the provision of training or in job search.

26. Levin et al., "Appropriating the Returns"; Cohen et al., "Protecting Their Intellectual Assets"; Arundel and Kabla, "What Percentage of Innovations Are Patented?"

## Chapter 2. The Skills of the Unskilled

1. Sokoloff, "Was the Transition . . . ?"; Bessen, "Was Mechanization De-Skilling?"; Mohanty, "Experimentation in Textile Technology." For example, studying Rhode Island weaving workshops during the late eighteenth century, Mohanty reports that "To make fabrics for early cloth manufacturers, weavers needed only rudimentary knowledge of their craft . . . the level of skill required of the

workshop weavers was no more than a craftsman might acquire during the first year of an apprenticeship" (pp. 9–10).

2. The following industries account for 58 percent of establishments with over 100 employees in the 1850 Census sample (Atack and Bateman, "U.S. Historical Statistics"): textiles, apparel, footwear, household furniture, meat, and dairy products. These goods had been produced previously largely within households (see Tryon, *Household Manufactures*).

3. The amount of cloth woven in households declined from 8.95 yards per person per year in 1825 to 0.27 yards per person per year in 1850 (Tryon, *Household Manufactures*, p. 306). Estimates of weavers in workshops is based on calculations from the IPUMS Census samples for 1850 and 1880 (Ruggles et al., Integrated Public Use Microdata Series). Scranton, *Proprietary Capitalism*, documents the vitality of workshop production into the latter nineteenth century.

4. Dickens, "General Appearance."

5. Morris, "Art, Wealth, and Riches."

6. Braverman, *Labor and Monopoly Capital*; Marglin, "What Do Bosses Do?"

7. Weaving apprenticeships had lasted only three years, but by the end of the eighteenth century, many artisans did not go through a formal apprenticeship; Mohanty, "Experimentation in Textile Technology."

8. Here I am studying the learning curves of individual workers, not of the mill as a whole. Some of the early research on Lowell looked at learning curves for the mills or even for the industry as a whole (see Davis and Stettler, "New England Textile Industry," and David, *Technical Choice*). Lazonick and Brush, in "Horndal Effect," pointed out that a variety of factors might influence productivity over the long time frames studied, such as the organization of the workforce and the level of effort extracted. They attempted to show the effects of these factors. Nevertheless, Lazonick and Brush's data do show individual learning curves. An individual in 1850 might begin learning at a different level than an individual in 1830 because of differences affecting the entire mill, but both individuals appear to improve performance dramatically within a year or two as the result of individual learning.

9. F. G. A., "Susan Miller."

10. For example, the cohorts shown in Figure 2.1 earned $8.54 on average during their first month on the job; female schoolteachers in Massachusetts earned $11.28 per month around this time. Most of the weavers could have taught school, and many did. See Bessen, "Technology and Learning," for more details.

11. Bessen, "Technology and Learning."

12. These estimates were obtained two different ways, using data on alternative wages and on skill premiums earned. See Bessen, "Technology and Learning," for details.

13. Shlakman, *Economic History*, p. 147.

14. Barnett, "Introduction of the Linotype"; Barnett, "Chapters"; Brown and Philips, "Craft Labor and Mechanization"; Chin, Juhn, and Thompson, "Techni-

cal Change"; Gordon, "Who Turned the Mechanical Ideal?"; Gray, "Taking Technology to Task"; Nelson, "Mass Production."

15. Sokoloff, "Was the Transition . . . ?"
16. Bresnahan and Greenstein, "Technical Progress and Co-invention."
17. Black and Lynch, "How to Compete"; Bresnahan, Brynjolfsson, and Hitt, "Information Technology"; Lynch, "Adoption and Diffusion."
18. Brynjolfsson and Hitt, "Beyond Computation," p. 27.
19. Brynjolfsson, Hitt, and Yang, "Intangible Assets."
20. Autor, Levy, and Murnane, "Skill Content."
21. Gawande, *Complications*, p. 19.
22. Darby and Zucker "Change or Die"; Darby, Zucker, and Welch, "Going Public"; Zucker, Darby, and Armstrong, "Geographically Localized Knowledge"; Zucker, Darby, and Armstrong, "Commercializing Knowledge"; Zucker, Darby, and Brewer, "Intellectual Human Capital"; Jensen and Thursby, "Proofs and Prototypes."
23. Bahk and Gort, "Decomposing Learning"; Jovanovic and Nyarko, "Bayesian Learning"; Argote and Epple, "Learning Curves."
24. Boston Consulting Group, *Perspectives on Experience*; Thompson, "Learning by Doing."
25. Bessen, "Productivity Adjustments." This study of thousands of plants also shows that ramp-up is associated with increases in "multifactor productivity." Multifactor productivity is a measure that attempts to account for changes in capital per worker and materials per worker.
26. Alternatively, employers might learn which workers are more productive and let the others go. In this case employers are learning, and there is another sort of human capital investment.
27. Rosenzweig, "Why Are There Returns to Schooling?"
28. Foster and Rosenzweig, "Microeconomics of Technology Adoption."
29. Abowd, Lengermann, and McKinney, "Measurement of Human Capital."
30. Much of the remaining variation in wages is explained by firm-specific characteristics and unobserved factors.
31. Lane, *Ships for Victory*, p. 202.
32. Thompson, "How Much?"

## Chapter 3. Revolutions in Slow Motion

1. Du Maurier, "Edison's Telephonoscope."
2. Kitch, "Nature and Function of the Patent System," using data from Jewkes, Sawers, and Stillerman, *Sources of Invention*.
3. Gort and Klepper, "Time Paths."
4. Auerswald et al., "Production Recipes Approach."
5. Rosenberg and Steinmueller, "Engineering Knowledge."
6. Bessen, "More Machines."

7. These times are rough estimates, but nevertheless illustrative of the remainder principle. See Bessen, "More Machines," for actual times.

8. If the development of the improvement or its implementation involved an indivisible fixed cost, then these costs would act as a threshold and improvements would not be made until they were sufficiently profitable to cover the fixed costs. If, on the other hand, the costs were not necessarily a large lump sum and/or there was substantial heterogeneity in these costs, then the effect of greater profitability on inventive activity would be more continuous. In either case, the remainder principle explains why the process is sequential over a period of time.

9. Draper, "Continued Development."

10. David Landes, in *The Unbound Prometheus*, described this pattern during the Industrial Revolution as one of "challenge and response" after Toynbee.

11. Baldwin and Clark, *Design Rules*.

12. Weavers were paid mainly on piece rates, so they would benefit directly from learning this skill. A weaver on an hourly rate would only benefit to the extent that her employer raised her pay for acquiring such skills.

13. Marx, *Capital*, vol. 1, ch. 15.

14. Autor, Levy, and Murnane, "Skill Content."

15. This is why new inventions so often come from skilled workers and managers: there is "user innovation." See Eric von Hippel, *Sources of Innovation*.

16. Thomson, "Learning by Selling."

17. This topic is explored in Rosenberg, "Technological Interdependence." The Corliss steam engine not only provided cheaper power, it also regulated the power supply in response to demand changes, which improved the ability to manufacture finer textiles. See Rosenberg and Trajtenberg, "General Purpose Technology."

18. This output is based on the amount of cotton processed per textile worker, not just weavers.

19. Moore's Law predicts that the number of transistors on a semiconductor chip (and, roughly, the processor speed) doubles about every two years. Both the exponential growth in textiles and in semiconductors can be viewed as the outcome of a process of coordination between a base technology and complementary knowledge/products.

20. David, "The Dynamo and the Computer."

21. Black and Lynch, "How to Compete"; Bresnahan, Brynjolfsson, and Hitt, "Information Technology"; Lynch, "Adoption and Diffusion."

22. See Chapter 11, and Bessen and Maskin, "Sequential Innovation."

## Chapter 4. Standard Knowledge

1. Students only needed to determine the atomic number of an element to determine its place in the periodic table, and from this they could infer chemical properties. For example, the rightmost column contains noble gases that are inert. The

next to last column contains halogens that are highly reactive; they will combine with hydrogen to form acids.

2. For example, Justus von Liebig's laboratory in Giessen had a dozen students early on. See Haber, *Chemical Industry*, p. 71.

3. Bensaude-Vincent, *History of Chemistry*.

4. Moser, "Do Patents Weaken the Localization of Innovations?"

5. Since the 1980s, economists have studied various aspects of technical standards, focusing mainly on compatibility standards, or those standards that allow different components of a system to work together, such as hardware and software. Compatibility standards give rise to interesting problems such as competition between standards and problems of "lock-in" to a given standard. But technical standards are only one way that technical knowledge is standardized, and these compatibility issues are only part of the role that technical standards play. For a review of this literature, see David and Greenstein, "Economics of Compatibility Standards," and Blind, *Economics of Standards*.

6. Dominique Foray defines codification as "expressed in a particular language and recorded on a particular medium" (Foray, *Economics of Knowledge*, p. 74). Foray reviews the literature on codification. Language puts knowledge in a standardized form that can be more readily understood by someone who reads that language. But standardized knowledge is not necessarily codified; a tacit skill can be limited to apply to a certain range of conditions, thus becoming standardized to a degree. For instance, surgeons are certified in certain standard techniques that are tacit knowledge learned through experience. Codification is often most beneficial when it is combined with other sorts of standardization. Thus, although chemical experiments were all documented (codified) before Mendeleev, the experimental knowledge became much easier to learn when essential findings were simplified in the form of the periodic table. Such simplification can make the knowledge easier to acquire. Although it's not necessary, codification facilitates the ease with which knowledge can be standardized, and it magnifies the ease of communicating standardized knowledge.

7. The notion of dominant designs is developed in Utterback and Abernathy, "Dynamic Model"; Utterback, *Mastering the Dynamics*; and Suárez and Utterback, "Dominant Designs." On QWERTY, see David, "Clio."

8. Nelson and Winter, *Evolutionary Theory*.

9. See a review of this literature in Besen and Farrell, "Choosing How to Compete."

10. Raymond Vernon first developed evidence that firms do not export a technology until it has matured and is relatively standardized. See Vernon, "International Investment." A significant body of subsequent research finds supporting evidence. The cost of transferring technologies overseas decreases with their age. David Teece, "Technology Transfer," documents that the cost of transferring mechanical technologies overseas by multinational firms decreases substantially

with the age of the technology. For chemical and petroleum refining plants, he finds that the age relationship is weaker, but the cost decreases with the novelty of the technology. Also, early-stage industries and patenting activity with new technologies tend to be geographically localized. Conversely, older industries and technologies tend to be more geographically dispersed. Using patent citations as a proxy for knowledge spillovers, Jaffe, Trajtenberg, and Henderson, "Geographic Localization," find that the localization of knowledge decreases with the age of a technology. Audretsch and Feldman, "R&D Spillovers," find that early-stage industries tend to be more highly localized, and Desmet and Rossi-Hansberg, "Spatial Growth," find that older manufacturing technologies are less localized. And Petra Moser, "Do Patents Weaken . . . ?," finds greater geographical dispersion of patenting after the periodic table. Note, however, that these differences are a matter of the degree of standardization. AnnaLee Saxenian, *New Argonauts*, finds that the export of semiconductor manufacturing processes to Taiwan also involved the export of experienced engineers who brought with them much knowledge that was not standardized.

11. John Markoff, "Battles Loom for Control of TV's Portal to Cable," *New York Times*, April 3, 1993.
12. Christensen, *The Innovator's Dilemma*.
13. Edmund L. Andrews, "Technology; Time Warner's Ordinary People Plug Interactive TV," *New York Times*, December 18, 1994.
14. "A Talk with Miss Margaret Kelly, Director of the U.S. Mint," *New York Times*, August 6, 1911.
15. Almost all female stenographers were also typists. See Fine, *Souls of the Skyscraper.*
16. Ker, *G. K. Chesterton*, p. 392.
17. Costa, "From Mill Town to Board Room."
18. Rockwell, *Shorthand Instruction and Practice.*
19. National Stenographer, "The New Hammond," p. 319.
20. David, "Clio."
21. Data are from Kwolek-Folland, *Engendering Business.*
22. Some manufacturers continued to produce alternative keyboard layouts into the 1920s. See the Hammond Multiplex in The Virtual Typewriter Museum, http://www.typewritermuseum.org/index.html. During the 1930s, the Dvorak Simplified Keyboard was introduced, claiming superior performance.
23. Suárez and Utterback, "Dominant Designs."
24. See Temin, *Iron and Steel*. This standard was developed largely by Alexander Holley. The plant design included, among other things, an arrangement where pairs of Bessemer converters were situated next to each other (they were on each side of a pit in the original Bessemer plants), and the converters were elevated so that molten metal could be poured at ground level rather than in a pit. Holley also devised a method for quickly replacing the refractory bottom of the converter, returning the equipment to production much faster. Almost all of the Bessemer

plants in the United States in 1880 used Holley's design. His refractory bottom was developed in 1869–1870 and patented in 1872.

25. Formally, there is an option value to waiting. See, for example, Bessen, "Waiting for Technology."

26. Employers might be willing to train their employees to use a typewriter with a specific keyboard layout, but they would have to recoup the benefits of that training while the typist remained employed. High employee turnover, not unusual in a newly emerging occupation, would impair the ability of the employer to recoup the investment. This situation could also limit the adoption of a new standard and hence the adoption of the technology itself.

27. Besen and Farrell, "Choosing How to Compete"; Farrell and Saloner, "Standardization, Compatibility, and Innovation." As the literature notes, this situation typically involves a network externality: when I adopt one keyboard layout, other typists and employers using that layout receive an indirect benefit.

28. Dosi, "Technological Paradigms"; Nelson and Winter, "In Search of Useful Theory."

29. Michael Gort and Steven Klepper studied forty-six major new technologies and found several empirical regularities: the number of innovations tends to be highest during the early phases, when many new firms enter the market; industry output tends to grow rapidly at first, then slows as the products mature; prices decline, initially faster than later; typically industry revenues (the product of price and output) grows rapidly at first, but slows and often declines as the technology matures.

    Some of these changes are related to standardization. Steven Klepper explains them with a model in which standardization plays a prominent role. During the early phases, products have relatively few standard features. Consequently firms have opportunities to enter the industry competitively based on feature innovations. However, competitors can imitate successful innovations, making them part of the standard product offering. That is, product knowledge becomes more standardized. When this happens, established producers who can produce the standard product more efficiently have an advantage over many new entrants. This drives less efficient entrants out of the market, causing a shakeout and eventually a stable mature phase. Thus the degree to which product knowledge is standardized affects the relative roles of entrants and established firms.

    This pattern is also related to Clayton Christensen's notion of "disruptive innovations." When a new technology competes with an older, mature technology, it may initially operate on a small scale, coexisting with the older technology. Later, when greater standardization facilitates large-scale production, it may disrupt the old technology, largely replacing it.

    See Gort and Klepper, "Time Paths"; Winter, "Schumpeterian Competition"; Klepper and Graddy, "Evolution of New Industries"; Klepper, "Entry, Exit, Growth, and Innovation"; and Christensen, *The Innovator's Dilemma*.

30. For example, Everett Rogers attributes a technology life cycle to the heterogeneous adoption of a new technology by consumers with different psychologi-
cal attitudes; see Rogers, *Diffusion of Innovations*.

## Chapter 5. When Does Technology Raise Wages?

1. Mantoux, *Industrial Revolution*.
2. Clark, *Farewell to Alms*.
3. There are other factors that contribute to growth, such as the amount of effort
workers exert, the organization of production, and the efficiency of markets. I
include effort along with skills and the organization of production with technology.
4. Abramovitz, "Resource and Output Trends"; Solow, "Technical Change."
5. As Abramovitz put it in "Resource and Output Trends," the productivity measurements are "some sort of measure of our ignorance about the causes of economic growth." For example, standard growth accounting assumes that technology
is "Hicks neutral." However, the mechanical inventions of the nineteenth century were largely labor saving: they changed the ratio of machines to workers for
a given set of wages and prices. Such change is not Hicks neutral. Also, many
implementations (see, for example, Maddison, *Dynamic Forces*) incorporate technology indirectly into capital by making adjustments for "embodied technical
change," which, as Maddison notes, makes it even more difficult to disentangle
the real sources of growth. The example of weaving shows the large magnitude
of differences between growth accounting and an approach based on an actual
engineering production function.
6. Diamond, McFadden, and Rodriguez, "Measurement."
7. Bessen, "More Machines."
8. Indeed, a standard growth accounting using capital and labor as factors of
production would attribute 43 percent of the growth to capital accumulation, based
on a growth rate of output per worker of 3.72 percent, a growth rate of capital per
worker of 2.89 percent, and capital share of output averaging 55 percent between
the beginning and ending periods. This calculation is, however, based on some
strong assumptions that don't apply, including one that technical change is neutral when it was actually labor saving. Given the importance of textiles to overall
productivity growth during the Industrial Revolution, this finding suggests that
standard multifactor productivity growth estimates understate the role of technology and overstate the role of capital accumulation.
9. Clark, *Farewell to Alms*, p. 233.
10. Romer, "Endogenous Technological Change."
11. Cowen, *Great Stagnation*; Gordon, "Demise of U.S. Economic Growth."
12. Brynjolfsson and McAfee, *Second Machine Age*.
13. Employee compensation does not include proprietor's income or indirect taxes
less subsidies, income that accrues at least partially to labor. Using slightly dif-

ferent measures that account for these sources, the trend still declines after 1980. See Jacobson and Occhino, "Behind the Decline."

14. Piketty, *Capital in the Twenty-First Century*, pp. 200–201.
15. Stiglitz, *Price of Inequality*.
16. Karabarbounis and Neiman ("Global Decline") compare trends across countries and find the declines are associated with lower equipment prices, driven by information technology. See also Yglesias, "Workers Are Losing Out Globally." For another explanation, see Lynn and Longman, "Who Broke America's Job Machine?"
17. Bronfenbrenner ("Note on Relative Shares") outlines a simple production function model where the constancy of income shares depends on an elasticity of substitution between labor and capital of about one, although he shows that income shares might not be too sensitive to this parameter. In his model, there is not technical change, but the capital labor ratio increases. Solow ("Contribution") provides a growth model with technical change that is assumed to be purely labor augmenting. In this model, the capital labor ratio grows indefinitely so that constancy of income shares depends again on the elasticity of substitution being just right. A large series of other growth models provide similar results with similar assumptions. Note also that these models ignore international trade and the possible existence of subsistence workers elsewhere in the world. Empirical studies of engineering production functions find a wide range of elasticities and departures from labor-augmenting change. See the discussion in Bessen, "More Machines."
18. The elasticity of substitution is a parameter characterizing the production function and is "high" or "low" depending on whether it is greater than or less than one, respectively. In some cases, a decrease in the relative price of capital goods only generates a small increase in capital per worker, implying a low elasticity of substitution. In this case, labor's share of income will tend to grow as more capital is accumulated per worker. On the other hand, when the elasticity of substitution is high, a small decrease in the relative price of capital goods generates a lot more investment and a declining labor share. Estimation of the elasticity of substitution depends on assumptions about technical change. Using careful measures and estimating techniques, Berndt ("Reconciling Alternative Estimates") found an elasticity of substitution of about one between capital and labor when he estimated a constant elasticity of substitution (CES) production function under assumed Hicks neutral technical change. But estimates using translog production functions, which allow variable elasticities of substitution, typically reject the Cobb-Douglas restrictions (see, for example, Berndt and Christensen, "Translog Function," or Griffin and Gregory, "Intercountry Translog Model"). And estimates that assume a constant elasticity of substitution but allow factor-augmenting technical change also reject the Cobb-Douglas form, finding elasticities of substitution between capital and labor well below one (David and Van de Klundert, "Biased Efficiency Growth," and Antras, "Is the U.S. Aggregate Production Function Cobb-Douglas?").

19. Goldin and Katz, *Race between Education and Technology*. Note that Goldin and Katz also hold that the early factories, despite having much more capital per worker than small manufacturing workshops, required *fewer* skilled workers; that is, the factory was de-skilling.

20. See for example Lucas, "Mechanics of Economic Development," and Jovanovic, "Vintage Capital and Inequality."

21. Part of this premium may be due to a selection effect. That is, employers may pay more once they learn which employees are best able to handle technology productively. Nevertheless, that pay premium represents learning about technical skills.

22. Abowd, Lengermann, and McKinney, "Measurement of Human Capital."

23. Lewis, *Unionism and Relative Wages*; Lewis, *Union Relative Wage Effects*. For a more recent update, see Blanchflower and Bryson, "Union Wage Premium."

24. Jardini, "From Iron to Steel"; Nuwer, "From Batch to Flow."

25. Jardini, "From Iron to Steel," pp. 293–294; Montgomery, *Fall of the House of Labor*, pp. 30–31. Jardini notes that Bessemer workers earned more than wrought-iron workers despite both being represented by the same union. Montgomery notes that steel unions did not have consistent successes. By 1885, all but three of fifteen steel rolling mills required nonunion oaths by their workers. And as Jardini notes, the unions of Carnegie Steel faced disastrous setbacks at the Duquesne Works in 1890 and the Homestead Works in 1892. Bessemer workers earned relatively high wages nevertheless.

26. Becker, *Human Capital*.

## Chapter 6. How the Weavers Got Good Wages

1. Robinson, *Loom and Spindle*.

2. Dublin, *Women at Work*, pp. 99–100.

3. Dublin (*Women at Work*, p. 101) finds some evidence that the strike brought benefits to some workers.

4. Allen, "Engels' Pause."

5. Engels, *Condition of the Working Class*, pp. 25–26.

6. The formal notion in economics that aggregate income inequality first rises with economic development and then falls is called the "Kuznets Curve" and is attributed to Simon Kuznets ("Economic Growth and Income Inequality"). Economists have measured these trends (see, for example, Williamson, *Did British Capitalism Breed Inequality?*). Much of this analysis has been at a macro-level, however, and therefore involves broader changes than those I analyze here, including the shifting composition of occupations and changing tax structures. See, for example, Acemoglu and Robinson, "Why Did the West Extend the Franchise?"

7. Wages during the Civil War might not have been representative of peacetime wages.

8. Layer, *Earnings of Cotton Mill Operatives*.

9. The unskilled male wage only grew 6 percent from 1830 to 1900, after adjusting for inflation (David and Solar, "Bicentenary Contribution").

10. Spinners, in fact, also had learning curves and hence some significant skills. However, their learning curves were lower, implying lower skill levels. See Leunig, "Piece Rates and Learning."

11. Bessen, "Technology and Learning."

12. Dublin, *Women at Work*, p. 10.

13. In 1834, after the first strike, the strikers were replaced by trainees who were soon as productive as the women they replaced. Given that the mills had excess inventory, the production lost from the walkout was not especially costly. In 1836, the strike was more costly because the mills were understaffed before the strike.

14. We can infer that a newly hired weaver has experience if, in the payroll records, we observe that she was put directly on piece rate pay without any training period. Inexperienced weavers were put on day wages for two or three weeks while training before earning piece rate wages. These figures come from the Lawrence Company in Lowell.

15. The market may also have been small because the mills of Lowell tried to avoid hiring from each other. This group of mills had overlapping ownership and set wages jointly (Dublin, *Women at Work*, p. 10) and might have avoided hiring away experienced weavers from one another. However, there were plenty of other mills operating in New England that had different ownership and competed for workers (McGouldrick, *New England Textiles*, p. 37). The lack of standardization appears to have limited competition much more than the control over the market exerted by the Lowell mills.

16. Gibb, *Saco-Lowell Shops*.

17. Rosen, "Economics of Superstars." Note, however, that the superstar model applies when there is a great economy of scale, such as for an entertainer whose work is replicated digitally. This is something that does not occur in most occupations, however.

18. There were a number of mill companies in Lowell, but because they had overlapping ownership and management, they set wages jointly and avoided "poaching" employees from one another. They acted effectively more like a single company so that weavers would have to relocate to another town to find comparable work.

19. Ware, *Early New England Cotton Manufacture*; and Kulik, Parks, and Penn, *New England Mill Village*.

20. Smith Wilkinson cited in Ware, *Early New England Cotton Manufacture*, p. 200.

21. In the language of human capital theory, the case with a limited market corresponds to "firm-specific" human capital while the case with the robust market is called "general" human capital. See Becker, *Human Capital*.

22. In economic theory, the provision of firm-specific human capital can be underprovided because firms cannot credibly commit to rewarding employees

for expending effort at learning. See Acemoglu and Autor, "Lectures in Labor Economics."

23. Marx, *Capital*, vol. 1, ch. 15, sec. 5.

24. Lyons, "Family Response."

25. Bessen, "More Machines."

26. Raw cotton used in textiles grew from about .027 bales per person in 1860 to .064 bales per person in 1920. After 1920, cotton consumption per capita exhibits no clear trend. Of course, the U.S. population grew substantially from 1830 to 1900, but not enough to offset the labor-saving effect of technology.

27. McKenzie and Smith, "Protectionism Warranted?" The number of cotton textile workers declined from about 450,000 in 1920, to about 300,000 in 1960, to about 50,000 in 2002 (Bureau of the Census, *Historical Statistics of the United States*; Becker, Gray, and Marvakov, NBER-CES Manufacturing Industry Database). Output per worker is estimated from the NBER-CES database; from 1958 to 2005, real output per employee has grown an average 3.2 percent per year in cotton textiles (SIC 2211). Some of the decline in cotton employment can also be attributed to offshoring and to shifts in consumer preferences to new fibers.

28. The price elasticity of demand will decline as price declines under some rather general conditions. Suppose, for example, that consumers' willingness to pay is distributed according to a distribution function. Let $F(p)$ be the cumulative distribution function with respect to price, $p$. Then demand will be proportional to $1 - F(p)$. It is straightforward to show that the elasticity of demand with respect to price will increase with price if $F$ is a lognormal distribution or a wide variety of other common distributions. Typical economic distributions, such as those for income or wealth, are lognormal.

29. Saxonhouse and Wright, "Technique, Spirit, and Form."

30. Clark, "Why Isn't the Whole World Developed?"

31. Zeitz, "Do Local Institutions Affect All Foreign Investors in the Same Way?"

32. Bloom et al., "Does Management Matter?"

33. Throughout the nineteenth century, the United States imported more textiles than it exported. Although the United States was the most efficient producer of coarse cloths, much of the imported cloth was fine and fancy product.

34. In 2012, the United States imported $5.7 billion in fabric and $1.4 billion in yarn. That year the United States exported $8.5 billion in fabric and $5.1 billion in yarn. Data is from the U.S. Commerce Department, International Trade Administration, Office of Textiles and Apparel, http://otexa.ita.doc.gov/msrpoint .htm.

35. Broadwoven cotton fabrics accounted for 35 percent of the woven and knit products made by U.S. textile mills in 1958; they accounted for only 15 percent of output in 2005. These estimates are by dollar volume from the NBER-CES database.

36. In 1929 there were 1.3 million textile workers, about one third of them producing cotton textiles; by 1973, there were 1.0 million textile workers, but only 15

percent were in cotton cloth and finishing; in 2005 there were only 274,000 textile workers, about 10 percent in cotton cloth and finishing.
37. McKenzie and Smith, "Protectionism Warranted?"
38. Leunig, "Piece Rates and Learning."
39. As noted previously, the QWERTY standard took two or three decades to emerge as the dominant standard. In steelmaking, Nuwer ("From Batch to Flow") sees high throughput production standards emerging during the period of 1880–1920; Jardini ("From Iron to Steel") finds wages doubling at one mill as it adopted this standardized technology.

## Chapter 7. The Transition Today

1. Original broadcast title "March of the Machines," which aired on January 13, 2013, and was rebroadcast on September 8, 2013. Steve Kroft, correspondent; Harry Radliffe and Maria Gavrilovic, producers, http://www.cbsnews.com/news/are-robots-hurting-job-growth-08-09-2013/.
2. Deloitte Consulting, "2014 MHI Annual Industry Report."
3. Gue et al., "U.S. Roadmap."
4. Gue et al., "U.S. Roadmap," p. 54.
5. Brynjolfsson and McAfee, *Second Machine Age*, p. 10.
6. Occupational data can be tricky to compare over time because occupational classification schemes change. The table presents some well-defined detailed occupations from an establishment (workplace) survey over an interval when the categories did not change. Unfortunately, the occupational data do not permit clear counts on warehouse occupations. While word processing, accounting software, etc., might have had a different effect prior to 1999, the claim is that these technologies are eliminating jobs now.
7. Gup, *The Future of Banking*.
8. Gup, *The Future of Banking*, p. 53.
9. The ATM data come from various publications of the Bank for International Settlements, Committee on Payment and Settlement Systems: "Payment System in Eleven Developed Countries," for 1980, 1985, and 1989; "Statistics on Payment System in Eleven Developed Countries," for 1990, 1991, and 1992; "Statistics on Payment System in the Group of Ten Countries," for 1993–1999; "Statistics on Payment and Settlement Systems in Selected Countries," for 2001–2008; and "Statistics on Payment and Settlement Systems in the CPMI Countries," for 2009. Using estimates from the Occupational Employment Survey from the Bureau of Labor Statistics, an establishment survey, the employment of tellers increased from 504,000 in 1984 to 576,580 in 2009. Using the household survey of the March Current Population Survey, tellers increased from 363,000 in 1976 to 469,000 in 2009, an increase of 29 percent. At the same time, the percentage of part-time tellers increased from 24 percent in 1976 to 29 percent in 2009. This makes the increase in "full-time equivalent" teller jobs 26 percent.

10. Hannan and Hanweck, "Recent Trends." The number of savings associations did not increase as rapidly, but the number of employees per branch at savings associations fell only slightly, from thirteen to twelve. The cost of operations was not the only factor influencing the increase in bank branches. Other factors included population growth and deregulation. However, Hannan and Hanweck find that the number of bank branches increased more in areas with greater decreases in employees per branch.

11. See, for example, De Paula, "Rising Teller Turnover"; Nalbantian and Szostak, "How Fleet Bank Fought Employee Flight"; and Frei, "Breaking the Trade-Off."

12. Ann Carrns, "An ATM, With a Real Teller on the Screen," New York Times, April 4, 2013.

13. Frey and Osborne, "Future of Employment."

14. In 1976, the median hourly wage for full-time typesetters and compositors was 15 percent above the median wage for all full-time workers.

15. William Glaberson, "Seeds of a Newspaper Struggle," New York Times, December 8, 1992. In England, the comparable dispute was much more bitter, leading to a yearlong battle during the 1980s between Rupert Murdoch of News International and the unions.

16. I use 1979 and 2007 as comparison years here and in the following discussion, because these years were at roughly comparable points in the business cycle. Comparing the number of designers over time is a bit difficult because the occupational categories were changing and because different surveys categorized designers differently. The March Current Population Survey (CPS), a monthly survey of households, reported 194,471 "designers" in 1979 and 897,728 in 2007. It is possible that this difference is exaggerated because the occupational categories used in this survey changed over time. The Occupational Employment Survey covers workplace establishments, and thus misses freelance designers, but it reports different types of designers and it uses more consistent occupational categories. In 2010, it reported 212,300 "graphic designers" and "desktop publishers." I estimate (from CPS data) that about 26 percent of graphic designers today are freelancers, implying a total workforce of about 287,000 graphic designers.

17. These estimates come from the Current Population Survey, which does not directly measure work experience. In this chapter, I use an approximation of experience commonly used by labor economists: max(min(age-years-of-schooling-7, age-17),0). Roughly, this measures the number of years that the person has been out of school, assuming he/she began school at age 7 and including some checks for bad data.

18. For all types of designers, the hourly pay of the 90th percentile has increased 14 percent relative to the median hourly pay from 1979 to 2007. Generally, designers' pay has become more unequal with greater variation from designer to designer. These trends, of course, are not unique to designers, but are seen in a wide range of occupations.

19. Using the March Current Population Survey sample comparing 1976–1980 to 2005–2009.
20. American Nurses Association, "American Nurses Association's First Position."
21. The ANA, of course, had some self-interest in doing so, since stricter requirements would help raise wages for its members. See Chapter 9.
22. Christensen, Grossman, and Hwang, *Innovator's Prescription*.
23. Autor, Dorn, and Hanson, "China Syndrome."
24. Acemoglu et al., "Return of the Solow Paradox?"
25. Autor, Levy, and Murnane, "Skill Content."
26. This assumes that computer skills are occupation specific, otherwise wages for workers with computer skills would be equalized across occupations. This assumption makes sense if the associated skills are for application-specific computer systems, not merely for computer use generally.
27. The measure of experience here is potential experience calculated as the age of the worker minus the years of schooling minus 7. The table is based on differences in the means of log hourly wages. A multiple regression analysis using a Mincer-type equation with dummy variables for different levels of schooling and experience, plus controls for gender and race, shows very similar estimates based on differences in regression coefficients.
28. Manpower Group, "Talent Shortage Survey."
29. Cappelli, *Why Good People Can't Get Jobs*.
30. Cappelli, *Why Good People Can't Get Jobs*, ebook location 313.
31. Kocherlakota, "Inside the FOMC."
32. For a more thorough discussion of the "skills gap" see Rothstein, "Labor Market."
33. Various statistics on computer and Internet use are available at http://www.census.gov/hhes/computer/publications/.
34. Bresnahan and Trajtenberg, "General Purpose Technologies 'Engines of Growth'?" For an overview, see Jovanovic and Rousseau, "General Purpose Technologies."
35. Bureau of the Census, *Historical Statistics of the United States*, table D765. Wages are deflated using the GDP deflator. Hours per week also fell. The real hourly wage grew 4 percent over this twenty-year interval.
36. Brynjolfsson and McAfee, *Second Machine Age*.
37. Rifkin, *End of Work*, p. 3.
38. Press conference, February 15, 1962, reported in Dunlop, *Automation and Technological Change*.
39. Keynes, "Economic Possibilities."
40. Marx, *Capital*, vol. 1, ch. 15, quoting Andrew Ure in *The Philosophy of Manufactures* (London: Charles Knight, 1835, p. 23).
41. Vinge, "Coming Technological Singularity."

42. Timothy B. Lee, "No, Artificial Intelligence Isn't Going to Take All of Our Jobs," *The Switch* (blog), *Washington Post*, October 23, 2013, http://www.washing tonpost.com/blogs/the-switch/wp/2013/10/23/no-artificial-intelligence-isnt-going -to-take-all-of-our-jobs/.

## Chapter 8. Does Technology Require More College Diplomas?

1. In Joe Klein, "Learning That Works," *Time*, May 14, 2012.
2. OECD, *Education at a Glance.*
3. Cappelli, "Schools of Dreams."
4. Freeman, *Overeducated American.*
5. The average college graduate earns 1,500 yuan per month while the average migrant worker earns 1,200 yuan. In one case, a city advertised for college graduates to fill eight positions collecting "night soil" and 1,100 applicants responded. Yasheng Huang et al., "What Is a College Degree Worth in China?," *New York Times*, December 2, 2010; Keith Bradsher, "Chinese Graduates Say No Thanks to Factory Jobs," *New York Times*, January 24, 2013.
6. Goldin and Katz, *Race between Education and Technology.*
7. Bessen, "Technology and Learning."
8. But the benefits to schooling only showed up in those regions where the seed varieties could be grown. See Rosenzweig, "Why Are There Returns to Schooling?" Note that with the weavers, education might have served to select the women who could learn the factory skills more rapidly. The women who made the effort to go to school might have been brighter and more able.
9. Nelson, Peck, and Kalachek, "Technology, Economic Growth, and Public Policy," pp. 144–145.
10. Bartel and Lichtenberg, "Comparative Advantage."
11. This distinction is frequently misunderstood. For example, the Center on Education and the Workforce at Georgetown University criticizes the Bureau of Labor Statistics (BLS) for being too rigid because occupations employ more college grads than the BLS estimates and those workers earn wage premiums. But precisely because college education prepares workers to learn on the job, they can earn higher wages even when the strictly technical requirements of the job do not require a college degree. See Center on Education and the Workforce, "Recovery."
12. Salzman, Kuehn, and Lowell, "Guestworkers."
13. Jonathan Rothwell, "The Silicon Valley Wage Premium," *The Avenue* (blog), Brookings Institution, August 6, 2014, http://www.brookings.edu/blogs/the -avenue/posts/2014/08/06-the-silicon-valley-wage-premium-rothwell.
14. See, for example, Catherine Rampell, "Data Reveal a Rise in College Degrees among Americans," *New York Times*, June 12, 2013: "'Think about jobs fifteen years ago that didn't need any college education,' said Sandy Baum, a senior fellow at the George Washington University Graduate School of Education. Many of

them now do, she added. 'Maybe you don't need a bachelor's to change bed-pans,' Ms. Baum said, 'but today if you're an auto mechanic, you really have to understand computers and other technical things.'"

15. My estimates from the Current Population Survey.

16. Salzman, Kuehn, and Lowell, "Guestworkers."

17. These percentages are for hourly wages taken from the Current Population Survey Merged Outgoing Rotation Group, and the author's calculations, comparing the mean hourly wage for workers with sixteen years of education (± 0.5) to that for workers with twelve years of education (± 0.5), excluding self-employed workers. The dashed line shows the mean for college-educated workers with less than five years of experience to all high school educated workers.

18. This association does not necessarily imply causality. For example, one famous economics paper found that wage increases also tended to occur in occupations that use pencils. However, it does seem plausible that at least part of the increase in college wages relative to high school wages can be attributed to technology.

19. Goldin and Katz, *Race between Education and Technology.*

20. In 1979, college-educated workers with less than five years experience earned 1 percent more than workers with only a high school diploma; in 2009, they earned 16 percent more. Note that the wages of inexperienced college-educated workers are more volatile with respect to the business cycle.

21. Stone, Van Horn, and Zukin, "Chasing the American Dream."

22. Abel, Deitz, and Su, "Are Recent College Graduates Finding Good Jobs?"

23. This difference arises because employers only have limited information on the abilities of job applicants. A college diploma provides information that the applicant might be better at learning on the job, but in many cases that "signal" will not be correct. Thus some college-educated workers will not be suitable where jobs require substantial learning on the job. Some will quit and some will be fired. Note that I am not arguing that a college diploma is purely about signaling (as some people do).

24. Using the March Current Population Survey, I compare top-level providers to mid-skill providers and technicians. Top-level providers include physicians, dentists, veterinarians, optometrists, and podiatrists; the second group includes registered nurses, pharmacists, dietitians, respiratory therapists, occupational therapists, physical therapists, speech therapists, therapists not elsewhere classified, physicians' assistants, clinical laboratory technologists and technicians, dental hygienists, health record technologists and technicians, radiologic technicians, licensed practical nurses, and health technologists and technicians not elsewhere classified. If the ratio of mid-skill providers to top-level providers had remained the same as in 1989, there would have been 1.96 million fewer mid-level jobs in 2009.

25. The administration has since announced some new initiatives in technical education, but funding levels have remained the same.

26. This is spending per full-time equivalent student. Desrochers and Wellman, "Trends."
27. Richard Vedder, "Princeton Reaps Tax Breaks as State Colleges Beg," *Bloomberg News*, March 18, 2012.
28. Century Foundation, *Bridging the Higher Education Divide*.
29. Holzer et al., "Where Are All the Good Jobs?," p. 41.
30. Appelbaum, Bernhardt, and Murnane, *Low-Wage America*.
31. Maggie Severns, "The Student Loan Debt Crisis in 9 Charts," *Mother Jones*, June 5, 2013, http://www.motherjones.com/politics/2013/06/student-loan-debt-charts.
32. See, for example, Greenstone and Looney, "Where Is the Best Place to Invest $102,000?"
33. In addition, these studies tend to ignore the risk that a student will not complete college, but nevertheless accumulate debt (only about half of college entrants obtain a diploma within six years), and they ignore the extent to which the people who complete college would also be able to earn more than the average high school graduate even without the diploma (because of greater drive or ability).

## Chapter 9. Whose Knowledge Economy?

1. Mokyr, *Gifts of Athena*.
2. Drucker, "Next Society."
3. Machlup, *Production and Distribution of Knowledge*.
4. Note that a declining share of employment does not imply a declining share of output. See Baumol, Blackman, and Wolff, *Productivity and American Leadership*.
5. Baumol, Blackman, and Wolff, *Productivity and American Leadership*, ch. 6.
6. Rowthorn and Ramaswamy, "Growth, Trade, and Deindustrialization." Specifically, they find that the relative share consumers spend on manufactured goods tends to increase in early stages of development and to decrease later on (that is, the income elasticity of manufactured goods is greater than one initially and less than one later on).
7. Manufacturing might be more affected by globalization because many services are not "offshorable." However, mature services are also increasingly being performed overseas today, thanks, in part, to information technologies; see Blinder, "How Many United States Jobs Might Be Offshorable?"
8. Baumol and Bowen, "On the Performing Arts."
9. See Baily and Bosworth, "U.S. Manufacturing"; Triplett and Bosworth, "Productivity Measurement Issues," claiming Baumol's disease has been cured.
10. U.S. Department of Commerce, "Benefits of Manufacturing Jobs."
11. My argument is consistent with the interpretation that manufacturing workers are paid "efficiency wages" in order to keep them from quitting (Krueger and Sum-

mers, "Efficiency Wages"). Because these workers have greater firm-specific knowledge, employers have greater incentives to reduce employee turnover. Moreover, while efficiency wages might also be paid to reduce shirking on the job, a worker's output is often easier to measure in manufacturing than the output of service workers, so shirking might not explain greater efficiency wages in manufacturing.

12. Bureau of Labor Statistics, "Employment by Summary Education."

13. Pisano and Shih, "Does America Really Need Manufacturing?"

14. Blinder, "How Many United States Jobs Might Be Offshorable?"

15. American Nurses Association, "American Nurses Association's First Position."

16. Kleiner and Kudrle, "Does Regulation Affect Economic Outcomes?"; Kleiner and Krueger, "Analyzing the Extent."

17. Graddy, "Toward a General Theory."

18. Fox-Grange, *Scope of Practice.*

19. It is important to distinguish licensure from certification in this regard. Many occupations have certification; practitioners can become certified by passing an exam or by meeting other requirements. Certification also serves as a means to verify the quality and safety of service that a practitioner provides. Licensure goes beyond certification by limiting who can practice the occupation.

20. Wanchek, "Dental Hygiene Regulation."

21. Kleiner with Kyoung Won Park, *Stages of Occupational Regulation,* ch. 6.

22. Kleiner and Kudrle, "Does Regulation Affect Economic Outcomes?"

23. Kleiner, *Licensing Occupations*; Kleiner, *Stages of Occupational Regulation.*

24. Kleiner, "Occupational Licensing"; Kleiner and Krueger, "Analyzing the Extent."

25. Liang and Ogur, "Restrictions on Dental Auxiliaries."

26. Kleiner et al., "Relaxing Occupational Licensing Requirements."

27. Wanchek, "Dental Hygiene Regulation."

28. Humphris, Kleiner, and Koumenta, "How Does Government Regulate Occupations?"

29. Using National Income and Product Accounts (NIPA) and Current Population Survey (CPS) data, there were approximately 13.5 million nonphysician health care workers in 2008. Assuming 76 percent were subject to licensing, licensing raised wages 15 percent, and the constant output labor demand elasticity was 0.3, this yields $13.5 \times .76 \times .15 \times 0.3 = 0.5$ million lost jobs. This estimate does not include limitations on jobs arising from restricted access to education or limitations on scope of practice.

30. See Lynn, "New Data." During this period my father was a physical metallurgist at one large steel company where he developed a new, advantageous rolling technology. Once the technology was proven at a pilot plant, the company chose to make a quick buck by selling the technology to a German steel firm rather than adopting the process itself.

31. Lenway, Morck, and Yeung, "Rent Seeking."

32. ArcelorMittal, "Steel Statistics," http://www.transformingarcelormittalusa.com/USASteelIndustry/AmericasSteelIndustryStatistics.aspx.
33. Moore, "Rise and Fall."
34. Lindsey, Griswold, and Lukas, "Steel 'Crisis.'"
35. Today, the Steel Manufacturers Association, the trade group representing minimills, calls for limits on China's unfair trade practices. See Steel Manufacturers Association, "Public Policy Statement 2013–2014," http://www.steelnet.org/docs/public_policy.pdf.
36. House Ways and Means, Subcommittee on Trade, "Problems of the U.S. Steel Industry," Serial 98-93, 1984, p. 286.
37. Barringer and Pierce, "Paying the Price."
38. Schorsch, "Why Minimills Give the U.S. Huge Advantages in Steel."

## Chapter 10. Procuring New Knowledge

1. Generally, economists recognize that private firms in competitive markets tend to underinvest in new technologies. This is because firms typically do not capture all of the value that new technologies bring to society and are thus not willing to invest as much as is socially optimal. This means that society can typically boost economic growth by providing additional incentives that encourage private firms to innovate.
2. Lerner, *Boulevard of Broken Dreams*.
3. Ruttan, *Is War Necessary for Economic Growth?*
4. Thomson, "Government and Innovation."
5. Olmstead and Rhode, *Creating Abundance*; David and Wright, "Increasing Returns"; Thomson, "Government and Innovation."
6. Gordon, "Who Turned the Mechanical Ideal into Mechanical Reality?"
7. Smith, "Army Ordnance"; Hounshell, *From the American System to Mass Production*.
8. Hounshell, *From the American System to Mass Production*. See also Thomson, *Structures of Change*.
9. Thomson, *Structures of Change*, pp. 54–59.
10. Thomson, *Structures of Change*, p. 57.
11. Thomson, "Government and Innovation."
12. West, "Commercializing Open Science." Andrew Viterbi, the inventor of the algorithm and one of the founders of Qualcomm, has said that they did not patent the algorithm because "if we had patented, it probably would have slowed down its acceptance, because no one patented in those days. AT&T and IBM patented for commercial reasons, but we were a small government contractor." (IEEE Global History Network, "Oral History: Andrew Viterbi," http://www.ieeeghn.org/wiki/index.php/Oral-History:Andrew_Viterbi.)
13. Mowery and Simcoe, "Is the Internet a U.S. Invention?" The World Wide Web was invented by Tim Berners-Lee at CERN in Switzerland.

14. The military also realized that a packet-switched network (the Internet is packet-switched) was resistant to nuclear attack.
15. Mowery and Simcoe, "Is the Internet a U.S. Invention?," p. 1371.
16. Mowery and Simcoe, "Is the Internet a U.S. Invention?," p. 1382.
17. U.S. federal agencies have long been encouraged to support voluntary industry consensus standards rather than unique government standards. This policy was set out by the Office of Management and Budget in 1980 (Circular A-119), but the policy preference had been in place long before then. See McKiel, "Circular Reasoning."
18. Eaglen and Pollak, "U.S. Military Technological Supremacy."
19. Mowery, "Public Procurement."
20. Stowsky, "Secrets to Shield or Share?"
21. These innovations include encryption, flat panel displays, and "smart highways."
22. See American Association for the Advancement of Science (AAAS), "Defense and Nondefense R&D, 1953–2014," http://www.aaas.org/page/guide-rd-funding-data-%E2%80%93-historical-data.
23. Stowsky, "Secrets to Shield or Share?," p. 258.
24. Alexander, "Adaptation to Change."
25. Of course, for these reasons a higher level of security also meets the needs of influence peddlers. In addition, congressional frustration with the cozy relationship between the defense industry and military has sometimes led to short-sighted attempts to restrict defense R&D only to projects that have direct short-term benefit to the military. See, for example, the Mansfield Amendment of 1969. Offered by Senator Mike Mansfield of Montana, it prohibited military funding of research that was not directly related to a specific military application; it became part of Public Law 91-121.
26. Lazowska and Patterson, "Endless Frontier Postponed."
27. Pine, "OPEN to Wild Ideas"; Amy O'Leary, "Worries over Defense Department Money for 'Hackerspaces,'" *New York Times*, October 5, 2012; DARPA, "Young Faculty Award," http://www.darpa.mil/Opportunities/Universities/Young_Faculty.aspx.
28. Simcoe and Toffel, "Public Procurement."
29. See Longman, "Best Care Anywhere," p. 38, citing the *New England Journal of Medicine, The Annals of Internal Medicine*, and the National Committee for Quality Assurance.
30. David Stires, "Technology Has Transformed the VA," *Fortune*, May 11, 2006.
31. Ezra Klein, "Veterans Aren't the Only Ones Waiting for Health Care." *Vox*, May 23, 2014, http://www.vox.com/2014/5/23/5745356/veterans-aren-t-the-only-ones-waiting-for-health-care.
32. Institute of Medicine, *To Err Is Human*.
33. For an example, see Atul Gawande, "The Hot Spotters," *The New Yorker*, January 24, 2011.

34. Hillestad et al., "Can Electronic Medical Record Systems Transform Healthcare?"
35. Sidorov, "It Ain't Necessarily So"; Milt Freudenheim, "The Ups and Downs of Electronic Medical Records," *New York Times*, October 8, 2012.
36. Dranove et al., "Trillion Dollar Conundrum."
37. Freudenheim, "The Ups and Downs of Electronic Medical Records."

## Chapter 11. The Forgotten History of Knowledge Sharing

1. Bagnall, *Textile Industries of the United States*, pp. 546–550.
2. Chesbrough, *Open Innovation*. What Chesbrough calls open innovation does not necessarily involve free sharing of knowledge, but could involve knowledge exchange with compensation.
3. Meyer, "Airplane as an Open Source Invention."
4. See an overview by Bessen and Nuvolari, "Knowledge Sharing." Patents are, of course, documents themselves, and so their role is relatively easier for historians to access, possibly giving rise to a biased view of their relative importance.
5. Allen, "Collective Invention."
6. Epstein, "Property Rights."
7. Allen, "Collective Invention"; Allen, *British Industrial Revolution*; Allen, "Industrial Revolution in Miniature"; Nuvolari, "Collective Invention during the British Industrial Revolution"; Nuvolari and Verspagen, "Lean's Engine Reporter"; MacLeod, *Inventing the Industrial Revolution*, pp. 104–105.
8. Bessen and Nuvolari, "Diffusing New Technology"; Mak and Walton, "Steamboats"; McGaw, *Most Wonderful Machine*; Temin, *Iron and Steel*; Meyer, "Episodes of Collective Invention"; Thomson, *Structures of Change*; Wallace, *Rockdale*.
9. Allen, *British Industrial Revolution*, pp. 68–74; Olmstead and Rhode, *Creating Abundance*.
10. Von Hippel, "Cooperation between Rivals"; Schrader, "Informal Technology Transfer"; West, "Commercializing Open Science"; Meyer, "Episodes of Collective Invention"; Von Hippel, *Democratic Innovation*.
11. Wallace, *Rockdale*.
12. Fritz, *Autobiography of John Fritz*, p. 160.
13. Stephen Wozniak, "Homebrew and How the Apple Came to Be," http://www.atariarchives.org/deli/homebrew_and_how_the_apple.php.
14. West, "Commercializing Open Science."
15. Scotchmer, *Innovation and Incentives*.
16. Patents are not the only means of preventing imitation. Aside from the pharmaceutical and chemical industries, most firms use other means (Levin et al., "Appropriating the Returns"). By being first to market with an innovation, they earn profits before rivals can enter. Other times they can gain an advantage through learning by doing: they can maintain a cost advantage relative to rivals with less

experience. And big companies often earn profits on complementary products. For example, computer companies once earned profits on the hardware even though the software was copied. Although firms often use alternative means to limit imitation, copying is still seen as the central concern: if imitation hurts profits, it will reduce innovation incentives.

17. Much of the historical material in this chapter is based on Bessen and Nuvolari, "Diffusing New Technology" and "Knowledge Sharing."

18. Gilroy, *Art of Weaving*, p. 416. John Ramsbottom and Richard Holt patented a version in 1834 in England, but they did not patent it in the United States, perhaps because of Gilroy's prior art.

19. Meyer, *Networked Machinists*; Thomson, *Structures of Change.*

20. Wallace, *Rockdale*, p. 216.

21. Zevin, "Growth of Cotton Textile Production."

22. The value of a patent is defined as including the value of selling the patent to another party, who will obtain value by excluding rivals from the market.

23. The Boston Manufacturing Company did have difficulty enforcing its patents for the double speeder (a machine used for winding cotton prior to spinning), in part because of faulty drafting of the patent. However, the power loom was the key invention, and it appears that the BMC had no difficulty getting $15 per loom for a patent license or $35 gross profit on manufactured looms through 1823. The persistence of this royalty through 1823 suggests that the BMC did not experience significant price competition from Rhode Island mechanics using other designs, including Gilmour's. Moreover, the patent royalty of $15 compares reasonably well with the $25 royalty that the powerful sewing machine patent pool was able to charge on a comparably priced piece of equipment.

24. Draper patented this device in 1816 and he obtained a patent on an improved version in 1829. In 1830, Draper's successor licensed the patent and also sold his own manufactured version for $2. By comparison, the loom temple saved cloth manufacturers about $35 each year on each loom in labor costs. As with the power loom, patents captured less than 1 percent of the value created. In a highly competitive market for textiles, a manufacturer without the least costly technology would lose money. Under these conditions, the independent inventor with sole rights to that technology has all the bargaining power and can demand full value. But when competition between the manufacturers was soft, independent inventors did not have as much bargaining power, and bargaining was more along the lines of what economists call a bilateral monopoly.

25. Bessen, "More Machines." The three minutes saved was from the loom temple, for which there were many designs, not all of them patented. Even ignoring the initial power loom invention, the reduction in labor time was about eight minutes per yard, so the majority of the reduction was still from unpatented improvements.

26. Lemley, "Myth of the Sole Inventor."

27. Merton, "Singletons and Multiples."

28. Mokyr, *Gifts of Athena*, p. 101. There are other explanations. For example, common innovations might arise from sharp changes in consumer demand or in the availability of general purpose technologies.

29. For example, Edwin Mansfield, "Technical Change," studied twelve innovations and only one of them was adopted by most of the firms in less than a decade.

30. See Bessen and Nuvolari, "Diffusing New Technology."

31. Darby and Zucker, "Change or Die"; Darby, Zucker, and Welch, "Going Public"; Zucker, Darby, and Armstrong, "Geographically Localized Knowledge"; Zucker, Darby, and Armstrong, "Commercializing Knowledge"; Zucker, Darby, and Brewer, "Intellectual Human Capital."

32. Darby, Zucker, and Wang, "Joint Ventures"; Lach and Schankerman, "Royalty Sharing."

33. Parker and Grimm, "Recognition."

34. Von Hippel, *Democratic Innovation*.

35. Mokyr, *British Industrial Revolution*, p. 43; Bessen and Meurer, *Patent Failure*, pp. 77–81. Some, such as Samuel Crompton, did not obtain patents. Others, such as Edmund Cartwright and Richard Roberts, inventor of a successful automatic spinning machine, did not profit from their patents. Some others, such as John Kay, inventor of the "flying shuttle" for weaving, lost money thanks to ruinous litigation trying to enforce their patents. And just a few, like James Watt, made out well.

36. Moser, "How Do Patent Laws Influence Innovation?"

37. MacLeod, *Inventing the Industrial Revolution*.

38. Cohen et al., "Industry and the Academy."

39. Saxenian, *Regional Advantage*.

40. Saxenian, *Regional Advantage*, pp. 2–3.

41. Gilson, "Legal Infrastructure"; Hyde, "High Velocity Labor Market."

42. Marx, Strumsky, and Fleming, "Mobility, Skills, and the Michigan Non-Compete Experiment"; Fallick, Fleischman, and Rebitzer, "Job-Hopping in Silicon Valley"; Garmaise, "Ties That Truly Bind"; Samila and Sorenson "Noncompete Covenants"; Lobel, *Talent*.

43. Noncompete agreements may have their most important impacts on investments in knowledge and on knowledge sharing but they also have other effects, including the disclosure of trade secrets to employees and the effect of labor mobility on the functioning of labor markets—in particular, on matching heterogeneous employers and employees.

44. Garmaise, "Ties That Truly Bind."

45. Png, "Trade Secrets."

46. These states have conformed their trade secret statutes with the Uniform Trade Secrets Act. See Samuels and Johnson, "Uniform Trade Secrets Act." As of this writing, the Uniform Trade Secrets Act has been adopted in most states.

47. Png, "Law and Innovation"; Png and Samila, "Trade Secrets Law."

48. Other policy changes affecting employee incentives include changes in the assignment of employee rights to inventions unrelated to work and federal criminal prosecution of trade secrecy violations. See Lobel, "New Cognitive Property." Health insurance policy also affects job mobility and employee incentives. Studies show that the lack of portable health insurance has created "job lock," reducing the willingness of talented people to change jobs or start new companies. See Gruber and Madrian, "Health Insurance and Job Mobility"; Fairlie, Kapur, and Gates, "Is Employer-Based Health Insurance a Barrier to Entrepreneurship?"

49. Marx, "Firm Strikes Back."

50. Steven Greenhouse, "Noncompete Clauses Increasingly Pop Up in Array of Jobs," *New York Times*, June 8, 2014.

51. Russell Beck, "Trade Secret and Noncompete Survey—National Case Graph 2014 [Preliminary Data], January 7, 2014, http://faircompetitionlaw.com/2014/01/07 /trade-secret-and-noncompete-survey-national-case-graph-2014-preliminary-data/.

52. Fisk, *Working Knowledge*.

53. Moscarini and Thomsson, "Occupational and Job Mobility." The authors note several other factors that might contribute to declining job mobility, including a reduction in the number of viable occupations due to outsourcing and perceived uncertainty in the labor market. Another possible factor might be the aging of the workforce. However, they argue that this factor cannot explain the decline since the mid-1990s.

## Chapter 12. Patents and Early-Stage Knowledge

1. Houze, Cooper, and Kornhauser, *Samuel Colt*.

2. Porter obituary, *Scientific American*, November 8, 1884.

3. Rufus Porter, *Scientific American* 1, no. 1 (August 28, 1845), p. 1. See http:// en.wikisource.org/wiki/Scientific_American/Series_1/Volume_1/Issue_1 /Front_page.

4. Khan, *Democratization of Invention*.

5. Lamoreaux and Sokoloff, "Inventors, Firms, and the Market." Note that a popular culture of invention also developed in Britain, despite its more expensive and cumbersome patent system. See MacLeod, *Heroes of Invention*.

6. Oz, "Acceptable Protection"; Samuelson, Denber, and Glushko, "Developments on the Intellectual Property Front."

7. For example, see Andy Baio, "A Patent Lie: How Yahoo Weaponized My Work," *Wired*, March 13, 2012, http://www.wired.com/business/2012/03/opinion-baio -yahoo-patent-lie/.

8. Chien, "Startups and Patent Trolls."

9. Tucker, "Patent Trolls."

10. Bessen and Meurer, "Direct Costs."

11. Bessen, Ford, and Meurer, "Private and Social Costs."

12. Cotropia and Lemley, "Copying."

13. Smeets, "Does Patent Litigation Reduce Corporate R&D?"

14. Feldman, "Patent Demands."

15. Tucker, "Effect of Patent Litigation."

16. Bessen, "Generation of Software Patents."

17. Graham et al., "High Technology Entrepreneurs."

18. Three-quarters of the biotech start-ups responding to the Berkeley survey had patents, for example.

19. Graham et al., "High Technology Entrepreneurs," p. 1318.

20. Kravets, "Do Patents Really Matter?," used matching software to identify firms in the TechCrunch database of start-ups that had published patent applications in the U.S. Patent Office database. It is possible that missed matches might cause the estimate of those with patent applications to be understated. Other studies have used surveys of venture-backed firms, but these studies suffer from possible response bias. Mann and Sager, "Patents, Venture Capital, and Software," found that 24 percent of venture-backed software firms had patents. Graham et al., "High Technology Entrepreneurs," found that 67 percent of venture-backed software firms had patent applications, as did 96 percent of venture-backed biotechnology firms. However, the sample of venture-backed software firms used in this study was small, possibly making the estimate unreliable and explaining why it differs from the other studies.

21. Venture funds appear to be mainly motivated here by "salvage value." That is, they want their funded companies to get patents so that if the company fails, the patents might be sold off to recoup some small portion of the venture capital investment. Some people argue, instead, that patents help a start-up "signal" its quality to potential investors. The idea is that investors lack information about which start-ups have high-quality technology, and a start-up with a patent might appear to have better technology. This factor seems to have limited explanatory power, however, in software technology. It seems that the majority of start-up patents are filed for after a firm is funded. Such signaling is apparently not important for investors in public equity markets. And it appears that, to some extent, venture funds looking for patents have been something of a fad—much of the activity seems to be concentrated among some of the most risk-averse funds, such as corporate venture funds, and the percentage of start-ups obtaining patents appears to be declining in recent years (Kravets, "Do Patents Really Matter?"). The value of signaling might be greater in biotech, where obtaining a patent is more central to the prospect of commercial success.

22. The list of permissible elements after "comprising" might include some elements that are not recited in the patent claim, while the permissible elements listed after "consisting of" constitute all of the possible elements.

23. Dennis Crouch, "Small Entity Status," *Patently-O* (blog), February 12, 2013, http://www.patentlyo.com/patent/2013/02/small-entity-status.html.

24. Risch, "Patent Troll Myths."

25. Bessen and Meurer, "Direct Costs."
26. Love, "Empirical Study"; Allison, Lemley, and Walker, "Extreme Value"; Price-WaterhouseCoopers, "Patent Litigation Study." Two researchers found that, nevertheless, some patents acquired by trolls had some indications of being good quality (Fischer and Henkel, "Patent Trolls on Markets for Technology").
27. Bessen, "Generation of Software Patents."
28. Boldrin and Levine, "Case against Patents."
29. Bessen and Meurer, *Patent Failure*, p. 191.
30. Miller, "Do 'Fuzzy' Software Patent Boundaries . . . ?"; Miller, "Where's the Innovation?"
31. Nard and Duffy, "Rethinking Patent Law's Uniformity Principle."
32. Moreover, the increase in the number of patents granted does not account for the increase in litigation. The number of lawsuits filed per patent within four years of the patent grant has tripled since the 1980s. Note also that the upward spike shown for the year 2012 is related to a change in the law. Beginning in 2012, the law made it more difficult to sue multiple defendants in one lawsuit. Because patent trolls tend to sue multiple defendants—sometimes over 100—in a single suit, the data for the years immediately preceding 2012 understate the number of defendants.
33. *Alice Corp. v CLS Bank International*, decided June 19, 2014, no. 13-298.
34. Magliocca, "Blackberries and Barnyards."
35. Machlup and Penrose, "Patent Controversy." This action apparently did not deter innovation in the Netherlands (see Moser, "How Do Patent Laws Influence Innovation?").

## Chapter 13. The Political Economy of Technical Knowledge

1. OECD, "Information Technology Outlook."
2. Minetaki and Motohashi, "Subcontracting Structure."
3. Arora, Branstetter, and Drev, "Going Soft."
4. Baba, Takai, and Mizuta, "User-Driven Evolution."
5. U.S. Congress, Office of Technology Assessment, "The Big Picture: HDTV and High Resolution Systems," OTA-BP-CIT-64 (Washington, DC: U.S. Government Printing Office, June 1990); Charles P. Lecht, "Tsunami," *Computerworld*, February 13, 1978.
6. Bob Johnstone, "Japan Tackles Its Software Crisis," *New Scientist*, January 30, 1986, pp. 60–62.
7. Baba et al., "User-Driven Evolution." See also Minetaki and Motohashi, "Subcontracting Structure," table 2, with 136 of 439 firms listed as independent.
8. Usselman, "Unbundling IBM."
9. With personal computers, it might have been possible to adopt U.S. standards (MSDOS, Wintel). The dominant firms, however, had an interest in maintaining proprietary versions of their operating systems even when they imported

MSDOS. Microsoft's software needed to be adapted to the Japanese language, and this work was done differently by different vendors. Additionally, Japan did not have strong copyright enforcement until 1986, making foreign software vendors reluctant to export. Of course, copyright posed no obstacle to computer vendors who bundled proprietary software with their hardware.

10. Cottrell, "Standards and the Arrested Development."
11. Chesbrough, "Organizational Impact"; Lynskey, "Determinants."
12. Eichengreen, Park, and Shin, "Growth Slowdowns Redux."
13. David, "Learning by Doing"; Bils, "Tariff Protection"; Temin, *Iron and Steel*, pp. 173–174 and 209–213.
14. Chandler, *Scale and Scope*.
15. Freeman, *Technology Policy*.
16. Mowery, "U.S. National Innovation System"; Chesbrough, "Organizational Impact."
17. There is some dispute about how much these firms would have unbundled on their own without antitrust enforcement. Regardless of the motivation, the U.S. outcome was very different from that in other countries. See Usselman, "Unbundling IBM."
18. For example, the vice president for electronic component development at Western Electric, which licensed out AT&T's semiconductor technology, explained, "We realized that if this thing [the transistor] was as big as we thought, we couldn't keep it to ourselves and we couldn't make all the technical contributions. It was to our interest to spread it around. If you cast your bread on the water, sometimes it comes back angel food cake." Tilton, *International Diffusion*, pp. 75–76.
19. Appleyard, "How Does Knowledge Flow?"
20. Khan, *Democratization of Invention*.
21. The U.S. auto industry long made "knowledge work" the sole domain of professional engineers. Engineers designed the cars, and factory workers made them. Many engineers never set foot on the factory floor; factory workers rarely had meaningful opportunity to correct design errors that made the cars harder to assemble and more prone to defects or reliability problems. In contrast, the Japanese auto industry, especially Toyota, recognized that ordinary factory workers acquired significant knowledge about design and manufacturability on the job. Assembly-line workers participate on Japanese design teams. Moreover, when an assembly worker detects a problem, the worker can stop the assembly line until it is solved; that sort of power was unheard of in Detroit. Japanese automotive engineers begin their employment working on the factory floor and subsequently spend one month a year rotating into alternative jobs. In this way they gain an understanding of the entire process of producing a car. Needless to say, this cultivation of knowledge learned through experience in production allowed the Japanese automakers to design cars faster with fewer engineering hours, to produce

them with less labor, and to make them of higher quality, all at the same time. See Womack, Jones, and Roos, *Machine That Changed the World*.

22. Mike Masnick, "Hacking Society: It's Time to Measure the Unmeasurable," *Techdirt* (blog), April 27, 2012.

23. This bias features prominently in the argument by Michele Boldrin and David K. Levine, "Case against Patents."

24. Litman, "Revising Copyright Law"; Litman, *Digital Copyright*.

25. Buchanan and Tullock, *Calculus of Consent*; Olson, *Logic of Collective Action*.

26. Paul Krugman, "Barons of Broadband." *New York Times*, February 16, 2014. http://www.nytimes.com/2014/02/17/opinion/krugman-barons-of-broadband .html?hp&rref=opinion&_r=1.

27. Scherer, "Political Economy"; Jaffe and Lerner, *Innovation and Its Discontents*; Henry and Turner, "Court of Appeals"; Nard and Duffy, "Rethinking Patent Law's Uniformity Principle"; Dourado and Tabarrok, "Public Choice and Bloomington School."

28. First Street, "Lobbying the America Invents Act," CQPress, 2011, http:// firststreetresearch.files.wordpress.com/2011/11/first-street-report-lobbying-the -america-invents-act.pdf.

29. Judge Paul Michel, speaking at the National Academy of Sciences on February 12, 2013, cited $300 million in lobbying and campaign contributions.

30. President Obama himself recognizes that the bill did not adequately deal with the problem of patent trolls; see http://www.whitehouse.gov/blog/2013/06/04 /taking-patent-trolls-protect-american-innovation.

31. See Zach Carter, "The Spoilsmen: How Congress Corrupted Patent Reform," *Huffington Post*, August 4, 2011, http://www.huffingtonpost.com/2011/08/04 /patent-reform-congress_n_906278.html?view=print&comm_ref=false. Subsequently, Senator Schumer recognized the value of this proceeding to other industries and introduced the Patent Quality Improvement Act (S.866), which would extend the same review proceeding to all business method patents, not just financial ones.

32. The America Invents Act (AIA) changed the rules to make it harder for patent trolls to file lawsuits against many unrelated defendants. This means that for some purposes the number of lawsuits might not be the best measure of patent troll activity. Another measure is the number of defendant firms sued. Although the number of defendants declined in 2012, after a sharp spike in 2011 as patent holders sought to file multi-defendant lawsuits prior to the AIA, the number of defendants also rose in 2013 again (by 11 percent), continuing the trend of the previous decade. See James Bessen, "Patent Trolling Was Up 11 Percent Last Year," *Washington Post*, *The Switch* (blog), January 31, 2014, http://www.wash ingtonpost.com/blogs/the-switch/wp/2014/01/31/patent-trolling-was-up-11 -percent-last-year/.

33. See James Bessen, "How Patent Trolls Doomed Themselves by Targeting Main Street," *Ars Technica*, September 12, 2013, http://arstechnica.com/tech-policy/2013/09/op-ed-how-patent-trolls-doomed-themselves-by-targeting-main-street/.

34. Executive Office of the President, "Patent Assertion and U.S. Innovation," June 2013, http://www.whitehouse.gov/sites/default/files/docs/patent_report.pdf.

35. Mullin, "How the Patent Trolls Won in Congress."

36. Graddy, "Toward a General Theory of Occupational Regulation."

37. Fox-Grange, "Scope of Practice."

38. Jen DiMascio, "Defense Goes All-in for Incumbents," *Politico*, September 27, 2010, http://www.politico.com/news/stories/0910/42733.html.

39. Center for Responsive Politics, "Defense: Background," http://www.opensecrets.org/industries/background.php?cycle=2014&ind=D.

40. American Association for the Advancement of Science (AAAS), "Federal Spending Bills Contain 2,526 R&D Earmarks, AAAS Analysis Finds," January 8, 2008, http://www.eurekalert.org/pub_releases/2008-01/aaft-fsb010808.php.

41. Center for Responsive Politics, "Interest Groups: Lawyers and Lobbyists," http://www.opensecrets.org/industries/indus.php?Ind=K.

42. Several bills have been proposed. One, the Defend Trade Secrets Act sponsored by Senators Chris Coons and Orrin Hatch, has the support of 3M, Abbott, AdvaMed, Boston Scientific, Caterpillar, Corning, DuPont, GE, Eli Lilly, Medtronic, Micron, Microsoft, Monsanto, Philips, P&G, and United Technologies. See http://www.coons.senate.gov/newsroom/releases/release/senators-coons-hatch-introduce-bill-to-combat-theft-of-trade-secrets-and-protect-jobs.

43. It is a tendency also seen in treaties that "harmonize" intellectual property law.

44. Callum Borchers, "DeLeo Plan Would Preserve Tech Noncompetes," *Boston Globe*, June 3, 2014; Dennis Keohane, "Mass Legislators Pass on Change to Noncompete Laws," *BetaBoston*, July 31, 2014, http://betaboston.com/news/2014/07/31/mass-legislators-pass-on-change-to-noncompete-laws/.

45. Hathaway and Litan, "Declining Business Dynamism in the United States."

46. Haltiwanger, Hathaway, and Miranda, "Declining Business Dynamism in the U.S. High-Technology Sector."

## Chapter 14. The Skills of the Many and the Prosperity of Nations

1. Comin and Ferrer, "If Technology Has Arrived Everywhere."

2. Foster and Rosenzweig, "Microeconomics of Technology Adoption."

3. Diamond, *Guns, Germs, and Steel*.

4. Weber, *Protestant Ethic*. Weber also saw the Protestant ethic helping the work ethic of ordinary workers.

5. Landes, *Wealth and Poverty*.

6. Acemoglu and Robinson, *Why Nations Fail*. These authors also see the importance of economic incentives affecting ordinary workers, for example, incen-

tives to acquire an education. However, entrepreneurs and inventors are central to their explanation of the link between institutions and technological innovation.

7. Goldin and Sokoloff, in "Relative Productivity Hypothesis," argue that young women were relatively less productive than adult men on the farm. More generally they had few other opportunities to make a living (see Lebergott, "Wage Trends").

8. Generally, women's economic equality is correlated with economic development. See Inglehart and Norris, *Rising Tide*.

9. Rossi, *Sex Life*.

10. Greif and Iyigun, "Social Organizations."

11. Acemoglu et al., "Income and Democracy."

12. Acemoglu and Robinson, *Why Nations Fail*.

13. Ezra Klein, "The Doom Loop of Oligarchy," *Vox*, April 11, 2014, http://www.vox.com/2014/4/11/5581272/doom-loop-oligarchy.

14. Piketty, *Capital*, p. 422: "Our democratic societies rest on a meritocratic worldview, or at any rate a meritocratic hope, by which I mean a belief in a society in which inequality is based more on merit and effort than on kinship and rents."

# BIBLIOGRAPHY

Abel, Jaison R., Richard Deitz, and Yaqin Su. 2014. "Are Recent College Graduates Finding Good Jobs?" Federal Reserve Bank of New York, *Current Issues in Economics and Finance* 20(1). http://www.newyorkfed.org/research/current_issues/ci20-1 .html.

Abowd, John M., Paul A. Lengermann, and Kevin L. McKinney. 2002. "The Measurement of Human Capital in the U.S. Economy." Longitudinal Employer-Household Dynamics Technical Paper 2002-09. Center for Economic Studies, U.S. Census Bureau, revised March 2003.

Abramovitz, Moses. 1956. "Resource and Output Trends in the United States since 1870." *American Economic Review: Papers and Proceedings* 46: 5–23.

Abramowicz, Michael, and John F. Duffy. 2008. "Intellectual Property for Market Experimentation." *New York University Law Review* 83: 337.

Acemoglu, Daron, and David Autor. 2011. "Lectures in Labor Economics." Manuscript. http://economics.mit.edu/files/4689.

Acemoglu, Daron, David Dorn, Gordon H. Hanson, and Brendan Price. 2014. "Return of the Solow Paradox? IT, Productivity, and Employment in U.S. Manufacturing." National Bureau of Economic Research Working Paper no. w19837.

Acemoglu, Daron, Simon Johnson, James A. Robinson, and Pierre Yared. 2008. "Income and Democracy." *American Economic Review* 3: 808–842.

Acemoglu, Daron, and James A. Robinson. 2000. "Why Did the West Extend the Franchise? Democracy, Inequality, and Growth in Historical Perspective." *Quarterly Journal of Economics* 115(4): 1167–1199.

———. 2012. *Why Nations Fail: The Origins of Power, Prosperity, and Poverty.* New York: Crown Business.

Alexander, Arthur J. 1990. "Adaptation to Change in the U.S. Machine Tool Industry and the Effects of Government Policy." No. RAND/N-3079-USJF/RC. Santa Monica, CA: Rand Corporation.

Allen, Robert C. 1983. "Collective Invention." *Journal of Economic Behavior and Organization* 4: 21.

———. 2009a. *The British Industrial Revolution in Global Perspective*. Cambridge: Cambridge University Press.

———. 2009b. "Engels' Pause: Technical Change, Capital Accumulation, and Inequality in the British Industrial Revolution." *Explorations in Economic History* 46(4): 418–435.

———. 2009c. "The Industrial Revolution in Miniature: The Spinning Jenny in Britain, France, and India." *Journal of Economic History* 69: 901–927.

Allison, John R., Mark A. Lemley, and Joshua Walker. 2009. "Extreme Value or Trolls on Top? The Characteristics of the Most Litigated Patents." *University of Pennsylvania Law Review* 158: 1–37.

American Nurses Association. 1965. "American Nurses Association's First Position on Education for Nursing." *American Journal of Nursing* 65(12): 106–111.

Antras, Pol. 2004. "Is the U.S. Aggregate Production Function Cobb-Douglas? New Estimates of the Elasticity of Substitution." *Contributions to Macroeconomics* 4(1). http://www.degruyter.com/view/j/bejm.2004.4.1/bejm.2004.4.1.1161/bejm.2004.4.1.1161.xml.

Appelbaum, Eileen, Annette Bernhardt, and Richard J. Murnane, eds. 2006. *Low-Wage America: How Employers Are Reshaping Opportunity in the Workplace*. New York: Russell Sage Foundation.

Appleton, Nathan. 1858. *Introduction of the Power Loom and Origin of Lowell*. Lowell, MA: Penhallow.

Appleyard, Melissa. 1996. "How Does Knowledge Flow? Interfirm Patterns in the Semiconductor Industry." *Strategic Management Journal* 17: 137–154.

Argote, Linda, and Dennis Epple. 1990. "Learning Curves in Manufacturing." *Science* 246(4945): 920.

Arora, Ashish, Lee G. Branstetter, and Matej Drev. 2011. "Going Soft: How the Rise of Software-Based Innovation Led to the Decline of Japan's IT Industry and the Resurgence of Silicon Valley." Global COE Hi-Stat Discussion Paper Series no. 199.

Arrow, Kenneth J. 1962a. "The Economic Implications of Learning by Doing." *Review of Economic Studies* 29(3): 155–173.

———. 1962b. "Economic Welfare and the Allocation of Resources for Invention." In *The Rate and Direction of Inventive Activity: Economic and Social Factors*. Cambridge, MA: National Bureau of Economic Research, 609–626.

Arundel, Anthony, and Isabelle Kabla. 1998. "What Percentage of Innovations Are Patented? Empirical Estimates for European Firms." *Research Policy* 27(2): 127–141.

Atack, Jeremy, and Fred Bateman. 1999. "U.S. Historical Statistics: Nineteenth Century U.S. Industrial Development Through the Eyes of the Census of Manufactures." *Historical Methods* 32(4): 177–188.

Audretsch, David B., and Maryann P. Feldman. 1996. "R&D Spillovers and the Geography of Innovation and Production." *American Economic Review* 86(3): 630–640.

Auerswald, Philip, Stuart Kauffman, José Lobo, and Karl Shell. 2000. "The Production Recipes Approach to Modeling Technological Innovation: An Application to Learning by Doing." *Journal of Economic Dynamics and Control* 24(3): 389–450.

Autor, David, H., David Dorn, and Gordon H. Hanson. 2012. "The China Syndrome: Local Labor Market Effects of Import Competition in the United States." National Bureau of Economic Research Working Paper no. w18054.

Autor, David H., Frank Levy, and Richard J. Murnane. 2003. "The Skill Content of Recent Technological Change: An Empirical Investigation." *Quarterly Journal of Economics* 118: 1279–1333.

Baba, Yasunori, Shinji Takai, and Yuji Mizuta. 1996. "The User-Driven Evolution of the Japanese Software Industry: The Case of Customized Software for Mainframes." In *The International Computer Software Industry: A Comparative Study of Industry Evolution and Structure*, edited by David Mowery. New York: Oxford University Press, 104–130.

Bagnall, William R. 1893. *The Textile Industries of the United States: Including Sketches and Notices of Cotton, Woolen, Silk, and Linen Manufacturers in the Colonial Period.* Vol. 1. Cambridge, MA: Riverside Press.

Bahk, Byong-Hong, and Michael Gort. 1993. "Decomposing Learning by Doing in New Plants." *Journal of Political Economy* 101(4): 561–583.

Baily, Martin Neil, and Barry P. Bosworth. 2014. "U.S. Manufacturing: Understanding Its Past and Its Potential Future." *Journal of Economic Perspectives* 28(1): 3–26.

Baldwin, Carliss Young, and Kim B. Clark. 2000. *Design Rules: The Power of Modularity.* Vol. 1. Cambridge, MA: MIT Press.

Bank for International Settlements, Committee on Payment and Settlement Systems. 1980–2009. "Statistics on Settlement Systems in Selected Countries." Basel, Switzerland.

Barnett, George. 1904. "Introduction of the Linotype." *Yale Review* 13: 251.

———. 1925. "Chapters on Machinery and Labor." *Quarterly Journal of Economics* 40(1): 111–133.

Barringer, William H., and Kenneth J. Pierce. 2000. "Paying the Price for Big Steel: $100 Billion in Trade Restraints and Corporate Welfare, 30 Years of the Integrated Steel Companies' Capture of U.S. Trade Policy." Washington, DC: American Institute for International Steel.

Bartel, Ann P., and Frank Lichtenberg. 1987. "The Comparative Advantage of Educated Workers in Implementing New Technology." *Review of Economics and Statistics* 69(1): 1–11.

Baumol, William J., Sue Anne Batey Blackman, and Edward N. Wolff. 1989. *Productivity and American Leadership: The Long View.* Cambridge, MA: MIT Press.

Baumol, William J., and William G. Bowen. 1965. "On the Performing Arts: The Anatomy of Their Economic Problems." *American Economic Review* 55(1–2): 495–502.

Becker, Gary S. 1964. *Human Capital: A Theoretical and Empirical Analysis with Special Reference to Education.* Cambridge, MA: National Bureau of Economic Research.

Becker, Randy, Wayne Gray, and Jordan Marvakov. 2013. NBER-CES Manufacturing Industry Database. http://www.nber.org/nberces/.

Bensaude-Vincent, Bernadette. 1996. *A History of Chemistry*. Cambridge, MA: Harvard University Press.

Berndt, Ernst. 1976. "Reconciling Alternative Estimates of the Elasticity of Substitution." *Review of Economics and Statistics* 58(1): 59–68.

Berndt, Ernst, and L. Christensen. 1973. "The Translog Function and the Substitution of Equipment, Structures, and Labor in U.S. Manufacturing." *Journal of Econometrics* 1: 81–113.

Besen, Stanley M., and Joseph Farrell. 1994. "Choosing How to Compete: Strategies and Tactics in Standardization." *Journal of Economic Perspectives* 8(2): 117–131.

Bessen, James. 1997. "Productivity Adjustments and Learning-by-Doing as Human Capital." Working Paper no. 97-17. Center for Economic Studies, U.S. Census Bureau.

———. 1999. "Waiting for Technology: Path Dependence as a Random Walk." Working paper. http://ssrn.com/abstract=192169.

———. 2003. "Technology and Learning by Factory Workers: The Stretch-Out at Lowell, 1842." *Journal of Economic History* 63: 33–64.

———. 2012a. "A Generation of Software Patents." *Boston University Journal of Science and Technology Law* 18(2): 241–261.

———. 2012b. "More Machines, Better Machines . . . or Better Workers?" *Journal of Economic History* 72(1): 44–74.

———. 2013. "Was Mechanization De-Skilling?" Boston University School of Law Working Paper no. 11-13.

Bessen, James, Jennifer Ford, and Michael J. Meurer. 2011. "The Private and Social Costs of Patent Trolls." *Regulation* 34(4): 26–35.

Bessen, James, and Eric Maskin. 2009. "Sequential Innovation, Patents, and Imitation." *RAND Journal of Economics* 40(4): 611–635.

Bessen, James, and Michael J. Meurer. 2008. *Patent Failure: How Judges, Bureaucrats, and Lawyers Put Innovators at Risk*. Princeton, NJ: Princeton University Press.

———. 2014. "The Direct Costs from NPE Disputes." *Cornell Law Review* 99(2): 387–424.

Bessen, James, and Alessandro Nuvolari. 2013. "Diffusing New Technology Without Dissipating Rents: Some Historical Case Studies of Knowledge Sharing." Working paper. http://www.ssrn.com/abstract=2433567.

———. forthcoming. "Knowledge Sharing among Inventors: Some Historical Perspectives." In *Revolutionizing Innovation: Users, Communities, and Open Innovation*, edited by Dietmar Harhoff and Karim Lakhani. Cambridge, MA: MIT Press.

Bils, Mark. 1984. "Tariff Protection and Production in the Early U.S. Cotton Textile Industry." *Journal of Economic History* 44(4): 1033–1045.

Black, Sandra E., and Lisa M. Lynch. 2001. "How to Compete: The Impact of Workplace Practices and Information Technology on Productivity." *Review of Economics and Statistics* 83(3): 434–445.

Blanchflower, David G., and Alex Bryson. 2004. "The Union Wage Premium in the U.S. and the U.K." Centre for Economic Performance Discussion Paper dp0612, London School of Economics and Political Science.

Blind, Knut. 2004. *The Economics of Standards: Theory, Evidence, Policy.* Cheltenham, UK: Edward Elgar.

Blinder, Alan. 2007. "How Many United States Jobs Might Be Offshorable?" Center for Economic Policy Studies (CEPS) Working Paper no. 142.

Bloom, Nicholas, Benn Eifert, Aprajit Mahajan, David McKenzie, and John Roberts. 2013. "Does Management Matter? Evidence from India." *Quarterly Journal of Economics* 128(1): 1–51.

Boldrin, Michele, and David K. Levine. 2013. "The Case against Patents." *Journal of Economic Perspectives* 27(1): 3–22.

Boston Consulting Group. 1972. *Perspectives on Experience.* Boston: Boston Consulting Group.

Braverman, Harry. 1974. *Labor and Monopoly Capital: The Degradation of Work in the Twentieth Century.* New York: Monthly Review Press.

Bresnahan, Timothy F., Erik Brynjolfsson, and Lorin M. Hitt. 2002. "Information Technology, Workplace Organization, and the Demand for Skilled Labor: Firm-Level Evidence." *Quarterly Journal of Economics* 117(1): 339–376.

Bresnahan, Timothy F., and Shane Greenstein. 1996. "Technical Progress and Co-Invention in Computing and in the Uses of Computers." Brookings Papers on Economic Activity. *Microeconomics*: 1–83.

Bresnahan, Timothy F., and Manuel Trajtenberg. 1995. "General Purpose Technologies 'Engines of Growth'?" *Journal of Econometrics* 65(1): 83–108.

Bronfenbrenner, Martin. 1960. "A Note on Relative Shares and the Elasticity of Substitution." *Journal of Political Economy* 68(3): 284–287.

Brown, Martin, and Peter Philips. 1986. "Craft Labor and Mechanization in Nineteenth-Century American Canning." *Journal of Economic History* 46(3): 743–756.

Brynjolfsson, Erik, and Lorin M. Hitt. 2000. "Beyond Computation: Information Technology, Organizational Transformation, and Business Performance." *Journal of Economic Perspectives* 14(4): 23–48.

Brynjolfsson, Erik, Lorin M. Hitt, and Shinkyu Yang. 2002. "Intangible Assets: Computers and Organizational Capital." Brookings Papers on Economic Activity. *Macroeconomics*: 137–198.

Brynjolfsson, Erik, and Andrew McAfee. 2014. *The Second Machine Age: Work, Progress, and Prosperity in a Time of Brilliant Technologies.* New York: W. W. Norton and Company.

Buchanan, James M., and Gordon Tullock. 1962. *The Calculus of Consent: Logical Foundations of Constitutional Democracy.* Ann Arbor: University of Michigan Press.

Bureau of the Census. 1975. *Historical Statistics of the United States: Colonial Times to 1970.* Washington, DC: U.S. Department of Commerce.

Bureau of Labor Statistics. 2014. "Employment by Summary Education and Training Assignment, 2012 and Projected 2022." http://www.bls.gov/emp/ep_table _education_summary.htm.

Cappelli, Peter. 2008. "Schools of Dreams: More Education Is Not an Economic Elixir." *Issues in Science and Technology* (Summer): 59–64.

———. 2012. *Why Good People Can't Get Jobs: The Skills Gap and What Companies Can Do about It*. Philadelphia: Wharton Digital Press.

Center on Education and the Workforce. 2013. "Recovery: Job Growth and Education Requirements through 2020." https://cew.georgetown.edu/recovery2020.

Century Foundation. 2013. *Bridging the Higher Education Divide*. New York: The Century Foundation Press. http://tcf.org/assets/downloads/20130523-Bridging_the_Higher_Education_Divide-REPORT-ONLY.pdf.

Chandler, Alfred D. 1990. *Scale and Scope*. Cambridge, MA: Belknap Press of Harvard University Press.

Chesbrough, Henry W. 1999. "The Organizational Impact of Technological Change: A Comparative Theory of National Institutional Factors." *Industrial and Corporate Change* 8(3): 447–485.

———. 2003. *Open Innovation: The New Imperative for Creating and Profiting from Technology*. Boston: Harvard Business School Press.

Chien, Colleen. 2012. "Startups and Patent Trolls." Santa Clara University School of Law Accepted Paper 09-12. http://ssrn.com/abstract=2146251.

Chin, Aimee, Chinhui Juhn, and Peter Thompson. 2006. "Technical Change and the Demand for Skills during the Second Industrial Revolution: Evidence from the Merchant Marine, 1891–1912." *Review of Economics and Statistics* 88(3): 572–578.

Christensen, Clayton M. 1997. *The Innovator's Dilemma: When New Technologies Cause Great Firms to Fail*. Boston: Harvard Business School Press.

Christensen, Clayton M., Jerome H. Grossman, and Jason Hwang. 2009. *The Innovator's Prescription: A Disruptive Solution for Health Care*. New York: McGraw-Hill.

Clark, Gregory. 1987. "Why Isn't the Whole World Developed? Lessons from the Cotton Mills." *Journal of Economic History* 47(1): 141–173.

———. 2008. *A Farewell to Alms: A Brief Economic History of the World*. Princeton, NJ: Princeton University Press.

Cohen, Wesley M., Richard Florida, Lucien Randazzese, and John P. Walsh. 1998. "Industry and the Academy: Uneasy Partners in the Cause of Technological Advance." In *Challenges to Research Universities*, edited by Roger Noll. Washington, DC: Brookings Institution Press, 171–200.

Cohen, Wesley M., Richard R. Nelson, and John P. Walsh. 2000. "Protecting Their Intellectual Assets: Appropriability Conditions and Why U.S. Manufacturing Firms Patent (or Not)." National Bureau of Economic Research Working Paper no. w7552.

Comin, Diego A., and Martí Mestieri Ferrer. 2013. "If Technology Has Arrived Everywhere, Why Has Income Diverged?" National Bureau of Economic Research Working Paper no. 19010.

Costa, Dora L. 2000. "From Mill Town to Board Room: The Rise of Women's Paid Labor." *Journal of Economic Perspectives* 14(4): 101–122.

Cotropia, Christopher Anthony, and Mark A. Lemley. 2009. "Copying in Patent Law." *North Carolina Law Review* 87: 1421–1466.

Cottrell, Thomas. 1996. "Standards and the Arrested Development of Japan's Microcomputer Software Industry." In *The International Computer Software Industry: A Comparative Study of Industry Evolution and Structure*, edited by David Mowery. New York: Oxford University Press.

Cowen, Tyler. 2011. *The Great Stagnation: How America Ate All the Low-Hanging Fruit of Modern History, Got Sick, and Will (Eventually) Feel Better*. New York: Penguin.

———. 2013. *Average Is Over: Powering America Beyond the Age of the Great Stagnation*. New York: Penguin.

Cringely, Robert X. 2012. "Steve Jobs: The Lost Interview." Documentary film. https://www.youtube.com/watch?v=2nMD6sjAe8I.

Darby, Michael R., and Lynne G. Zucker. 2001. "Change or Die: The Adoption of Biotechnology in the Japanese and U.S. Pharmaceutical Industries." *Research on Technological Innovation, Management and Policy* 7: 85–125.

Darby, Michael R., Lynne G. Zucker, and Andrew Wang. 2004. "Joint Ventures, Universities, and Success in the Advanced Technology Program." *Contemporary Economic Policy* 22(2): 145–161.

Darby, Michael R., Lynne G. Zucker, and I. I. Welch. 2001. "Going Public When You Can in Biotechnology." National Bureau of Economic Research Working Paper no. 8954.

David, Paul A. 1970. "Learning by Doing and Tariff Protection: A Reconsideration of the Case of the Antebellum United States Cotton Textile Industry." *Journal of Economic History* 30(3): 521–601.

———. 1975. *Technical Choice Innovation and Economic Growth: Essays on American and British Experience in the Nineteenth Century*. Cambridge: Cambridge University Press.

———. 1985. "Clio and the Economics of QWERTY." *American Economic Review* 75(2): 332–337.

———. 1990. "The Dynamo and the Computer: An Historical Perspective on the Modern Productivity Paradox." *American Economic Review* 80(2): 355–361.

David, Paul A., and Shane Greenstein. 1990. "The Economics of Compatibility Standards: An Introduction to Recent Research." *Economics of Innovation and New Technology* 1(1–2): 3–41.

David, Paul A., and Peter Solar. 1977. "A Bicentenary Contribution to the History of the Cost of Living in America." *Research in Economic History* 2: 1–80.

David, Paul A,. and Theo Van de Klundert. 1965. "Biased Efficiency Growth and Capital-Labor Substitution in the U.S., 1899–1960." *American Economic Review* 55: 357–393.

David, Paul A., and Gavin Wright. 1997. "Increasing Returns and the Genesis of American Resource Abundance." *Industrial and Corporate Change* 6: 203–245.

Davis, Lance, and H. Louis Stettler III. 1966. "The New England Textile Industry 1825–1860." In *Output, Employment, and Productivity in the United States after 1800*. Cambridge, MA: National Bureau of Economic Research, 213–238.

Deloitte Consulting. 2014. "The 2014 MHI Annual Industry Report: Innovations That Drive Supply Chains."

De Paula, Matthew. 2005. "With Rising Teller Turnover, Banks Aim to Retain: Is Your Bank Keeping Its Tellers Happy?" *American Banker, January 2, 2005*.

Desmet, Klaus, and Esteban Rossi-Hansberg. 2009. "Spatial Growth and Industry Age." *Journal of Economic Theory* 144: 2477–2502.

Desrochers, Donna M., and Jane V. Wellman. 2011. *Trends in College Spending 1999–2009*. Washington, DC: Delta Project on Postsecondary Education Costs, Productivity, and Accountability. http://www.deltacostproject.org/sites/default/files/products/Trends2011_Final_090711.pdf.

Diamond, Jared M. 1997. *Guns, Germs, and Steel*. New York: W. W. Norton.

Diamond, Peter, Daniel McFadden, and Miguel Rodriguez. 1978. "Measurement of the Elasticity of Factor Substitution and Bias of Technical Change." In *Production Economics: A Dual Approach to Theory and Applications*, edited by Melvyn Fuss and Daniel MacFadden. Vol. 2. Amsterdam: North-Holland, 125–147.

Dickens, Charles. 1842. "General Appearance of Mill Workers." *American Notes*.

Dosi, Giovanni. 1982. "Technological Paradigms and Technological Trajectories." *Research Policy* 11: 147–162.

Dourado, Eli, and Alex Tabarrok. 2013. "Public Choice and Bloomington School Perspectives on Intellectual Property." Mercatus Center Working Paper no. 13-23. George Mason University.

Dranove, David, Chris Forman, Avi Goldfarb, and Shane M. Greenstein. 2012. "The Trillion Dollar Conundrum: Complementarities and Health Information Technology." National Bureau of Economic Research Working Paper no. w18281.

Draper, William F. 1903. "Continued Development of the Northrop Loom." *Transactions of the National Association of Cotton Manufacturers* 74: 163.

Drucker, Peter. 2001. "The Next Society." *The Economist*, November 1. http://www.economist.com/node/770819.

Dublin, Thomas. 1979. *Women at Work: The Transformation of Work and Community in Lowell, Massachusetts, 1826–1860*. New York: Columbia University Press.

Du Maurier, George. 1878. "Edison's Telephonoscope (Transmits Light as well as Sound)." *Punch*, December 9, 1878.

Dunlop, John T. 1962. *Automation and Technological Change: Report of the Twenty-first American Assembly*. Englewood Cliffs, NJ: Prentice-Hall.

Eaglen, Mackenzie, and Julia Pollak. 2012. "U.S. Military Technological Supremacy under Threat." American Enterprise Institute. http://www.aei.org/papers/foreign-and-defense-policy/defense/us-military-technological-supremacy-under-threat/.

Edwards, Alba M. 1943. *Comparative Occupation Statistics of the United States, 1870 to 1940*. 16th Census of the United States, Population, U.S. Department of Commerce. Washington, DC: Government Printing Office, tables 9 and 10.

Eichengreen, Barry, Donghyun Park, and Kwanho Shin. 2013. "Growth Slowdowns Redux: New Evidence on the Middle-Income Trap." National Bureau of Economic Research Working Paper no. w18673.

Engels, Friedrich. 1892. *The Condition of the Working Class in England in 1844*. London: George Allen and Unwin.

Epstein, Stephen. 2004. "Property Rights to Technical Knowledge in Premodern Europe, 1300–1800." *American Economic Review* 94: 382–387.

Fairlie, Robert W., Kanika Kapur, and Susan Gates. 2011. "Is Employer-Based Health Insurance a Barrier to Entrepreneurship?" *Journal of Health Economics* 30(1): 146–162.

Fallick, Bruce, Charles A. Fleischman, and James B. Rebitzer. 2006. "Job-Hopping in Silicon Valley: Some Evidence Concerning the Microfoundations of a High-Technology Cluster." *Review of Economics and Statistics* 88(3): 472–481.

Farrell, Joseph, and Garth Saloner. 1985. "Standardization, Compatibility, and Innovation." *RAND Journal of Economics* 16(1): 70–83.

Feldman, Robin. 2013. "Patent Demands and Startup Companies: The View from the Venture Capital Community." Working paper. http://ssrn.com/abstract=2346338.

F. G. A. 1841. "Susan Miller." *Lowell Offering*, August 1841.

Fine, Lisa M. 1990. *The Souls of the Skyscraper: Female Clerical Workers in Chicago, 1870–1930.* Philadelphia: Temple University Press.

Fischer, Timo, and Joachim Henkel. 2012. "Patent Trolls on Markets for Technology: An Empirical Analysis of NPEs' Patent Acquisitions." *Research Policy* 41(9): 1519–1533.

Fisk, Catherine L. 2009. *Working Knowledge: Employee Innovation and the Rise of Corporate Intellectual Property, 1800–1930.* Chapel Hill: University of North Carolina Press.

Foray, Dominique. 2004. *The Economics of Knowledge.* Cambridge, MA: MIT Press.

Foster, Andrew D., and Mark R. Rosenzweig. 2010. "Microeconomics of Technology Adoption." *Annual Review of Economics* 2(1): 395–424.

Fox-Grange, Wendy. 1995. *Scope of Practice: An Overview of 1995 Legislative Activity.* Washington, DC: Intergovernmental Health Policy Project.

Freeman, Christopher. 1987. *Technology Policy and Economic Performance: Lessons from Japan.* London: Pinter Publishers.

Freeman, Richard B. 1976. *The Overeducated American.* New York: Academic Press.

Frei, Frances X. 2006. "Breaking the Trade-Off between Efficiency and Service." *Harvard Business Review* 84(11): 93–101.

Frey, Carl Benedikt, and Michael A. Osborne. 2013. "The Future of Employment: How Susceptible Are Jobs to Computerisation?" Oxford Martin Programme on the Impacts of Future Technology working paper. http://www.futuretech.ox.ac.uk/sites/futuretech.ox.ac.uk/files/The_Future_of_Employment_OMS_Working_Paper_1.pdf.

Fritz, John. 1912. *The Autobiography of John Fritz.* New York: American Society of Mechanical Engineers.

Garmaise, Mark J. 2011. "Ties That Truly Bind: Noncompetition Agreements, Executive Compensation, and Firm Investment." *Journal of Law, Economics, and Organization* 27(2): 376–425.

Gartner, Scott Sigmund, Michael R. Haines, Alan L. Olmstead, Richard Sutch, and Gavin Wright. 2006. *Historical Statistics of the United States.* Edited by Susan B. Carter. New York: Cambridge University Press.

Gawande, Atul. 2002. *Complications: A Surgeon's Notes on an Imperfect Science.* New York: Picador.

Gibb, George. 1950. *The Saco-Lowell Shops: Textile Machinery Building in New England, 1813–1949.* New York: Russell & Russell.

Gilroy, Clinton G. 1844. *The Art of Weaving by Hand and by Power.* New York: George D. Baldwin.

Gilson, Ronald J. 1999. "The Legal Infrastructure of High Technology Industrial Districts: Silicon Valley, Route 128, and Covenants Not to Compete." *New York University Law Review* 74: 575.

Goldin, Claudia D., and Lawrence F. Katz. 2008. *The Race between Education and Technology.* Cambridge, MA: Harvard University Press.

Goldin, Claudia, and Kenneth Sokoloff. 1984. "The Relative Productivity Hypothesis of Industrialization: The American Case, 1820 to 1850." *Quarterly Journal of Economics* 99(3): 461–487.

Gordon, Robert B. 1988. "Who Turned the Mechanical Ideal into Mechanical Reality?" *Technology and Culture* 29(4): 744–778.

Gordon, Robert J. 2014. "The Demise of U.S. Economic Growth: Restatement, Rebuttal, and Reflections." National Bureau of Economic Research Working Paper no. w19895.

Gort, Michael, and Steven Klepper. 1982. "Time Paths in the Diffusion of Product Innovations." *Economic Journal* 92(367): 630–653.

Graddy, Elizabeth. 1991. "Toward a General Theory of Occupational Regulation." *Social Science Quarterly* 72(4): 676–695.

Graham, Stuart, Robert Merges, Pamela Samuelson, and Ted Sichelman. 2009. "High Technology Entrepreneurs and the Patent System: Results of the 2008 Berkeley Patent Survey." *Berkeley Technology Law Journal* 24(4): 255–327.

Gray, Rowena. 2013. "Taking Technology to Task: The Skill Content of Technological Change in Early Twentieth Century United States." *Explorations in Economic History* 50(3): 351–367.

Greenstone, Michael, and Adam Looney. 2011. "Where Is the Best Place to Invest $102,000—In Stocks, Bonds, or a College Degree?" The Hamilton Project. http://www.brookings.edu/research/papers/2011/06/25-education-greenstone-looney.

Greif, Avner, and Murat Iyigun. 2013. "Social Organizations, Violence, and Modern Growth." *American Economic Review* 103(3): 534–538.

Griffin, James M., and Paul R. Gregory. 1976. "An Intercountry Translog Model of Energy Substitution Responses." *American Economic Review* 66: 845–857.

Gruber, Jonathan, and Brigitte C. Madrian. 1994. "Health Insurance and Job Mobility: The Effects of Public Policy on Job-Lock." *Industrial and Labor Relations Review* 48(1): 86–102.

Gue, Kevin, Elif Akcali, Alan Erera, William Ferrell, and Gary Forger. 2014. "U.S. Roadmap for Material Handling and Logistics." http://www.mhlroadmap.org/index.html.

Gup, Benton E. 2003. *The Future of Banking.* Westport, CT: Quorum Books.

Haber, Ludwig F. 1969. *The Chemical Industry during the Nineteenth Century: A Study of the Economic Aspect of Applied Chemistry in Europe and North America.* Oxford: Clarendon Press.

Haltiwanger, John, Ian Hathaway, and Javier Miranda. 2014. "Declining Business Dynamism in the U.S. High-Technology Sector." Kansas City, MO: Ewing Marion Kauffman Foundation.

Hannan, Timothy H., and Gerald A. Hanweck. 2008. "Recent Trends in the Number and Size of Bank Branches: An Examination of Likely Determinants." Finance and Economics Discussion Series no. 2008-02. Federal Reserve Board.

Hathaway, Ian, and Robert Litan. 2014. "Declining Business Dynamism in the United States: A Look at States and Metros." Economic Studies at Brookings, May. Brookings Institution. http://www.brookings.edu/~/media/research/files/papers/2014/05/declining%20business%20dynamism%20litan/declining_business_dynamism_hathaway_litan.pdf.

Henry, Matthew D., and John L. Turner. 2006. "The Court of Appeals for the Federal Circuit's Impact on Patent Litigation." *Journal of Legal Studies* 35(1): 85–117.

Hillestad, R., J. Bigelow, A. Bower, F. Girosi, R. Meili, R. Scoville, and R. Taylor. 2005. "Can Electronic Medical Record Systems Transform Healthcare? An Assessment of Potential Health Benefits, Savings, and Costs." *Health Affairs* 24(5): 1103–1117.

Hollander, Samuel. 1965. *The Sources of Increased Efficiency: A Study of Dupont Rayon Plants*. Cambridge, MA: MIT Press.

Holzer, Harry J., Julia I. Lane, David B. Rosenblum, and Fredrik Andersson. 2011. *Where Are All the Good Jobs Going?* New York: Russell Sage Foundation.

Hounshell, David Allen. 1979. *From the American System to Mass Production: The Development of Manufacturing Technology in the United States, 1850–1920*. Newark: University of Delaware Press.

Houze, Herbert G., Carolyn C. Cooper, and Elizabeth Mankin Kornhauser. 2006. *Samuel Colt: Arms, Art, and Invention*. New Haven, CT: Yale University Press.

Humphris, Amy, Morris M. Kleiner, and Maria Koumenta. 2011. "How Does Government Regulate Occupations in the U.K. and U.S.? Issues and Policy Implications." In *Employment in the Lean Years: Policy and Prospects for the Next Decade*, edited by David Marsden. Oxford: Oxford University Press, 87–101.

Hyde, Alan. 1998. "Silicon Valley's High Velocity Labor Market." *Journal of Applied Corporate Finance* 11(2): 28–37.

Inglehart, Ronald, and Pippa Norris. 2003. *Rising Tide: Gender Equality and Cultural Change around the World*. Cambridge: Cambridge University Press.

Institute of Medicine. 2000. *To Err Is Human: Building a Safer Health System*. Washington, DC: National Academy Press.

Jacobson, Margaret, and Filippo Occhino. 2012. "Behind the Decline in Labor's Share of Income." *Economic Trends*, February 3. Federal Reserve Bank of Cleveland. http://www.clevelandfed.org/research/trends/2012/0212/01gropro.cfm.

Jaffe, Adam B., and Josh Lerner. 2004. *Innovation and Its Discontents: How Our Broken Patent System Is Endangering Innovation and Progress, and What to Do about It*. Princeton, NJ: Princeton University Press.

Jaffe, Adam B., Manuel Trajtenberg, and Rebecca Henderson. 1993. "Geographic Localization of Knowledge Spillovers as Evidenced by Patent Citations." *Quarterly Journal of Economics* 108(3): 577–598.

Jardini, David. 1995. "From Iron to Steel: The Recasting of the Jones and Laughlins Workforce between 1885 and 1896." *Technology and Culture* 36(2): 271–301.

Jensen, Richard, and Marie Thursby. 2001. "Proofs and Prototypes for Sale: The Licensing of University Inventions." *American Economic Review* 91(1): 240–259.

Jewkes, John, David Sawers, and Richard Stillerman. 1969. *The Sources of Invention.* New York: W. W. Norton.

Jovanovic, Boyan. 1995. "Learning and Growth." National Bureau of Economic Research Working Paper no. w5383.

———. 1998. "Vintage Capital and Inequality." *Review of Economic Dynamics* 1(2): 497–530.

Jovanovic, Boyan, and Yaw Nyarko. 1995. "A Bayesian Learning Model Fitted to a Variety of Empirical Learning Curves." Brookings Papers on Economic Activity. *Microeconomics*: 247–305.

Jovanovic, Boyan, and Peter L. Rousseau. 2005. "General Purpose Technologies." In *Handbook of Economic Growth*, edited by Philippe Aghion and Steven Durlauf. Amsterdam: Elsevier, 1181–1224.

Karabarbounis, Loukas, and Brent Neiman. 2014. "The Global Decline of the Labor Share." *Quarterly Journal of Economics* 129(1): 61–103.

Kennedy, John F. 1962. Press conference, February 15. Reported in *Automation and Technological Change: Report of the Twenty-first American Assembly*, edited by John T. Dunlop. Englewood Cliffs, NJ: Prentice-Hall.

Ker, Ian. 2012. *G. K. Chesterton: A Biography.* Oxford: Oxford University Press.

Keynes, John Maynard. 1933. "Economic Possibilities for Our Grandchildren (1930)." *Essays in Persuasion*: 358–373.

———. 1936. *The General Theory of Employment, Interest and Money.* New York: Harcourt Brace.

Khan, Zorina B. 2005. *The Democratization of Invention: Patents and Copyrights in American Economic Development, 1790–1920.* New York: Cambridge University Press.

Kieff, F. Scott. 2000. "Property Rights and Property Rules for Commercializing Inventions." *Minnesota Law Review* 85: 697.

Kitch, Edmund W. 1977. "The Nature and Function of the Patent System." *Journal of Law and Economics* 20(2): 265–290.

Kleiner, Morris M. 2000. "Occupational Licensing." *Journal of Economic Perspectives* 14(4): 189–202.

———. 2006. *Licensing Occupations: Ensuring Quality or Restricting Competition?* Kalamazoo, MI: W. E. Upjohn Institute for Employment Research.

———. 2013. *Stages of Occupational Regulation: Analysis of Case Studies.* Kalamazoo, MI: W. E. Upjohn Institute for Employment Research.

Kleiner, Morris M., and Alan B. Krueger. 2013. "Analyzing the Extent and Influence of Occupational Licensing on the Labor Market." *Journal of Labor Economics* 31(2): S173–S202.

Kleiner, Morris M., and Robert T. Kudrle. 2000. "Does Regulation Affect Economic Outcomes? The Case of Dentistry." *Journal of Law and Economics* 43(2): 547–582.

Kleiner, Morris M., Allison Marier, Kyoung Won Park, and Coady Wing. 2014. "Relaxing Occupational Licensing Requirements: Analyzing Wages and Prices for a Medical Service." National Bureau of Economic Research Working Paper no. 19906.

Klepper, Steven. 1996. "Entry, Exit, Growth, and Innovation over the Product Life Cycle." *American Economic Review* 86(3): 562–583.

Klepper, Steven, and Elizabeth Graddy. 1990. "The Evolution of New Industries and the Determinants of Market Structure." *RAND Journal of Economics* 21(1): 27–44.

Kocherlakota, Narayana. 2010. "Inside the FOMC." Speech in Marquette, Michigan, August 17.

Kravets, Leonid. 2012. "Do Patents Really Matter to Startups? New Data Reveals Shifting Habits." *TechCrunch*, June 21, 2012. http://techcrunch.com/2012/06/21/do-patents-really-matter-to-startups-new-data-reveals-shifting-habits/.

Krueger, Alan B., and Lawrence H. Summers. 1988. "Efficiency Wages and the Inter-Industry Wage Structure." *Econometrica* 56(2): 259–293.

Kulik, Gary, Roger N. Parks, and Theodore Z. Penn. 1982. *The New England Mill Village, 1790–1860*. Cambridge, MA: MIT Press.

Kuznets, Simon. 1955. "Economic Growth and Income Inequality." *American Economic Review* 45(1): 1–28.

Kwolek-Folland, Angel. 1994. *Engendering Business: Men and Women in the Corporate Office, 1870–1930*. Baltimore: Johns Hopkins University Press.

Lach, Saul, and Mark Schankerman. 2004. "Royalty Sharing and Technology Licensing in Universities." *Journal of the European Economic Association* 2(2–3): 252–264.

Lamoreaux, Naomi R., and Kenneth L. Sokoloff. 1999. "Inventors, Firms, and the Market for Technology in the Late Nineteenth and Early Twentieth Centuries." In *Learning by Doing in Markets, Firms, and Countries*. Chicago: University of Chicago Press, 19–60.

Landes, David S. 1969. *The Unbound Prometheus: Technological Change and Industrial Development in Western Europe from 1750 to the Present*. Cambridge: Cambridge University Press.

———. 1999. *The Wealth and Poverty of Nations: Why Some Are So Rich and Some So Poor*. New York: W. W. Norton.

Lane, Frederic C. 1951. *Ships for Victory: A History of Shipbuilding under the U.S. Maritime Commission in World War II*. Baltimore: Johns Hopkins University Press.

Larcom, Lucy. 1889. *A New England Girlhood*. Vol. 9. Boston: Houghton, Mifflin.

Layer, Robert George. 1955. *Earnings of Cotton Mill Operatives, 1825–1914*. Cambridge, MA: Committee on Research in Economic History.

Lazonick, William, and Thomas Brush. 1985. "The "Horndal Effect" in Early U.S. Manufacturing." *Explorations in Economic History* 22(1): 53–96.

Lazowska, Edward D., and David A. Patterson. 2005. "An Endless Frontier Postponed." *Science* 308(5723): 757.

Lebergott, Stanley. 1960. "Wage Trends, 1800–1900." In *Trends in the American Economy in the Nineteenth Century*. Princeton, NJ: Princeton University Press, 449–500.

Lemley, Mark A. 2011. "The Myth of the Sole Inventor." *Michigan Law Review* 110: 709.

Lenway, Stefanie, Randall Morck, and Bernard Yeung. 1996. "Rent Seeking, Protectionism, and Innovation in the American Steel Industry." *Economic Journal* 106(435): 410–421.

Lerner, Josh. 2009. *Boulevard of Broken Dreams: Why Public Efforts to Boost Entrepreneurship and Venture Capital Have Failed—and What to Do about It*. Princeton, NJ: Princeton University Press.

Lessig, Lawrence. 2011. *Republic, Lost: How Money Corrupts Congress—and a Plan to Stop It*. New York: Twelve.

Leunig, Timothy. 2003. "Piece Rates and Learning: Understanding Work and Production in the New England Textile Industry a Century Ago." Working paper no. 22360. London School of Economics and Political Science, Department of Economic History.

Levin, Richard C., Alvin K. Klevorick, Richard R. Nelson, Sidney G. Winter, Richard Gilbert, and Zvi Griliches. 1987. "Appropriating the Returns from Industrial Research and Development." *Brookings Papers on Economic Activity* 3: 783–831.

Lewis, H. Gregg. 1963. *Unionism and Relative Wages in the United States*. Chicago: University of Chicago Press.

———. 1986. *Union Relative Wage Effects: A Survey*. Chicago: University of Chicago Press.

Liang, I. Nellie, and Jonathan D. Ogur. 1987. "Restrictions on Dental Auxiliaries: An Economic Policy Analysis." Bureau of Economics Staff Report. Washington, DC: Federal Trade Commission.

Lindsey, Brink, David T. Griswold, and Aaron Lukas. 1999. "The Steel 'Crisis' and the Costs of Protectionism." Washington, DC: Center for Trade Policy Studies, Cato Institute.

Litman, Jessica. 1996. "Revising Copyright Law for the Information Age." *Oregon Law Review* 75: 19.

———. 2006. *Digital Copyright*. Amherst, NY: Prometheus Books.

Lobel, Orly. 2014. *Talent Wants to Be Free*. New Haven, CT: Yale University Press.

———. Forthcoming. "The New Cognitive Property: Human Capital Law and the Reach of Intellectual Property." *Texas Law Review*.

Longman, Phillip. 2005. "The Best Care Anywhere." *Washington Monthly*. http://www.washingtonmonthly.com/features/2005/0501.longman.html.

Love, Brian J. 2013. "An Empirical Study of Patent Litigation Timing: Could a Patent Term Reduction Decimate Trolls without Harming Innovators?" *University of Pennsylvania Law Review* 161: 1309.

Lucas, Robert E. 1988. "On the Mechanics of Economic Development." *Journal of Monetary Economics* 22(1): 3–42.

Lyman, Henry B. 1861. "Transaction of the Rhode Island Society for the Encouragement of Domestic Industry." Cited in William R. Bagnall, *The Textile Industries of the*

*United States: Including Sketches and Notices of Cotton, Woolen, Silk, and Linen Manufacturers in the Colonial Period.* Vol. 1. Cambridge, MA: Riverside Press, 1893.

Lynch, Lisa M. 2007. "The Adoption and Diffusion of Organizational Innovation: Evidence for the U.S. Economy." Institute for the Study of Labor Discussion Paper no. 2819.

Lynn, Barry C., and Phillip Longman. 2010. "Who Broke America's Jobs Machine?" *Washington Monthly* (March/April). http://www.washingtonmonthly.com/features /2010/1003.lynn-longman.html.

Lynn, Leonard. 1981. "New Data on the Diffusion of the Basic Oxygen Furnace in the U.S. and Japan." *Journal of Industrial Economics* 30(2): 123–135.

Lynskey, Michael J. 2004. "Determinants of Innovative Activity in Japanese Technology-Based Start-Up Firms." *International Small Business Journal* 22(2): 159–196.

Lyons, John. 1989. "Family Response to Economic Decline: Handloom Weavers in Early Nineteenth-Century Lancashire." *Research in Economic History* 12: 45–91.

Machlup, Fritz. 1962. *The Production and Distribution of Knowledge in the United States.* Vol. 278. Princeton, NJ: Princeton University Press.

Machlup, Fritz, and Edith Penrose. 1950. "The Patent Controversy in the Nineteenth Century." *Journal of Economic History* 10(1): 1–29.

MacLeod, Christine. 1988. *Inventing the Industrial Revolution: The English Patent System, 1660–1800.* Cambridge: Cambridge University Press.

———. 1998. "James Watt, Heroic Invention and the Idea of the Industrial Revolution." In *Technological Revolutions in Europe: Historical Perspectives*, edited by Maxine Berg and Kristine Bruland. Cheltenham, UK: Edward Elgar, 109–110.

———. 2007. *Heroes of Invention: Technology, Liberalism, and British Identity, 1750–1914.* Cambridge: Cambridge University Press.

Maddison, Angus. 1991. *Dynamic Forces in Capitalist Development: A Long-Run Comparative View.* Oxford: Oxford University Press.

Magliocca, Gerard N. 2006. "Blackberries and Barnyards: Patent Trolls and the Perils of Innovation." *Notre Dame Law Review* 82: 1809.

Mak, James, and Gary M. Walton. 1972. "Steamboats and the Great Productivity Surge in River Transportation." *Journal of Economic History* 32: 619–640.

Mann, Ronald J., and Thomas W. Sager. 2007. "Patents, Venture Capital, and Software Start-Ups." *Research Policy* 36(2): 193–208.

Manpower Group. 2013. "Talent Shortage Survey Research Results." http:// www.manpowergroup.com/wps/wcm/connect/587d2b45-c47a-4647-a7c1 -e7a74f68fb85/2013_Talent_Shortage_Survey_Results_US_high+res .pdf?MOD=AJPERES.

Mansfield, Edwin. 1961."Technical Change and the Rate of Imitation." *Econometrica* 29(4): 741–766.

Mantoux, Paul. 1983. *The Industrial Revolution in the Eighteenth Century: An Outline of the Origins of the Modern Factory System in England.* London: Methuen and Co.

Marglin, Stephen. 1974. "What Do Bosses Do?" *Review of Radical Political Economics* 6(2): 60–112.

Marx, Karl. (1867) 1990. *Capital.* London: Penguin.

Marx, Matt. 2011. "The Firm Strikes Back: Non-compete Agreements and the Mobility of Technical Professionals." *American Sociological Review* 76(5): 695–712.

Marx, Matt, Deborah Strumsky, and Lee Fleming. 2009. "Mobility, Skills, and the Michigan Non-Compete Experiment." *Management Science* 55(6): 875–889.

McGaw, Judith A. 1987. *Most Wonderful Machine: Mechanization and Social Change in Berkshire Paper Making, 1801–1885.* Princeton, NJ: Princeton University Press.

McGouldrick, Paul F. 1968. *New England Textiles in the Nineteenth Century: Profits and Investment.* Cambridge, MA: Harvard University Press.

McKenzie, Richard B., and Stephen D. Smith. 1987. "Protectionism Warranted?" *Cato Journal* 6(3): 731–746.

McKiel, Mary. 2012. "Circular Reasoning." *Defense Standardization Program Journal* (October/December): 8–13. http://www.dsp.dla.mil/APP_UIL/content/newsletters/journal/DSPJ-10-12.pdf.

Meisenzahl, Ralf, and Joel Mokyr. 2011. *The Rate and Direction of Invention in the British Industrial Revolution: Incentives and Institutions.* National Bureau of Economic Research Working Paper no. w16993.

Merton, Robert K. 1961. "Singletons and Multiples in Scientific Discovery: A Chapter in the Sociology of Science." *Proceedings of the American Philosophical Society* 105(5): 470–486.

Meyer, David R. 2006. *Networked Machinists: High-Technology Industries in Antebellum America.* Baltimore: Johns Hopkins University Press.

Meyer, Peter. 2003. "Episodes of Collective Invention." U.S. Bureau of Labor Statistics Working Paper no. 368.

———. 2013. "The Airplane as an Open Source Invention." *Revue Economique* 64(1): 115–132.

Miller, Shawn P. 2012. "Where's the Innovation? An Analysis of the Quantity and Qualities of Anticipated and Obvious Patents." Working paper. Social Science Research Network, February 10. http://ssrn.com/abstract=2029263.

———. forthcoming. "Do 'Fuzzy' Software Patent Boundaries Explain High Claim Construction Reversal Rates?" *Stanford Technology Law Review* 17.

Minetaki, Kazunori, and Kazuyuki Motohashi. 2009. "Subcontracting Structure and Productivity in the Japanese Software Industry." *Review of Socionetwork Strategies* 3: 51–65.

Mohanty, Gail Fowler. 1988. "Experimentation in Textile Technology, 1788–1790, and Its Impact on Handloom Weaving and Weavers in Rhode Island." *Technology and Culture* 29(1): 1–31.

Mokyr, Joel. 1999. *The British Industrial Revolution.* 2nd ed. Boulder, CO: Westview Press.

———. 2002. *The Gifts of Athena: Historical Origins of the Knowledge Economy.* Princeton, NJ: Princeton University Press.

———. 2009. *The Enlightened Economy: An Economic History of Britain, 1700–1850.* New Haven, CT: Yale University Press.

Montgomery, David. 1989. *The Fall of the House of Labor: The Workplace, the State, and American Labor Activism, 1865–1925.* Cambridge: Cambridge University Press.

Montgomery, James. 1840. *A Practical Detail of the Cotton Manufacture of the United States of America.* Glasgow: John Niven.

Moore, Michael O. 1996. "The Rise and Fall of Big Steel's Influence on U.S. Trade Policy." In *The Political Economy of Trade Protection,* edited by Anne O. Krueger. Chicago: University of Chicago Press, 15–34.

Morris, William. 1883. "Art, Wealth, and Riches: An Address Delivered at a Joint Conversazione of Manchester Societies at The Royal Institution Manchester 6th March 1883." In *The Collected Works of William Morris* (1915). London: Longmans, Green and Company, 143–163.

Moscarini, Giuseppe, and Kaj Thomsson. 2007. "Occupational and Job Mobility in the U.S." *Scandinavian Journal of Economics* 109(4): 807–836.

Moser, Petra. 2005. "How Do Patent Laws Influence Innovation? Evidence from Nineteenth Century World's Fairs." *American Economic Review* 95(4): 1214–1236.

———. 2011. "Do Patents Weaken the Localization of Innovations? Evidence from World's Fairs." *Journal of Economic History* 71(2): 363–382.

Mowery, David. 1992. "The U.S. National Innovation System: Origins and Prospects for Change." *Research Policy* 21(2): 125–144.

———. 2013. "Public Procurement and Innovation in the Post-1945 U.S. Economy." Report for the Expert Group on Innovation and Growth, European Commission.

Mowery, David, and Timothy Simcoe. 2002. "Is the Internet a U.S. Invention?—An Economic and Technological History of Computer Networking." *Research Policy* 31(8): 1369–1387.

Mullin, Joe. 2014. "How the Patent Trolls Won in Congress." *Ars Technica,* May 23. http://arstechnica.com/tech-policy/2014/05/how-the-patent-trolls-won-in-congress/.

Nalbantian, Haig R., and Anne Szostak. 2004. "How Fleet Bank Fought Employee Flight." *Harvard Business Review* (April): 116–125.

Nard, Craig Allen, and John F. Duffy. 2007. "Rethinking Patent Law's Uniformity Principle." *Northwestern University Law Review* 101: 1619.

National Stenographer. 1890. "The New Hammond." *National Stenographer* 1 (August 1890): 319.

Nelson, Daniel. 1987. "Mass Production and the U.S. Tire Industry." *Journal of Economic History* 47(2): 329–339.

Nelson, Richard R., Merton J. Peck, and Edward D. Kalachek. 1967. *Technology, Economic Growth, and Public Policy: A Rand Corporation and Brookings Institution Study.* Washington, DC: Brookings Institution.

Nelson, Richard R., and Sidney G. Winter. 1977. "In Search of a Useful Theory of Innovation." *Research Policy* 6: 36–76.

———. 1982. *An Evolutionary Theory of Economic Change.* Cambridge, MA: Belknap Press of Harvard University Press.

Nuvolari, Alessandro. 2004. "Collective Invention during the British Industrial Revolution: The Case of the Cornish Pumping Engine." *Cambridge Journal of Economics* 28(3): 347–363.

Nuvolari, Alessandro, and Bart Verspagen. 2007. "Lean's Engine Reporter and the Development of the Cornish Engine: A Reappraisal." *Transactions of the Newcomen Society* 77: 167–189.

Nuwer, Michael. 1988. "From Batch to Flow: Production Technology and Work-Force Skills in the Steel Industry, 1880–1920." *Technology and Culture* 29(4): 808–838.

OECD. 2006. "Information Technology Outlook 2006." Paris: OECD Publishing.

———. 2013. *Education at a Glance 2013: OECD Indicators.* Paris: OECD Publishing. http://dx.doi.org/10.1787/eag-2013-en.

Olmstead, Alan L., and Paul W. Rhode. 2008. *Creating Abundance.* Cambridge: Cambridge University Press.

Olson, Mancur. 1965. *The Logic of Collective Action: Public Goods and the Theory of Groups.* Cambridge, MA: Harvard University Press.

Oz, Effy. 1998. "Acceptable Protection of Software Intellectual Property: A Survey of Software Developers and Lawyers." *Information & Management* 34(3): 161–173.

Parker, Robert P., and Bruce T. Grimm. 2000. "Recognition of Business and Government Expenditures for Software as Investment: Methodology and Quantitative Impacts, 1959–98." Bureau of Economic Analysis working paper no. 0002. http://www.bea.gov/papers/pdf/software.pdf.

Piketty, Thomas. 2014. *Capital in the Twenty-first Century.* Cambridge, MA: Harvard University Press.

Pine, Art. 2011. "OPEN to Wild Ideas." *ASEE Prism* 20(5): 29–33.

Pisano, Gary P., and Willy C. Shih. 2012. "Does America Really Need Manufacturing? Yes, When Production Is Closely Tied to Innovation." *Harvard Business Review* 90(3): 94.

Png, Ivan. 2012a. "Law and Innovation: Evidence from State Trade Secrets Laws." Working paper. Social Science Research Network, June 15. http://ssrn.com/abstract =1755284.

———. 2012b. "Trade Secrets, Non-Competes, and Mobility of Engineers and Scientists: Empirical Evidence." Working paper, Social Science Research Network, August 21. http://ssrn.com/abstract=1986775.

Png, Ivan, and Sampsa Samila. 2013. "Trade Secrets Law and Engineer/Scientist Mobility: Evidence from 'Inevitable Disclosure.'" Working paper. https://www.law .northwestern.edu/research-faculty/searlecenter/events/entrepreneur/documents /Png_Samila_Inevitable_Disclosure.pdf.

PriceWaterhouseCoopers. 2013. "Patent Litigation Study." http://www.pwc.com/us /en/forensic-services/publications/2013-patent-litigation-study.jhtml.

Rifkin, Jeremy. 1995. *The End of Work: The Decline of the Global Labor Force and the Dawn of the Post-Market Era.* New York: Putnam.

Risch, Michael. 2012. "Patent Troll Myths." *Seton Hall Law Review* 42: 457.

Robinson, Harriet Hanson. 1898. *Loom and Spindle or Life amongst the Early Mill Girls.* Carlisle, MA: Applewood Books.

Rockwell, Julius Ensing. 1893. *Shorthand Instruction and Practice*. Bureau of Education, Circular of Information no. 1, 1893, Whole number 192. Washington, DC: U.S. Government Printing Office.

Rodgers, Daniel T. 1978. *The Work Ethic in Industrial America, 1850–1920*. Chicago: University of Chicago Press.

Rogers, Everett M. 1962. *Diffusion of Innovations*. New York: Simon and Schuster.

Romer, Paul M. 1990. "Endogenous Technological Change." *Journal of Political Economy* 98(5): S71–102.

Rosen, Sherwin. 1981. "The Economics of Superstars." *American Economic Review* 71(5): 845–858.

Rosenberg, Nathan. 1979. "Technological Interdependence in the American Economy." *Technology and Culture* 20(1): 25–50.

———. 1982. *Inside the Black Box: Technology and Economics*. Cambridge: Cambridge University Press.

Rosenberg, Nathan, and W. E. Steinmueller. 2012. "Engineering Knowledge." Stanford Institute for Economic Policy Research Discussion Paper no. 11-022.

Rosenberg, Nathan, and Manuel Trajtenberg. 2004. "A General Purpose Technology at Work: The Corliss Steam Engine in the Late-Nineteenth-Century United States." *Journal of Economic History* 64(1): 61–99.

Rosenzweig, Mark R. 1995. "Why Are There Returns to Schooling?" *American Economic Review* 85(2): 153–158.

Rossi, William A. 1977. *The Sex Life of the Foot and Shoe*. London: Routledge & K. Paul.

Rothstein, Jesse. 2012. "The Labor Market Four Years into the Crisis: Assessing Structural Explanations." National Bureau of Economic Research Working Paper no. w17966.

Rowthorn, Robert, and Ramana Ramaswamy. 1998. "Growth, Trade, and Deindustrialization." International Monetary Fund Working Paper no. 98/60.

Ruggles, Steven, J. Trent Alexander, Katie Genadek, Ronald Goeken, Matthew B. Schroeder, and Matthew Sobek. 2010. Integrated Public Use Microdata Series: Version 5.0 [Machine-readable database]. Minneapolis: University of Minnesota.

Ruttan, Vernon W. 2006. *Is War Necessary for Economic Growth? Military Procurement and Technology Development*. Oxford: Oxford University Press.

Saez, Emanuel, and Thomas Piketty. 2003. "Income Inequality in the United States, 1913–1998." *Quarterly Journal of Economics* 118(1): 1–39.

Salzman, Hal, Daniel Kuehn, and B. Lindsay Lowell. 2013. "Guestworkers in the High-Skill U.S. Labor Market: An Analysis of Supply, Employment, and Wage Trends." Economic Policy Institute Briefing Paper no. 359.

Samila, Sampsa, and Olav Sorenson. 2011. "Noncompete Covenants: Incentives to Innovate or Impediments to Growth." *Management Science* 57(3): 425–438.

Samuels, Linda B., and Bryan K. Johnson. 1990. "The Uniform Trade Secrets Act: The States' Response." *Creighton Law Review* 24: 49–98.

Samuelson, Pamela, Michel Denber, and Robert J. Glushko. 1992. "Developments on the Intellectual Property Front." *Communications of the ACM* 35(6): 33–39.

Saxenian, AnnaLee. 1996. *Regional Advantage: Culture and Competition in Silicon Valley and Route 128*. Cambridge, MA: Harvard University Press.

————. 2006. *The New Argonauts: Regional Advantage in a Global Economy*. Cambridge, MA: Harvard University Press.

Saxonhouse, Gary, and Gavin Wright. 1984. "Two Forms of Cheap Labor in Textile History." In *Technique, Spirit and Form in the Making of the Modern Economies: Essays in Honor of William N. Parker*, edited by Gary Saxonhouse and Gavin Wright. Greenwich, CT: JAI Press, 271–300.

Scherer, Frederic M. 2009. "The Political Economy of Patent Policy Reform in the United States." *Journal on Telecommunications and High Technology Law* 7: 167.

Schorsch, Louis L. 1996. "Why Minimills Give the U.S. Huge Advantages in Steel." *McKinsey Quarterly* 2: 44–55.

Schrader, Stephan. 1991. "Informal Technology Transfer between Firms: Cooperation through Information Trading." *Research Policy* 10: 153–170.

Scotchmer, Suzanne. 1991. "Standing on the Shoulders of Giants: Cumulative Research and the Patent Law." *Journal of Economic Perspectives* 5: 29–41.

————. 2004. *Innovation and Incentives*. Cambridge, MA: MIT Press.

Scranton, Philip. 1984. *Proprietary Capitalism: The Textile Manufacture at Philadelphia, 1800–1885*. New York: Cambridge University Press.

Shlakman, Vera. (1935) 1969. *Economic History of a Factory Town: A Study of Chicopee, Massachusetts*. New York: Octagon Books.

Sichelman, Ted. 2009. "Commercializing Patents." *Stanford Law Review* 62: 341.

Sidorov, Jaan. 2006. "It Ain't Necessarily So: The Electronic Health Record and the Unlikely Prospect of Reducing Health Care Costs." *Health Affairs* 25(4): 1079–1085.

Simcoe, Timothy, and Michael W. Toffel. 2012. "Public Procurement and the Private Supply of Green Buildings." Harvard Business School Working Paper no. 13-030.

Smeets, Roger. 2014. "Does Patent Litigation Reduce Corporate R&D? An Analysis of U.S. Public Firms." Working paper. Social Science Research Network, April 28. http://papers.ssrn.com/sol3/papers.cfm?abstract_id=2443048.

Smith, Merritt Roe. 1985. "Army Ordnance and the 'American System' of Manufacturing, 1815–1861." In *Military Enterprise and Technological Change*, edited by Merritt Roe Smith. Cambridge, MA: MIT Press, 39–86.

Sokoloff, Kenneth. 1984. "Was the Transition from the Artisanal Shop to the Non-Mechanized Factory Associated with Gains in Efficiency? Evidence from the U.S. Manufacturing Censuses of 1820 and 1850." *Explorations in Economic History* 21 (October): 351–382.

Solow, Robert M. 1956. "A Contribution to the Theory of Economic Growth." *Quarterly Journal of Economics* 70(1): 65–94.

————. 1957. "Technical Change and the Aggregate Production Function." *Review of Economics and Statistics* 39(3): 312–320.

Stiglitz, Joseph. 2013. *The Price of Inequality: How Today's Divided Society Endangers Our Future*. New York: W. W. Norton and Company.

Stone, Charley, Carl Van Horn, and Cliff Zukin. 2012. "Chasing the American Dream: Recent College Graduates and the Great Recession." Worktrends Report, Rutgers University.

Stowsky, Jay. 2004. "Secrets to Shield or Share? New Dilemmas for Military R&D Policy in the Digital Age." *Research Policy* 33(2): 257–269.

Suárez, Fernando F., and James M. Utterback. 1995. "Dominant Designs and the Survival of Firms." *Strategic Management Journal* 16(6): 415–430.

Teece, David J. 1977. "Technology Transfer by Multinational Firms: The Resource Cost of Transferring Technological Know-How." *Economic Journal* 87(346): 242–261.

Temin, Peter. 1964. *Iron and Steel in Nineteenth-Century America: An Economic Inquiry.* Cambridge, MA: MIT Press.

Thompson, Peter. 2001. "How Much Did the Liberty Shipbuilders Learn? New Evidence for an Old Case Study." *Journal of Political Economy* 109(1): 103–137.

———. 2009. "Learning by Doing." In *Handbook of Economics of Technical Change,* edited by Bronwyn Hall and Nathan Rosenberg. Amsterdam: Elsevier/North-Holland, 429–476.

Thomson, Ross. 1987. "Learning by Selling and Invention: The Case of the Sewing Machine." *Journal of Economic History* 47(2): 433–445.

———. 2009. *Structures of Change in the Mechanical Age: Technological Innovation in the United States, 1790–1865.* Baltimore: Johns Hopkins University Press.

———. 2012. "The Government and Innovation in the United States: Insights from Major Innovators." *Business and Economic History Online* 10. http://www.thebhc .org/publications/BEHonline/2012/thomson.pdf.

Tilton, John. 1971. *The International Diffusion of Technology: The Case of Transistors.* Washington, DC: Brookings Institution Press.

Triplett, Jack, and Barry Bosworth. 2003. "Productivity Measurement Issues in Service Industries: 'Baumol's Disease' Has Been Cured." *Federal Reserve Bank of New York Economic Policy Review* (September).

Tryon, Rolla Milton. 1917. *Household Manufactures in the United States, 1640–1860.* Chicago: University of Chicago Press.

Tucker, Catherine. 2011. "Patent Trolls and Technology Diffusion." Working paper. http://ebusiness.mit.edu/research/papers/2011.12_Tucker_Patent%20trolls%20 and%20Techonology%20Diffusion_305.pdf.

———. 2014. "The Effect of Patent Litigation and Patent Assertion Entities on Entrepreneurial Activity." Working paper. Social Science Research Network, June 22. http://papers.ssrn.com/sol3/papers.cfm?abstract_id=2457611.

U.S. Department of Commerce. 2012. "The Benefits of Manufacturing Jobs." Economics and Statistics Administration (ESA) Issue Brief no. 01-12. http://www .esa.doc.gov/sites/default/files/reports/documents/1thebenefitsofmanufacturing jobsfinal5912.pdf.

Usselman, Steven W. 2009. "Unbundling IBM: Antitrust and the Incentives to Innovation in American Computing." In *The Challenge of Remaining Innovative: Insights from Twentieth Century American Business,* edited by Sally H. Clarke, Naomi

Lamoreaux, and Steven W Usselman. Stanford, CA: Stanford University Press, 249–279.

Utterback, James M. 1996. *Mastering the Dynamics of Innovation*. Boston: Harvard Business School Press.

Utterback, James M., and William J. Abernathy. 1975. "A Dynamic Model of Process and Product Innovation." *Omega* 3(6): 639–656.

Vernon, Raymond. 1966. "International Investment and International Trade in the Product Cycle." *Quarterly Journal of Economics* 80(2): 190–207.

Vinge, Vernor. 1993. "The Coming Technological Singularity: How to Survive in the Post-Human Era." Originally published in *Vision-21: Interdisciplinary Science and Engineering in the Era of Cyberspace*, edited by G. A. Landis. NASA Publication CP-10129, 11–22. http://www.rohan.sdsu.edu/faculty/vinge/misc/singularity.html.

von Hippel, Eric. 1987. "Cooperation between Rivals: Informal Know-How Trading." *Research Policy* 16(6): 291–302.

———. 1988. *The Sources of Innovation*. New York: Oxford University Press.

———. 2005. *Democratic Innovation*. Cambridge, MA: MIT Press.

von Tunzelmann, G. N. 1978. *Steam Power and British Industrialization to 1860*. Vol. 295. Oxford: Clarendon Press.

Wadsworth, Alfred P., and Julia De Lacy Mann. 1931. *The Cotton Trade and Industrial Lancashire, 1600–1780*. Manchester: Manchester University Press.

Wallace, Anthony F. C. 1978. *Rockdale: The Growth of an American Village in the Early Industrial Revolution*. New York: Alfred A. Knopf.

Wanchek, Tanya. 2010. "Dental Hygiene Regulation and Access to Oral Healthcare: Assessing the Variation across the U.S. States." *British Journal of Industrial Relations* 48(4): 706–725.

Ware, Caroline F. 1931. *The Early New England Cotton Manufacture: A Study in Industrial Beginnings*. Boston: Houghton Mifflin.

Warsh, David. 2007. *Knowledge and the Wealth of Nations: A Story of Economic Discovery*. New York: W. W. Norton.

Weber, Max. 1930. *The Protestant Ethic and the Spirit of Capitalism*. Translated by Talcott Parsons. London: George Allen and Unwin.

West, Joel. 2008. "Commercializing Open Science: Deep Space Communications as the Lead Market for Shannon Theory, 1960–73." *Journal of Management Studies* 45(8): 1506–1532.

Williamson, Jeffrey G. 1985. *Did British Capitalism Breed Inequality?* Boston: Allen and Unwin.

Winter, Sidney G. 1984. "Schumpeterian Competition in Alternative Technological Regimes." *Journal of Economic Behavior and Organization* 5: 287–320.

Womack, James P., Daniel T. Jones, and Daniel Roos. 1990. *The Machine That Changed the World: The Story of Lean Production: How Japan's Secret Weapon in the Global Auto Wars Will Revolutionize Western Industry*. New York: Rawson Associates.

Wright, Gavin. 2007. "Historical Foundations of American Technology." Economics Program Working Papers 08-10. The Conference Board. http://web.stanford.edu/~write/papers/Historical%20FoundationsR.pdf.

Yglesias, Matthew. 2012. "Workers Are Losing Out Globally." *Slate*, December 11. http://www.slate.com/blogs/moneybox/2012/12/11/workers_are_losing_out_globally .html.

Zeitz, Peter. 2013. "Do Local Institutions Affect All Foreign Investors in the Same Way? Evidence from the Interwar Chinese Textile Industry." *Journal of Economic History* 73(1): 117–141.

Zevin, Robert. 1971. "The Growth of Cotton Textile Production after 1815." In *The Reinterpretation of American Economic History*, edited by Robert Fogel and Stanley Engerman. New York: Harper and Row, 122–147.

Zucker, Lynne G., Michael R. Darby, and Jeff S. Armstrong. 1998. "Geographically Localized Knowledge: Spillovers or Markets?" *Economic Inquiry* 36(1): 65–86.

———. 2001. "Commercializing Knowledge: University Science, Knowledge Capture, and Firm Performance in Biotechnology." National Bureau of Economic Research Working Paper no. 8499.

Zucker, Lynne G., Michael R. Darby, and M. B. Brewer. 1998. "Intellectual Human Capital and the Birth of U.S. Biotechnology Enterprises." *American Economic Review* 88(1): 290–306.

# INDEX

*Note*: Page numbers followed by *f* and *t* indicate figures and tables.